Frommer's®

PORTABLE
Aruba, Bonaire & Curaçao

5th Edition

by Christina P. Colón, Ph.D.

Here's what critics say about Frommer's:

"Amazingly easy to use. Very portable, very complete."
—**BOOKLIST**

"Detailed, accurate, and easy-to-read information for all price ranges."
—**GLAMOUR MAGAZINE**

Wiley Publishing, Inc.

Published by:

WILEY PUBLISHING, INC.

111 River St.
Hoboken, NJ 07030-5774

ISBN 978-0-470-49737-1

Editor: Jennifer Polland
Production Editor: Jana M. Stefanciosa
Cartographer: Anton Crane
Photo Editor: Richard Fox
Production by Wiley Indianapolis Composition Services

Front cover photo: Divi Divi Tree on Eagle Beach © Chris Ballentine/Paul
Thompson Images/Alamy Images

For information on our other products and services or to obtain technical
support, please contact our Customer Care Department within the U.S. at
877/762-2974, outside the U.S. at 317/572-3993 or fax 317/572-4002.

Wiley also publishes its books in a variety of electronic formats. Some content that appears in print may not be available in electronic formats.

Manufactured in the United States of America

5   4   3   2   1

CONTENTS

LIST OF MAPS

ACKNOWLEDGMENTS

I would like to thank Felisa Mahabal, for her accurate and lightning-fast fact-checking, and Heidi Sarna, for her ongoing inspiration. Thanks to Fern Pochettino of the AGA, for her dining insight; Rayon Koolman with ATA, who served as tour guide, social planner, and friend while in Aruba; Rolando Marin at TCB, whose endless patience and unsurpassed knowledge make every trip to Bonaire a pleasure; the dedicated staff of STINAPA; Stephen Brodbar for his research input; and Chernov Rozier at CTB, who helped me explore Curacao, the largest and most cosmopolitan of the ABC islands. Stateside, I'd like to thank the good people at The Coral Reef Alliance and the Born Free Foundation, for their insight and expertise into conservation issues. On a personal note, I'd like to thank Rick Lopez for his investigation into the nightlife of Aruba and stunt-man driving skills, and Gretchen Heldring, for braving the depths of Bonaire's waters and the heights of its cliffs.

ABOUT THE AUTHOR

Through travel writing, **Christina P. Colón** has merged her three greatest passions in life: conservation, education, and travel. With a Ph.D. in ecology and an M.A. in environmental conservation education, she has explored the jungles of Borneo, forests of Belize, shores of Bora Bora, and woodlands of the Bronx. In addition to authoring academic publications, she has produced videos, enriched websites, and authored or contributed to numerous travel guides, including *Frommer's Caribbean Ports of Call, Frommer's Caribbean Cruises & Ports of Call, Frommer's Caribbean, Cruise Vacations For Dummies, The New York Times Guide to New York City,* and several *Fodor's USA Guides.*

HOW TO CONTACT US

In researching this book, we discovered many wonderful places—hotels, restaurants, shops, and more. We're sure you'll find others. Please tell us about them, so we can share the information with your fellow travelers in upcoming editions. If you were disappointed with a recommendation, we'd love to know that, too. Please write to:

Frommer's Portable Aruba, Bonaire & Curaçao, 5th Edition
Wiley Publishing, Inc. • 111 River St. • Hoboken, NJ 07030-5774

AN ADDITIONAL NOTE

Please be advised that travel information is subject to change at any time—and this is especially true of prices. We therefore suggest that you write or call ahead for confirmation when making your travel plans. The authors, editors, and publisher cannot be held responsible for the experiences of readers while traveling. Your safety is important to us, however, so we encourage you to stay alert and be aware of your surroundings. Keep a close eye on cameras, purses, and wallets, all favorite targets of thieves and pickpockets.

FROMMER'S STAR RATINGS, ICONS & ABBREVIATIONS

Every hotel, restaurant, and attraction listing in this guide has been ranked for quality, value, service, amenities, and special features using a **star-rating system.** In country, state, and regional guides, we also rate towns and regions to help you narrow down your choices and budget your time accordingly. Hotels and restaurants are rated on a scale of zero (recommended) to three stars (exceptional). Attractions, shopping, nightlife, towns, and regions are rated according to the following scale: zero stars (recommended), one star (highly recommended), two stars (very highly recommended), and three stars (must-see).

In addition to the star-rating system, we also use **seven feature icons** that point you to the great deals, in-the-know advice, and unique experiences that separate travelers from tourists. Throughout the book, look for:

(Finds) Special finds—those places only insiders know about

(Fun Facts) Fun facts—details that make travelers more informed and their trips more fun

(Kids) Best bets for kids and advice for the whole family

(Moments) Special moments—those experiences that memories are made of

(Overrated) Places or experiences not worth your time or money

(Tips) Insider tips—great ways to save time and money

(Value) Great values—where to get the best deals

The following **abbreviations** are used for credit cards:

AE American Express	**DISC** Discover	**V** Visa
DC Diners Club	**MC** MasterCard	

TRAVEL RESOURCES AT FROMMERS.COM

Frommer's travel resources don't end with this guide. Frommer's website, **www. frommers.com,** has travel information on more than 4,000 destinations. We update features regularly, giving you access to the most current trip-planning information and the best airfare, lodging, and car-rental bargains. You can also listen to podcasts, connect with other Frommers.com members through our active-reader forums, share your travel photos, read blogs from guidebook editors and fellow travelers, and much more.

Planning Your Trip to Aruba

So many islands, so little time. With all the tropical
paradises you could visit, why would you pick Aruba for your Caribbean vacation?

Well, there's the reliably near-perfect weather. If you have only a
week away from the job, why not guarantee yourself 7 days of ideal
tanning conditions—unwaveringly sunny skies, warm temperatures,
and cooling breezes. And because the island's more of a desert than a
rainforest, the humidity's low and it hardly ever rains. Hurricanes?
Schmurricanes. There's rarely one within hundreds of miles. Aruba is
far south of the tropical-storm belt.

You like beaches? Aruba's got beaches, some of the best in the Caribbean . . . in the world, for that matter. The photos only look as if they've
been doctored. What you see is what you get: miles of white, sugary
sand; warm, gentle surf; turquoise and aqua seas; and plenty of space.

When you tire of lolling on the beach, there's scuba diving, snorkeling, great windsurfing, and all the other watersports you expect
from a sun-and-sea vacation. On land, you can golf, ride a horse,
hike, or drive an all-terrain vehicle over the island's wild and woolly
outback. Away from the beach, Aruba is a desert island full of cacti,
iguanas, and strange boulder formations. Contrasting sharply with
the resort area's serene beaches, the north coast features craggy limestone cliffs, sand dunes, and crashing breakers.

And such nice places to stay. You can choose from luxury resorts,
all-inclusives, cozy boutique hotels, and modest budget spots. They're
all well maintained and chock-full of bells and whistles to meet the
whims of most travelers. With all the package tours available, they can
be surprisingly affordable, too.

If you're a foodie, you may be surprised at how well you can eat in
Aruba. Unlike the generally standard fare in most of the Caribbean,
Aruba's culinary offerings are diverse, inventive, and often very good.

After the sun sets, there's plenty to do besides eat. You can try your
luck at one of the island's dozen casinos, take in a live Vegas-style show,
or listen to some amazing live music, including Latin jazz and Caribbean sounds such as the island's own Tumba music. Bars, clubs, booze
cruises, you name it—if you're looking for a party, you'll find it.

Learning the Local Lingo

Although English is spoken throughout Aruba, Bonaire, and Curaçao, learning a few words of the native tongue, Papiamento, can be fun.

Bon bini.	bahn *bee*-nee	Welcome.
Bon dia.	bahn *dee*-a	Good morning.
Bon tardi.	bahn *tar*-dee	Good afternoon.
Bon nochi.	bahn *no*-chee	Good evening.
Danki/Di nada.	*dahn*-kee	Thank you.
Na bo ordo.	nah bo *or*-doe	You are welcome.
Kon ta bai?	kahn tah *bye*	How are you?
Bon.	*bahn*	Good/nice.
Dushi.	*doo*-shee	Sweet/sweetheart.
Te otro biaha.	tay oh-tro bee-*ah*-ha	Until next time.

You'll find the overwhelming majority of Arubans to be genuinely friendly and welcoming. Sure, the island's totally dependent on tourism, but nobody learns to be this nice. With little history of racial or cultural conflicts, the island has no cause for animosity. As the license plates say, it's "One Happy Island." And, although Dutch is the official language, almost everyone speaks English. You'll also hear Spanish and Papiamento, the local tongue (a mix of several European, African, and Native American languages), now recognized as an official language, along with Dutch.

While safety is always a concern, Aruba enjoys one of the region's lowest crime rates, fueled in part by high employment. Though it's not uncommon to see solo senior tourists as well as solo 20-something women, it's always safer—not to mention more fun—to travel with a friend.

Enough of the good points: What's the downside? Well, if you're looking to stay in an old, converted, family-run sugar mill or immerse yourself in rich colonial history or pre-Columbian culture, you could do better elsewhere. From day one, Aruba's been pretty much of a backwater. It's still part of the Netherlands, so there's a Dutch influence, which adds a slight European flavor. A few small museums highlight the island's past and some centuries-old indigenous rock glyphs and paintings, but nobody visits Aruba for culture or history.

The people who do visit, though, come back. With 60% of visitors coming back for more, Aruba has the highest repeat-visitor rate in the Caribbean; the highest hotel-occupancy figures, too. Honeymooners, families, and couples of all ages and types fill the resorts during the

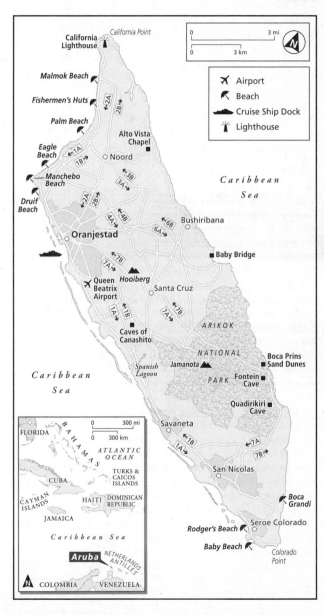

winter high season and in the traditionally quieter summer months as well. More than 70% come from the United States, and a fair number hail from Canada. Others come from Holland and South America, especially nearby Venezuela and Colombia.

The bottom line? Aruba's determined to make sure you have a good time. It's a great place to unwind, and few islands work as hard to make you feel as special and pampered. You'll learn your first Papiamento phrase when you arrive—*bon bini* (welcome!). The last words from your lips as you board your plane back home will probably be in the local dialect, too—*masha danki, Aruba* (thank you, Aruba).

Aruba is a tiny island. Only 32km (20 miles) long and 9.7km (6 miles) across at its widest point, it's slightly larger than Washington, D.C. (70 sq. miles). It's the westernmost of the Dutch ABC islands—Aruba, Bonaire, and Curaçao—and less than 32km (20 miles) north of Venezuela.

In a place as small as Aruba, it's easy to get your bearings, especially since just about everything for tourists centers on the two biggest beaches. Remember Mercury, the messenger god from Roman mythology? Aruba's shaped like his winged foot: toes to the east, heel to the west. Aruba's capital and largest city, **Oranjestad** (pronounced "oh-*rahn*-juh-stahd" or "oh-*rahn*-yay-stahd"), is on the island's southern coast, pretty far to the west, where Mercury's heel would be. The island's hotels stretch along the back-to-back shores of **Eagle Beach** and **Palm Beach,** a couple of miles west of Oranjestad, or up the god's Achilles tendon. One of the island's landmarks, the **California Lighthouse,** stands at the wing on Mercury's foot, while **San Nicolas,** once Aruba's largest city and home of the island's oil refinery, steps on his toes. Between Oranjestad and San Nicolas on the south coast, Savaneta is Aruba's oldest town and major fishing center.

If you're like most visitors, you'll be staying in one of three areas: in Oranjestad, in the Low-Rise hotel area along Eagle Beach, or a little farther from town in the High-Rise hotel area on Palm Beach. The three locations have distinct atmospheres, so where you stay will determine the tone of your vacation. Would you rather be in the city or at the seaside? Are casinos and nightclubs important, or do you prefer quiet strolls along the beach? Are you looking for a casual beach town or a glamorous resort strip?

Let's start in the thick of the action. **Oranjestad** is Aruba's only town of any size or sophistication. If you want an "urban" environment with a variety of restaurants, nightclubs, and casinos, this is the place for you. The entire island has fewer than 100,000 residents, but most seem to live or work around the capital. Its waterfront bustles with cruise ships, yachts, fishing boats, and cargo carriers. Fueled by the boutiques, restaurants, bars, and casinos radiating from the docks, vehicular and pedestrian traffic in town is heavy much of the day and night. Contributing to the congestion, Arubans cruise the main boulevard to see and be seen, giving the strip an *American Graffiti* flavor on weekend nights. The presence of a professional race-car track, the Aruba International Raceway, on the island has resulted in the appearance of a surprisingly high number of hot rods and souped-up macho machines. For more information on upcoming races, to see pictures of past events, and for directions and ticket prices, buckle your seat belt and log on to www.arubaraceway.com.

Much of the architecture combines Dutch gables and baroque ornamentation with such Caribbean colors as pistachio, ocher, pink, and aqua. The result is a sun-drenched gingerbread confection with a touch of theme-park squeaky cleanliness. Walk 5 or 6 blocks away from the waterfront, though, and Oranjestad becomes a nondescript, workaday town with neighborhoods ranging from tony to shabby. Staying in town doesn't necessarily mean sacrificing beach time: The best beaches are only minutes away, and one hotel (the Renaissance) even has its own nearby island replete with private beaches, a restaurant and bar, a spa, and a tennis court.

In sharp contrast to Oranjestad, but only a 20-minute walk west, the **Low-Rise** hotel area feels like a laid-back summer beach town. This district stretches over several contiguous strands with such names as Bushiri, Druif, Manchebo, and Eagle, but it's hard to see where one ends and another begins, and most people refer to the entire area as Eagle Beach. As the Low-Rise name implies, the dozen or so complexes here seldom climb above three or four stories. Some are directly on the beach; others are located across a relatively sleepy road. The small boutique hotels, quiet timeshares, and sprawling resorts (including several all-inclusives) attract a diverse group of people. A couple of the smaller hotels cater to couples, while the timeshares have a generally quieter, older clientele (with kids and grandkids appearing at certain times of the year). The all-inclusives and larger hotels boast all kinds of guests with an especially large number of families and children. Many apartment-style accommodations feature full kitchens, living rooms, and guest rooms, facilities attractive to families and groups of friends who want to save a bit by eating in from time to time (large supermarkets are a $6 taxi ride or 15-min. walk away). But plenty of restaurants are in the area and a couple of large casinos too. Low Risers are quick to point out that Eagle Beach is wider, quieter, and less crowded than Palm Beach, and they prefer the comfortable, casual ambience.

On the flip side, the **High-Rise** area begins about a quarter of a mile after Eagle Beach ends. Stretching along Palm Beach, this strip of glitzy High-Rise resorts is Aruba's Waikiki. The dozen or so hotels

Frommer's Favorite Aruba Experiences

Bake on the beach. This is why you came: powdery white sand, turquoise water, and soothingly monotonous waves. Whether basking at Palm, Eagle, Manchebo, or Druif Beach, close your eyes and feel the stress evaporate. You're a beach potato; use sunscreen or you'll be a fried potato.

Get dirty. If you love the rugged outdoors, spend the better part of a day hiking, biking, driving, horseback riding, or off-roading through expansive Arikok National Park to marvel at Aruba's diverse ecosystems and rural past. Ramble over hills strewn with boulders and cacti, visit old farms (known as *cunucus*), spelunk through caves in search of Indian rock glyphs, and slide down sand dunes. Along the way, you'll meet hummingbirds, hawks, iguanas, goats, and donkeys.

Chow down. Dining in Aruba is a daily ritual of indulgence and romance. Most restaurants have picturesque settings, with both indoor and outdoor seating, often on or overlooking the water. The service is consistently good and the food is among the best in the Caribbean. Whether you opt for a local favorite on the cheap, or a French classic that breaks the bank, you are guaranteed to stagger back to your hotel

here tend to be swanky, self-contained resorts that ramble over acres of lushly landscaped grounds. Most boast splashy casinos, numerous restaurants and bars, and endless amenities and services. Some hotels here are definitely upscale, and others are perfectly middle class: Whether you're a big cheese or small potato, there's a place here to suit your budget. These hotels, unlike the Low Risers, are full-fledged glamour destinations. And if you're totally focused on sun time, you'll appreciate that all but a couple of the resorts are directly on the beach (the others are just across the street). The area also offers more places to eat, drink, and gamble, and its piers are a hubbub of dive boats and motorized watersports. However, with the increased number of amenities and giant resorts, Palm Beach doesn't offer the Low-Rise area's beach-town simplicity, and it's comparatively crowded.

room sated and happy as a stuffed clam marinated in a dry martini.

Play Jacques Cousteau. Aruba has some of the best wreck dives in the Caribbean. In fact, Aruba boasts the largest sunken vessel in the Caribbean and has some of the most haunting and accessible sunken ships this side of the *Titanic.* If you'd rather not get wet, you can still descend 45m (148 ft.) below the surface to make friends with a variety of marine critters from the comfort of a tiptop submarine or semisubmersible boat.

Come sail away. The turquoise Caribbean water that surrounds Aruba is even more captivating when you are sailing across it. Whether you choose a sleek catamaran, teak schooner, teeny trimaran, or a windsurf board or kiteboard, as the saying goes: *Just do it!*

Toast the setting sun. Aruba's picture-perfect days almost invariably melt into picture-perfect sunsets. What better way to round off the day than with a tropical drink at sunset; so grab a front-row seat at one of the many stylish bars on the beach, or on the water, or overlooking the harbor and drink up while you drink in the view.

Aside from the big three, you have a couple of other options when deciding where to stay. Next to the island's championship golf course **Tierra del Sol,** condominiums and free-standing villas appeal to vacationers who prefer time on the links to hours on the beach. This complex looks and feels like a desert resort in Arizona, and short-term rentals are available.

For the serious budget option, a handful of **motels** can be found a 10- to 20-minute walk inland from the beaches. They lack the glamour of the larger resorts, but they make Aruba affordable for almost everyone.

Away from the hotels and the capital, Aruba features splendid, if modest, natural wonders, more great beaches, and a handful of authentically native towns. But more about exploring the island later in the book.

THE WEATHER

Almost invariably, the weather is wonderful—warm, sunny, dry, and breezy. There's no monsoon season and no threat of tropical storms—the island is far outside the hurricane belt. The average annual temperature is 82°F (28°C), and no month of the year has an average high temperature lower than 85°F (29°C) or higher than 89°F (32°C). Lows range from 76°F (24°C) to 80°F (27°C).

The sun can be hot, and its reflection off the white sandy beaches is blinding. Fortunately, the almost-constant trade winds make it easy to forget just how warm it is. Usually a godsend, these pleasant, gentle breezes can occasionally escalate to surprising gusts or sustained winds, so hold onto your hat. Better yet, buy one with a chin strap, and no they're not all dorky. With the right attitude, anyone can pull off a straw cowboy hat; these hats are readily available at most souvenir shops. In September, though, you'll wish the breezes were back. Tropical storms plaguing less-fortunate islands far to the north suck away the trade winds during that back-to-school month, making Aruba as hot as any other spot in the Caribbean. Unless you fancy relentless heat with no relieving breezes, avoid visiting in September.

The wind provides a collateral perk, too. It blows away annoying mosquitoes and other flying pests. That said, with the creation of so many new High-Rise hotels, the breezes aren't nearly as strong as they once were. So when the breezes wane, it's time to bring out the insect repellent. Aruba's dry, though, so you'll never encounter the number of bugs that infest more lush islands.

Rainfall averages about 46 centimeters (18 in.) a year, with most precipitation falling from October through January. Even then rains tend to be erratic and brief and it's rare for the sun not to shine most of the day.

Another plus: The humidity is less oppressive in Aruba than in most of the Caribbean. Although not exactly Arizona, the island's more dusty than sultry.

HURRICANES The curse of much of the Caribbean, hurricanes are something you can gleefully ignore if you're vacationing in Aruba. The island is miles and miles from the storms that wreak havoc on much of the region from June to November. On rare occasions, storm activity far to the north is so violent that it causes wave action to ripple in Aruba. Some damage has occurred over the years, but it's relatively negligible.

THE HIGH SEASON & THE OFF SEASON

Because the weather is consistently nice year-round, Aruba's high and low seasons reflect climates in the United States and Canada rather than the weather on the island itself. When it's cold and wintery in North America, demand for Aruba's warmth and sunshine peaks. Roughly speaking, the island's high season runs from mid-December to mid-April. During this period, hotels charge their highest prices, and you'll need to reserve a room well in advance—months in advance if you want to bask on the beach over Christmas or in the depths of February. Guests during the high season tend to be older and wealthier, although there are plenty of families. The national mix weighs heavily toward Americans and Canadians.

The off season—roughly from mid-April to mid-December (although it varies from hotel to hotel)—is one big summer sale. All resorts routinely slash their room rates, which means you can get the same accommodations in the low season for 20% to 50% less than you would in darkest winter.

But if you think Aruba's a ghost town in the summer, think again. The deals are so attractive, and the season dovetails so nicely with Europe's traditional vacation time and South America's winter, that the island's resorts are still pretty full. The mix of visitors shifts in the summer toward families, Europeans (especially Dutch), South Americans, and the more budget conscious from everywhere. Americans still make up the largest national group.

Some activities and attractions scale back a bit in the summer, but not much. For example, instead of six excursions a day, a tour operator may offer only three; restaurants might close an hour earlier; and hotels may use the "downtime" for new construction or renovation (ask if work is scheduled; if it's potentially disturbing, request a room far away from the noise).

If you're single and want crowds, don't worry. Lots of potential playmates are around in the summer, too.

Because the difference in high-season and low-season rates at most hotels is drastic, I've included both in chapter 2. See for yourself how much you can save if you wait a bit for your fun in the sun.

Since the global economic downturn in early 2009, the travel industry worldwide has suffered, because people are more reluctant to indulge in a vacation. Aruba's tourist-based economy has at times been hit hard. But there is a silver lining; in uncertain times, fearless, opportunistic travelers can find significant bargains. For example, many restaurants are now offering early-bird specials, prix-fixe meals, and free appetizers or cocktails with a coupon. Some even let children eat for free. The offerings change weekly. When times are lean, keep an eye out for these deals, which are advertised in tourism brochures and fliers and on websites.

HOLIDAYS

Most stores and restaurants close on official holidays. If you stay near the resort areas, however, you may not be affected at all. Here's a list of Aruba's holidays: January 1 (New Year's Day); January 25 (Betico Croes Day); February 15, 2010 (Carnival Monday); February 24, 2010 (Fat Tuesday); February 25, 2010 (Ash Wednesday); March 18 (National Anthem and Flag Day); April 2, 2010 (Good Friday); April 10, 2010 (Easter Sunday); April 30 (Queen's Birthday); May 1 (Aruba's Labor Day); May 13, 2010 (Ascension Day); December 25 (Christmas Day); and December 26 (Boxing Day).

ARUBA CALENDAR OF EVENTS

For an updated list of events, and specific dates, times, and locations, contact the **Aruba Tourism Authority** (© **800/TO-ARUBA** [862-7822]; www.aruba.com/ourpeopleplaces/events.aspx) or check http://events.frommers.com, where you'll find a searchable, up-to-the-minute roster of what's happening in cities all over the world.

JANUARY

Dande. For almost 200 years, roaming troubadours have marked the end of the old year and the beginning of the new in Aruba. As the clock strikes midnight, groups of musicians go from house to house serenading each family with good wishes for the coming year. If the dande group misses your home, you'll have nothing but bad luck in the coming year. Some families set off fireworks after they've been serenaded, and the mother of the house often sweeps out the "old spirit." January 1.

Betico Croes Day. G. F. "Betico" Croes, Aruba's seminal political leader, was instrumental in the island's fight for "Status Aparte"—semi-independence from Holland and autonomy from the other Dutch islands in the Caribbean. Low-key patriotic observances mark the holiday. January 25.

Carnival. Highlights of Aruba's version of pre-Lenten revelry include the Children's Parade (toddlers, dwarfed by their elaborate costumes, dance down the street) and the Grand Carnival parades in Oranjestad and San Nicolas (calypso, marching, and drumming contests accompanied by monstrous sound systems). During the Tivoli Lighting Parade, thousands of miniature lights blanket the costumes and floats. Representatives of the island's various districts vie for the title of carnival queen, and unsuspecting tourists, whisked off their planes, help decide the winner. The parties, dancing, and music begin in January, culminating on the weekend before Ash Wednesday. Early January to late February.

MARCH

National Anthem and Flag Day. In celebration of Aruba's flag, anthem, and autonomy, nationalistic exhibits, folkloric presentations, and fireworks displays take place islandwide. Children sing the national anthem—on the streets, on television, and on the radio—*ad infinitum* and off-key. March 18.

APRIL

Queen's Birthday. To celebrate the birthday of Queen Beatrix of the Netherlands, kite contests, sporting events, and cultural programs are held around the island. April 30.

MAY

Aruba Food & Wine Festival. The annual food and wine tasting event features a pastry extravaganza with famous chefs showcasing their talents. This 3-day culinary event concludes with a concert highlighting the celebration of a renowned international musical band or artist. Late May.

Soul Beach Music Festival. This star-studded event (www.soul beach.net) takes place over Memorial Day weekend. Performers in the past have included Wyclef Jean, Sean Paul, Chaka Khan, and other renowned rhythm-and-blues performers. Held at the Havana Beach Club, this festival also includes comedy, beach parties, and plenty of nightclub action. Memorial Day weekend.

JUNE

Dera Gai (St. John's Day). Centuries ago, after harvesting crops, the island's indigenous people built bonfires, and then challenged one another to jump over them. Storytelling, music, dancing, and food and drink fueled the merriment. Later a rooster was buried up to its neck and covered with a calabash gourd. Blindfolded men with sticks had three chances to "find" the rooster; the winner kept the fowl for dinner. Today a dummy rooster is used, but the music and dancing persist. Crop remnants and other disposable items are buried in a symbolic soul cleansing. June 24.

International Triathalon. Competitors from around the world participate in a triathlon including a 1.5K swim, 40K bike race, and a 10K run. More than 100 athletes usually participate in the event, hosted by the Aruba Triathlon Association. Late June.

JULY

Hi-Winds World Challenge. Windsurfers and kiteboarders from multiple countries gather at Hadicurari, or Fishermen's Huts, just north of the High-Rise hotels, for one of the most popular competitions in the Caribbean (www.aruba-hiwinds.org). Early July.

Aruba Music Festival, Oranjestad. Bands from around the Caribbean perform in a free concert. First week of July.

Aruba Reef Care Project. Joining forces to raise awareness of the marine environment, certified divers, snorkelers, and topsiders clean up beaches and underwater sites. First weekend in July.

AUGUST

Aruba International Pro-Am Golf Tournament. Professional and amateur golfers team up in this 2-day, 36-hole tournament that features prizes, special events, and parties. Late August.

SEPTEMBER

Caribbean Sea Jazz Festival. This outdoor festival features international and local musicians at Cas di Cultura (www.caribbean seajazz.com). Early September.

Ultimatebet.com Aruba Poker Classic and Blackjack Tournament. This no-limit Texas hold 'em poker tournament brings together players from all over the world to compete for millions of dollars (www.ultimatebet.com). Late September.

OCTOBER

Annual Aruba Music Festival. This annual event features musical heavyweights—past performers include Crosby, Stills, and Nash; Jackson Brown; John Mayer; and Chicago. Columbus Day weekend.

NOVEMBER

Aruba Heinekin Catamaran Regatta. This international catamaran regatta decorates Aruba's waters with the colorful sails of catamarans from Europe. The event represents a great opportunity for experienced yacht racers as well as recreational sailors. For more information visit www.arubaregatta.com. Early November.

Aruba Beach Tennis International Championship. Aruba is one of the first countries to host an international tournament in the new sport of beach tennis (www.arubabeachtennis.com). International beach tennis pros come down to play, and a large number of amateurs participate as well. Competitions are held at Moomba Beach. Mid-November.

DECEMBER

Sint Nicolaas Day, Oranjestad. Sint Nicolaas arrives at Paardenbaai Harbor in Oranjestad to greet Aruba's children and reward them with gifts for their good behavior during the year. December 5.

2 ENTRY REQUIREMENTS

PASSPORTS

U.S. and Canadian citizens need a valid passport to enter Aruba. Citizens of a member country of the European Union need a passport and an E.U. Travel Card. A valid passport is required of all other nationalities. When you arrive in Aruba, be prepared to show an onward or return ticket or proof of sufficient funds for your stay.

Before leaving home, make two copies of your passport, driver's license, airline ticket, and hotel vouchers. Leave one copy with someone at home; carry the other with you separately from your passport. If you lose your papers, you'll be glad you took the trouble.

VISAS

Americans, Canadians, Australians, New Zealanders, and E.U. nationals can stay in Aruba for up to 1 month without a visa. Timeshare and home owners are allowed to stay on island up to 180 days. If you plan to stay longer, get a visa application from the **Institute of Vigilance & Security Aruba (IASA)** in Aruba (© **297/587-7444;** fax 297/587-1077) or at a Dutch embassy or consulate.

For information on obtaining a visa, please see "Fast Facts," on p. 190.

CUSTOMS

Aruba Customs regulations allow incoming visitors to bring articles for personal use. Persons 19 and over can also bring in 2.25 liters of wine, 3 liters of beer, or 1 liter of liquor and 200 cigarettes, 25 cigars, and 250 grams of tobacco.

For information on what you're allowed to take home, contact one of the following agencies:

U.S. Citizens: U.S. Customs & Border Protection (CBP), 1300 Pennsylvania Ave., NW, Washington, DC 20229 (© **877/287-8667;** www.cbp.gov).

Canadian Citizens: Canada Border Services Agency (© **800/ 461-9999** in Canada, or 204/983-3500; www.cbsa-asfc.gc.ca).

U.K. Citizens: HM Customs & Excise (© **0845/010-9000;** or 020/8929-0152 from outside the U.K.; www.hmce.gov.uk).

Australian Citizens: Australian Customs Service (© **1300/363-263;** www.customs.gov.au).

New Zealand Citizens: New Zealand Customs, the Customhouse, 17–21 Whitmore St., Box 2218, Wellington (© **04/473-6099** or 0800/428-786; www.customs.govt.nz).

MEDICAL REQUIREMENTS

There are no vaccinations required for entry to Aruba, Bonaire, or Curaçao. For more information see "Health" on p. 21.

---

3 GETTING THERE & GETTING AROUND

GETTING TO ARUBA
By Plane

Aruba's airport, **Queen Beatrix International Airport** (airport code AUA; www.airportaruba.com) is clean, modern, and organized. Unless your flight arrives with several others (it may on weekends), the lines through Immigration and Customs move rapidly. Luggage won't make it to the conveyer belts as fast as you'd like, but once it arrives there are plenty of free luggage carts available. The terminal has a bank and an ATM, a cellphone kiosk, and tourism desk. Most stores are in the departing passenger lounges, but in the courtyard to your left as you leave the U.S. arrivals building, a handful of small shops sell books, souvenirs, and snacks.

As of 2009, there are seven airlines that make regularly scheduled nonstop flights to Aruba from the U.S. and Europe. American Airlines once dominated the route, but Continental, Delta, United, and US Airways have joined the fray. There are even nonstop flights from Canada via Air Canada. Although the number of flights generally increases during the high season, airlines may alter service depending on demand (and their own financial condition). There are also chartered flights from the U.S., U.K., and Australia, so ask your travel agent if you can get in on one of those.

Charter flights offer an alternative for both Canadians and Americans. If you've booked a package through a large tour operator, your flight might be a charter anyway. Charters serve Atlanta, Baltimore, Boston, Charlotte, Chicago, Cincinnati, Cleveland, Dallas, Detroit, Hartford, Louisville, Memphis, Milwaukee, Minneapolis, Nashville, New York, Philadelphia, Pittsburgh, St. Louis, and Toronto.

To find out which airlines travel to Aruba, please see "Airline, Hotel & Car Rental Websites," p. 193.

Getting into Town from the Airport

In the interest of protecting cabdrivers' livelihood, Aruban law precludes hotels from picking up guests at the airport. If you've come on a package tour, your ground transportation voucher gives you a seat on one of the privately operated, air-conditioned buses that take arriving passengers to the hotels. Otherwise, you can take a cab.

> ## ⓘ Tips Hassle-Free Return to the States
>
> You just arrived, but remember this for later. Because U.S. Customs and Immigration agents are stationed at Aruba's airport, formalities for reentry to the United States are taken care of before you board your plane for home. Though that means no long lines to wait in when you get back to the U.S., it can mean a considerable wait before you board, so be sure to arrive at the Aruba airport 3 hours before your plane is scheduled to depart.

Fixed, regulated fares are $13 to Oranjestad, $17 to the Low-Rise hotels, $20 to the High Rises, and $25 or so to Tierra del Sol. Taxis line up outside the terminal and can accommodate up to five passengers. If you want to get behind the wheel of your own car, 20 or so car-rental kiosks await you on the other side of the taxis (see "Airline, Hotel & Car Rental Websites," p. 193). The drive from the airport to the hotels is usually 10 to 30 minutes, depending on traffic and the time of day.

By Cruise Ship

In 2009, 285 cruise ships brought 500,000 visitors to Aruba. Royal Caribbean and Princess ships begin itineraries in Aruba, and Celebrity, Crystal, Holland America, Fred Olsen, Norwegian, P&O Cruises, Princess, and Royal Caribbean all have ships that make port calls here.

Cruisers arrive at the **Aruba Ports Authority** (www.arubaports. com), a modern terminal with a tourist information booth, ATMs, and plenty of shops. From the pier, it's a 5-minute walk to the immediately evident shopping districts of downtown Oranjestad. If you're not taking a shore excursion, you can make your way around on your own, allowing some time for the beach (just a 5- to 10-min. taxi ride away), lunch, and shopping. Taxis line up to take cruisers to the beach; if you want to save money, the bus terminal is practically as close as the cabs: After you've walked to the main harborfront road, look for the large pastel bus shelter to your right. Most buses serve the resort areas, but before boarding, ask your driver if he's headed your way. The trip to the Low-Rise area takes about 15 minutes; to the High-Rise area, add another 5 to 10 minutes. Same-day round-trip fare between the beach hotels and the Oranjestad station is $2; a one-way ride is $1.15 to $1.25. Make sure you have exact change.

Still a large cargo port, Oranjestad is separating its cruise and cargo facilities and beefing up passenger terminal services. For more information, contact the **Cruise Tourism Authority,** Royal Plaza Mall, Ste. 230, L.G. Smith Blvd. 94, Oranjestad (© **297/583-3648;** www.arubabycruise.com).

GETTING AROUND

BY RENTAL CAR   It's easy to rent a car in Aruba. Decent roads connect major tourist attractions, and all the major rental companies honor valid U.S., British, Australian, and Canadian driver's licenses, provided you are at least 23 and have had a valid license for at least 3 years. Most major U.S. car-rental companies and a variety of reputable local operators maintain offices at the airport and at major hotels; others have free delivery and pickup service. There's no tax on car rentals, but even if you purchase a collision-damage waiver, you're responsible for the first $300 to $500 worth of damage. Rental rates for cars, usually Suzukis, Toyotas, Kias, Hyundais, or Jeeps, vary from season to season and from dealer to dealer. Gas is expensive compared to North America. All service stations charge the same price, and there's no discount for self-service.

Is it necessary to rent a car? It depends. If you want to explore the island, go ahead and get one for a day or two or three; many of the local agencies have 3-day specials. If you have no intention of leaving your resort except to dine, gamble, and shop, it's cheaper to take cabs or the reliable buses. Or you can book a half-day jeep, ATV, or dune buggy excursion that will allow you to explore the island as part of an off-road caravan, where you get to see the wild side of Aruba but not worry about getting lost.

(Tips)   Rules of the Road

As in the U.S. and Canada, driving is on the right side of the road. Traffic signs use international symbols; most are self-explanatory, but some aren't. Ask your car-rental agency for a sheet of the symbols, and take a few minutes to familiarize yourself with them. There are no right turns on red. Car speedometers are in kilometers and mph. The speed limit in urban areas is 25 mph and out of town it's 50 mph, unless otherwise posted. Much of Oranjestad's traffic is one-way; at intersections where there are no road signs, traffic from your right has the right of way. An increase in the number of cars on the islands means traffic can become a little congested just before 9am and just after 5pm on weekdays. Saturday night in Oranjestad can rival traffic in Times Square.

| (Tips) **Driving Hazards**

Most of Aruba's roads are pretty good, but the traffic signs leave much to be desired. Few streets outside of Oranjestad are marked, and signs to major tourist attractions look as if they were made by neighborhood kids decades ago. Try to keep your eye on the road, though, because iguanas and goats pose unusual traffic hazards. Arubans are considerate, cautious drivers for the most part, although they seem to drive either too fast or too slow. For a small town, Oranjestad has big-city traffic much of the day. Seat-belt laws exist but are often ignored, as are drunk-driving laws. Headgear is required by law for all two-wheel vehicles, but be warned; some rental helmets bear the following caveat: THIS HELMET IS A NOVELTY ITEM; AND IS NOT INTENDED FOR USE AS PROTECTIVE HEADGEAR.

To rent a car, try **Avis** at the cruise terminal, Schotlandstraat 85 (© **800/331-1212** in the U.S., or 297/582-7202 in Aruba; www. avis.com); **Budget** at the airport (© **800/472-3325** in the U.S., or 297/582-8600 in Aruba; www.budget.com); **Dollar** at the airport (© **800/800-3665** in the U.S. or 297/583-3101 in Aruba; www. dollar.com); **Hertz** has multiple locations, including the airport and Oranjestad (© **800/654-3001** in the U.S., or 297/588-7570 in Aruba; www.hertz.com); **National** at the airport (© **800/227-3876** in the U.S., or 297/582-5451 in Aruba; www.nationalcar.com); or **Thrifty Car Rental** at the airport (© **800/THRIFTY** [847-4389], or 297/583-5335 in Aruba; www.thrifty.com). During the high season, expect to pay $60 to $65 per day for a compact car, $90 per day for a four-wheel-drive vehicle. During the low season, rates drop to $40 to $45 for a compact, $60 to $85 for a jeep.

For a better deal, try one of the reputable local agencies, such as **Explore Car Rental,** Schotlandstraat 85 (© **297/582-7202;** www. explorecarrental.com); **Economy Car Rental,** Bushiri 27 (© **866/ 978-5780** or 297/583-0200; www.economyaruba.com); or **Amigo Rent-a-Car,** Schotlandstraat 56 (© **297/583-8833;** www.amigocar. com). You can make reservations online; look for online specials.

For more information on car rental companies in Aruba, please see "Airline, Hotel & Car Rental Websites," p. 193.

BY BUS Aruba has an excellent public bus system, with regular, reliable service. Buses run roughly every 20 minutes from 8am to 6pm and every hour from 6pm to midnight, Monday through Saturday. On Sunday and holidays, service is less frequent: every half-hour between 6am and 6pm and every 2 hours between 8pm and midnight. A same-day one-way ride is about $1.20, or $2.30 round-trip. It's best to have exact change. Schedules are available at the **Arubus** office (© **297/588-2300** or 588-0617 after 4pm; www.arubus.com) at the central terminal on Zoutmanstraat in Oranjestad, but your hotel's reception desk will know when buses pass by. You'll seldom wait more than 20 minutes for the next coach or minibus. The trip into town takes 10 to 20 minutes. There's a stop in front of most hotels.

BY TAXI Taxis are nonmetered but rates are fixed, and every cab has a copy of the official rate schedule. Tell the driver where you're going and ask the fare before you get in. Hailing a taxi on the street is difficult, but you'll find plenty of cabs at hotels. To return to your resort from dinner, have the restaurant call for a car. The dispatch office is inland from the Low Rises on Pos Abou, behind the Eagle Bowling Palace on the Sasaki road (© **297/582-2116**). Tip 10% to 15%. Because it's next to impossible to find a taxi in remoter parts of the island, ask the driver who dropped you off to return for you at a certain time. Most drivers speak good English and are willing, even eager, to give you a tour of the island. Expect to pay $45 per hour for a maximum of five passengers. Following are rates for the most common routes:

- From High-Rise hotels: $8 to Low-Rise hotels; $10 to Noord restaurants and Oranjestad; $20 to the airport
- From Low-Rise hotels: $8 to High-Rise hotels; $10 to Noord restaurants and Oranjestad; $17 to the airport
- From Oranjestad hotels: $8 to Low-Rise hotels; $10 to Noord restaurants and High-Rise hotels; $13 to the airport

A surcharge of $3 is added on Sunday, holidays, and after midnight. The minimum fare is $5. Waiting time is $3 per 5 minutes. A surcharge of $2 is also levied for additional pieces of luggage over one per person. Shirtless, wet, or damp passengers are not allowed, and you're charged $50 for seat damage from wet clothing or sharp objects.

BY MOTORCYCLE & SCOOTER Because Aruba's roads are good and the terrain is flat, mopeds and motorcycles are another transit option. They're available at **George's Cycle Center,** L.G. Smith Blvd. 124 (© **297/993-2202**). Scooters rent for $40 per day, motorcycles for $70 to $120. For $150 a day or $95 for 4 hours during the high season ($100 or $85 in the off season), you can go hog-wild and rent a Harley (HOG members get a $10 discount during the high season). **Big Twin Aruba,** L.G. Smith Blvd. 124A (© **297/582-8660;** www. harleydavidson-aruba.com) offers half-day tours for $130 and full-day tours for $163.

4 MONEY & COSTS

Let's face it, Aruba ain't cheap. Well-known for its glitzy hotels, exclusive boutique resorts, and over-the-top restaurants, Aruba has a few bargains to offer. Keep in mind, everything has to be flown in and almost no food is produced on the island. For this reason, and because it's marketed to an upscale audience, prices are easily on par with those in similarly ranked restaurants in New York or London. Bank machines are readily available in shopping malls, and in addition to a couple of bucks for fees, you will likely pay a currency conversion fee. Banks may have slightly better prices, but since U.S. dollars are widely accepted, if you have these, you are better off using them and asking for dollars back when you are given change.

Aruba is not a bargain shopper's paradise compared to cheaper Caribbean destinations such as Mexico or the Dominican Republic. The upside is that the standard of living among Arubans is fairly high, and the island lacks grim scenes of abject poverty or hopelessness. There are also some easy ways to save cash. While a taxi to the airport or into town will cost you $15 or $20 dollars, you can ride the clean local buses for about $1.25. A cup of coffee may cost you the usual $3 but most hotels have beverage makers and you don't need to use bottled water since the island has some of the cleanest water in the world. While a three-course dinner at even a moderate restaurant (sans alcohol) can set you back $50, the portions are so enormous that you can easily share one appetizer, main course, and dessert between two people and be sated. Most hotel rooms will run you about $150 and up, but if you opt for a small inn catering to locals that is a short walk or bus ride to the beach, you can probably find a deal under $50.

CASH/CURRENCY The U.S. dollar is as widely accepted as the **Aruban florin (AWG),** and most items and services are priced in both currencies.

The AWG is divided into 100¢. Silver coins come in denominations of 5¢, 10¢, 25¢, and 50¢ as well as 1, 2$^1/_2$, and 5 florins. The 50¢ piece, the square *yotin,* is Aruba's best-known coin. Paper currency comes in denominations of 5, 10, 25, 50, and 100 florins. At press time, the (fairly stable) exchange rate was 1.78 AWG to $1 (1 AWG is worth about US56¢). Hotels, restaurants, and stores accept dollars at rates of between 1.75 and 1.80 AWG; supermarkets and gas stations use a conversion rate of 1.75 AWG to the dollar.

The currency used in the neighboring Dutch islands of Curaçao and Bonaire, the Netherlands Antillean florin (NAf), is not accepted in Aruba.

Note: Since U.S. dollars are accepted almost everywhere in Aruba, prices are quoted in U.S. dollars throughout this book.

The Value of the Aruban Florin (AWG) vs. Other Popular Currencies

AWG	US$	C$	UK£	Euro €	A$	NZ$
1.00	0.56	0.65	0.36	0.39	0.73	0.94

ATMS   Aruba has plenty of cash machines—at the airport; in Oranjestad, in Noord, at the Allegro, Holiday Inn, Hyatt, Marriott Playa Linda, and Radisson in the High-Rise area; and at La Cabana in the Low-Rise area. Your hotel can steer you in the right direction, and an ATM is never far away. Most dispense both florins and dollars. Since you can expect to pay a fee of about $3 per transaction, take out as much as you estimate you'll really need rather than taking out a small amount and planning to go back later.

CREDIT CARDS   Major credit cards are almost universally accepted in Aruba. Visa and MasterCard seem to dominate the landscape, with Discover making a comeback and American Express being at times shunned due to the alleged fees it charges. Diners Club is rarely accepted. In any case, you'll still need good old paper money for small purchases, cabs, and the occasional restaurant or small shop. Luckily, U.S. dollars are often accepted and you can request them when getting change as well.

If your credit card is lost or stolen, contact your credit card company immediately. In Aruba, both **MasterCard** and **Visa** cardholders can visit branches of **Aruba Bank** (© **800/325-3678**) or **Caribbean Mercantile Bank** (© **954/846-1585**) for cash advances or to report a lost or stolen card. **Discover** cardholders can get assistance by calling © **800/DISCOVER** (347-2683), or 801/902-3100 in Aruba (www.discover.com). **American Express** cardholders and traveler's check holders should call © **800/221-7282** for assistance.

If you lose your card, chances are slim that the police will find it. Notify them anyway: Lots of credit card companies and insurers require a police-report number.

TRAVELER'S CHECKS   Traveler's checks are becoming relics now that ATMs make cash accessible 24/7. If you want to avoid ATM service charges, though, or if you just want the security of knowing you can get a refund if your wallet's stolen, go ahead and get traveler's checks. You'll have to show identification every time you cash one. Most banks sell them, and most Aruban businesses accept them. Be sure to keep a record of the serial numbers (separate from the checks, of course). You'll need the numbers to get a refund if your checks are lost or stolen.

Tips **Arm Yourself with Small Bills**

Before you leave home, amass a bundle of small bills to make for easy tipping and small purchases.

You can get **American Express** traveler's checks by calling ⓒ **800/ 221-7282** or visiting www.americanexpress.com. Traveler's checks are also offered through **Thomas Cook Currency Services** (ⓒ **800/223-9920**).

TAXES, SERVICE CHARGES & TIPPING   Aruba has a 3% sales tax, but it is unclear whether merchants will charge that when you make a purchase or simply incorporate it into their prices, so its best to ask before you buy. Hotels charge an 11% government tax on rooms, and most routinely add 5% to 7% for "service." A few resorts may also charge an energy surcharge of $4 to $8 per unit per night.

Most, but not all, restaurants charge 10% to 15% for service, but not all of this goes to the service staff. Some restaurants keep a percentage for overhead, while the rest is distributed among all restaurant personnel; so you are generally expected to leave a little extra cash on the table (say 10%). If no charge is included in your tab, leave 15%, or 20% if the service was excellent.

Taxi drivers expect 10% to 15%, and porters should get about $2 per bag. Some of the hotel service charge should trickle down to the chambermaids, but if you're staying in a nice place, leave $2 per day for the housekeeper anyway. For spa treatments, if a service charge is not included, leave 15%.

5 HEALTH

STAYING HEALTHY

Keep the following suggestions in mind when traveling in Aruba:

- You can relax about water. Aruba's tap water is completely safe to drink and tastes fine. In fact, it's among the best in the world.
- Aruba's sun can be brutal. Wear sunglasses and a hat (with a strap—remember the wind) and use high SPF sunscreen liberally. The best sunscreens contain zinc oxide, titanium dioxide, or avobenzone (check "active ingredients" on the label). Limit your time on the beach in the first day or two, or wear a coverup. If you get burned, stay out of the sun until you recover and get some locally made aloe gel.

- The wind is usually strong enough to blow mosquitoes away, but the pests can sometimes be a nuisance anyway. Malaria's not a concern, but bring insect repellent for your own comfort.
- Food is generally safe in Aruba. Be careful if you encounter street vendors. Make sure that what you get is hot and that it hasn't been sitting out for any length of time.
- The **United States Centers for Disease Control and Prevention (CDC; ✆ 800/CDC-INFO** [232-4636]; www.cdc.gov/travel) provides up-to-date information on necessary vaccines and health hazards by region or country. Unfortunately, its information on Aruba is lumped with the other Caribbean islands, most of which lack Aruba's generally modern and sanitary conditions.
- Pack prescription medications in your carry-on luggage. Carry written prescriptions with generic names, not brand names, and dispense all medications from their originally labeled vials.

WHAT TO DO IF YOU GET SICK

Finding a good doctor in Aruba is not a problem, and all speak good English. Hotels have physicians on call, and the modern **Horacio Oduber Hospital,** L.G. Smith Boulevard, near Eagle Beach (✆ 297/ 587-4300,** also the number to call in case of a medical emergency; www.arubahospital.com), has excellent medical facilities, including a new recompression chamber. If you have an emergency while you're on the eastern end of the island, San Nicolas has a medical center, the **Centro Médico,** Avicenastraat 16 (✆ 297/588-5548). Consulting hours are limited, but emergency assistance is available 24 hours a day, 7 days a week. **Labco Medical and Homecare Service,** Fergusonstraat 52, P.O. Box 1147 (✆ 297/582-6651), rents wheelchairs, walkers, crutches, bedpans, and other medical equipment. If your emergency cannot be handled locally, **Air Ambulance** (✆ 297/582-9197) service is available to Curaçao, Venezuela, and all U.S. cities. The island's dental facilities are good; make appointments through your hotel.

---

6 SAFETY

Aruba is one of the Caribbean's safest destinations. Don't leave your valuables unattended on the beach or in an unlocked car, though. All hotels have safes, most of which will fit a laptop. Place electronics as well as airline tickets, jewelry, and passports inside.

Since the drinking age is 18 in Aruba, parents with teenage children should lay down clear ground rules about drinking before the trip. Young women are at times encouraged to drink too much, particularly on booze cruises or other venues where the alcohol is included, so it's recommended that such outings be enjoyed by groups of three or more, with the understanding that no one leaves the group, even if that hunky bartender is absolutely irresistible.

Full-moon parties and other ravelike beach bashes are increasingly common, and while they are mostly harmless fun, keep in mind that a density of people plied with alcohol and subjected to deafening music is a perfect venue for pickpockets, pickup lines, and the occasional drunken hookup.

There are few scammers or petty criminals, although drinking and driving is fairly common, so take care when driving on unfamiliar roads late at night. That said, in some remote areas, you are more likely to encounter a donkey or a ditch than an oncoming vehicle, but these can be just as treacherous, so proceed with caution.

7 SPECIALIZED TRAVEL RESOURCES

In addition to the destination-specific resources listed below, please visit Frommers.com for additional specialized travel resources.

GAY & LESBIAN TRAVELERS

Arubans seem genuinely confounded when asked about homophobia on the island. People here pride themselves on Aruba's diversity, and most are gentle and remarkably nonjudgmental, certainly of tourists, but also of their gay and lesbian neighbors. Compared to notoriously homophobic Jamaica and Grand Cayman Island, Aruba is truly gay friendly. Homosexuality is a nonissue here.

Some Arubans are out, especially those under age 40; others aren't. Those who are live pretty much like their straight friends and family. Gay visibility, especially in the hotel, restaurant, and entertainment industries, is undeniable. The influx of no-apologies gay Latinos over the past few years has increased gay visibility significantly. And if it's any indication, the island's top show for almost a decade was a drag-queen extravaganza.

Hyatt, Renaissance, and Bucuti Beach are all approved as gay-friendly lodgings by the Travel Alternative's Group or TAG. For additional information on traveling and staying at gay-friendly destinations, log on to www.tagapproved.com.

TRAVELERS WITH DISABILITIES

Traveling with a disability is seldom a piece of cake, and like most places, Aruba could do more to welcome vacationers with disabilities.

1

Queen Beatrix International Airport was renovated in 2000, yet facilities compliant with the Americans with Disabilities Act (ADA) weren't part of the overhaul. Instead, the facility has a truck to transfer wheelchair passengers from planes to the terminal using a special ramp and door.

Many resorts boast ADA-compliant facilities, including the Marriott, Holiday Inn, Hyatt Regency, Marriott's Aruba Ocean Club, Radisson, and Divi Phoenix. The Costa Linda even has a beach wheelchair. Many other hotels are equipped for wheelchairs, including the Aruba Grand, Renaissance, Costa Linda, and Tamarijn.

If you need special equipment while you're on the island, **Labco Medical and Home Healthcare Services** (𝓒 **297/582-6651;** fax 297/582-6567; www.labcomedical.com) specializes in oxygen-delivery systems, but it also sells and rents medical and home healthcare products, such as oxygen concentrators, tanks, commodes, scooters, crutches, wheelchairs, walkers, shower chairs, and lifts.

FAMILY TRAVEL

Aruba remains one of the safest and most reliably storm-free Caribbean destinations. With the creation of one water park on De Palm Island and another new park close to Oranjestad, Aruba is even more kid friendly than ever. Most hotels and resorts have well-run children's programs as well as special activities for young guests that include introductions to snorkeling and underwater exploration and supervised participation in other outdoor watersports and games.

To locate accommodations, restaurants, and attractions that are particularly kid friendly, refer to the "Kids" icon throughout this guide. Some top kid pleasers include:

- Windsurfing lessons in Lac Bay (best for the over 10 set)
- The Donkey Sanctuary
- The Blue Parrotfish Water Park on De Palm Island (best for tots)
- Morgan's Island water park
- The Ostrich Farm
- The Butterfly Farm
- Miniature golf and paddle boats at Adventure Golf
- Atlantis Submarine
- Snorkeling on any catamaran sail
- Land sailing on the flats near Sourbon

Family Travel Forum (www.familytravelforum.com) regularly prints articles about destinations including Aruba, Bonaire, and Curaçao and also offers discounts, deals, and trip-planning consultants to guide parents to appropriate vacation destinations for the entire family. Some good books on the market that address specific concerns of traveling with kids are Open Road's *Caribbean with Kids*

SENIOR TRAVEL

Aruba's a great place for wise and seasoned travelers. In fact, a hefty portion of the island's guests, especially during the high season, are people over 50. If you're looking for a quiet environment with a more mature clientele, think about renting a unit in a timeshare. Most large hotels have plenty of seniors, too. If you're revolted by the idea of being segregated from the youngsters, fear not: No resort, hotel, or timeshare caters to one type of person only. Most feature a nice mix of families and couples of all ages.

Mention your age when you begin planning your trip; many hotels and most airlines and cruise lines offer senior discounts. And don't hesitate to ask for discounts after you're on the island. Just be sure to have some kind of ID, such as a driver's license, especially if no one believes you're a day over 45.

8 SUSTAINABLE TOURISM

Aruba has a few pluses and minuses in its sustainability record. A growing number of hotels participate in the **Green Globe Initiative,** started by Amsterdam Manor and soon followed by the Bucuti Beach Resort, both of which remain the island's leaders in sustainable tourism and environmental conservation. They not only reduce their energy output and waste, but also promote awareness and sponsor activities such as beach and reef cleanups.

Other hotels are less conservation oriented, particularly those targeting the American market where amenities such as air-conditioning and bottled water are assumed. This is in stark contrast to even the most upscale hotels that target Dutch or other European guests, where air-conditioning is rarely on in rooms and where bottled water and disposable travel-size toiletries are just as often absent. Water conservation is a big issue on the island since it is wildly expensive to desalinate seawater, but you wouldn't know it based on the lush poolside gardens in most big resorts.

Most tour operators seem woefully unaware of conservation issues, or at best they merely pay lip service to the topic. They are equally willing to offer high-speed rides on banana boats and jet skis as they are to take you kayaking in the mangroves or off-roading in an ATV. Unfortunately, many tour operators do not promote low-impact

General Resources for Green Travel

In addition to the resources for Aruba listed above, the following websites provide valuable wide-ranging information on sustainable travel. For a list of even more sustainable resources, as well as tips and explanations on how to travel greener, visit www.frommers.com/planning.

- **Responsible Travel** (www.responsibletravel.com) is a great source of sustainable travel ideas; the site is run by a spokesperson for ethical tourism in the travel industry. **Sustainable Travel International** (www.sustainable travelinternational.org) promotes ethical tourism practices, and manages an extensive directory of sustainable properties and tour operators around the world.

- In the U.K., **Tourism Concern** (www.tourismconcern.org. uk) works to reduce social and environmental problems connected to tourism. The **Association of Independent Tour Operators** (**AITO;** www.aito.co.uk) is a group of specialist operators leading the field in making holidays sustainable.

- In Canada, **www.greenlivingonline.com** offers extensive content on how to travel sustainably, including a travel and transport section and profiles of the best green shops and services in Toronto, Vancouver, and Calgary.

- In Australia, the national body which sets guidelines and standards for ecotourism is **Ecotourism Australia** (www. ecotourism.org.au). The **Green Directory** (www.thegreen directory.com.au), **Green Pages** (www.thegreenpages. com.au), and **Eco Directory** (www.ecodirectory.com.au) offer sustainable travel tips and directories of green businesses.

activities, like horseback riding, biking, or hiking. One ecofriendly tour operator is **Aruba Nature Sensitive Hiking and Jeep Tours** (p. 96; ✆ **297/594-5017;** www.sensitivehikers.com), which offers easy or challenging hikes in Arikok National Park, various caves, old gold mines, or sand dunes.

When inside **Arikok National Park** (p. 105), there is a clear mandate that the park and its species are to be protected—this job is taken seriously. However, when park rangers are asked by tourists to show them the bats or other delicate species that reside in protected areas,

- **Carbonfund** (www.carbonfund.org), **TerraPass** (www. terrapass.org), and **Carbon Neutral** (www.carbonneutral. org) provide info on "carbon offsetting," or offsetting the greenhouse gas emitted during flights.
- **Greenhotels** (www.greenhotels.com) recommends green-rated member hotels around the world that fulfill the company's stringent environmental requirements. **Environmentally Friendly Hotels** (www.environmentally friendlyhotels.com) offers more green accommodations ratings. The **Hotel Association of Canada** (www.hac greenhotels.com) has a Green Key Eco-Rating Program, which audits the environmental performance of Canadian hotels, motels, and resorts.
- **Sustain Lane** (www.sustainlane.com) lists sustainable eating and drinking choices around the U.S.; also visit **www.eatwellguide.org** for tips on eating sustainably in the U.S. and Canada.
- For information on animal-friendly issues throughout the world, visit **Tread Lightly** (www.treadlightly.org). For information about the ethics of swimming with dolphins, visit the **Whale and Dolphin Conservation Society** (www.wdcs.org).
- **Volunteer International** (www.volunteerinternational. org) has a list of questions to help you determine the intentions and the nature of a volunteer program. For general info on volunteer travel, visit **www.volunteer abroad.org** and **www.idealist.org**.

there is a tendency to oblige the request, despite the potentially harmful impact these visits may have on the species or the habitat.

The bottom line is the tourist dictates what the tour operators offer. You can set an example by asking for low-impact activities or requesting that the boat operator not handle or capture marine life to entertain passengers. You can even mention when you tip them that you wish to leave the island as beautiful as it was upon your arrival and thank them for preserving it intact for when you return.

Do-gooders rejoice. Now you can merrily merge your desire to frolic in the Caribbean surf with your inclination to make the world a better place. *Voluntourism* is the fastest-growing segment of the world's travel industry, and Aruba is keeping pace with demand by offering a spectrum of volunteer opportunities to accommodate everyone from the ecoseeker to the critter cuddler. The possibilities range from reef and beach cleanups to pitching in at the donkey sanctuary. Here is a sampling of the opportunities available in Aruba:

- **Annual Aruba Reef Care Project:** This annual cleanup of the island's beaches is Aruba's largest volunteer environmental initiative. Hundreds of participants snorkel, scuba dive, or comb the beaches grabbing and bagging litter. This event usually occurs in July; call ✆ **297/582-3777** for more information.

- **Sponsor-A-Mile:** The Eagle Beach Area Coalition for Aruba's Sustainable Tourism sponsors a monthly drive to keep the beaches clean by letting visitors "adopt" a mile of beach and keep it clear of debris during their stay. Participating resorts include the Divi Phoenix, Amsterdam Manor, Costa Linda, Bucuti Beach, Manchebo Beach, the Mill, Aruba Marriott, and the Renaissance; contact any of these resorts for more information.

- **"Salba Nos Buriconan" (Save Our Donkeys) Foundation:** Animal lovers can volunteer at the donkey sanctuary to help feed, care for, and teach visitors about the island's donkeys. Visit www.arubandonkey.org for more information.

- **Dive for Earth Week:** In support of Earth Day, Aruba encourages volunteers to help to clear the shorelines and surf of garbage and debris. Sponsors provide transportation, tools, and refreshments. Contact the Aruba Tourism Authority at ✆ **297/582-3777.**

9 OUTDOOR PURSUITS

BIRDING In the High-Rise area, the **Bubali Bird Sanctuary** attracts more than 80 ornithological species to its nutrient-rich ponds and wetlands. How many brown pelicans, black olivaceous cormorants, herons, and egrets can you spot? Farther afield, **Arikok National Park** (✆ **297-585-1234**) features several diverse ecosystems in a compact area. Birds here include hummingbirds (common emerald and ruby-topaz), rufous-collared sparrows, tropical mockingbirds, ospreys, yellow orioles, American kestrels, black-faced grassquit, yellow warblers, Caribbean parakeets, long-tongued bats, common ground doves, troupials, crested caracaras, and Aruban burrowing owls. The Wyndham, Radisson, Hyatt, and Renaissance offer close encounters with a variety of showy tropical species such as toucans, cockatoos, and macaws.

FISHING   Local fishermen use simple hand lines (fishing line, hooks, and lead weights) to bring up red snapper and dolphin fish. Most activity takes place along the southwest coast, although some anglers occasionally venture to the north coast, where the rough seas trap fish in small pools carved out of the limestone bluffs. To try your hand at deep-sea fishing, charter one of the many skippered boats. Typical catches include barracuda, amberjack, sailfish, wahoo, blue and white marlin, kingfish, bonito, and black- and yellow-fin tuna. A few restaurants will even cook and serve up your day's catch.

GOLF   On the island's northern tip, **Tierra del Sol** (www.tierra delsol.com) is one of the Caribbean's best golf courses. The championship 18-hole, par-71 course was designed by Robert Trent Jones II and features stupendous views of the ocean and the California Lighthouse. Bunkers, cacti, and coral rock come into play throughout the course, while water hazards are confined to holes 13, 14, and 15. Gusting to speeds of 64kmph (40 mph), the wind is the real challenge, though. The only competition is from the **Links at Divi Aruba** (www.divigolf.com), near Druif Beach, a picturesque 9-hole course surrounded by landscaped water traps, lakes, and lagoons, and boasting a camera that captures your final shot so you can review the tape over drinks in the clubhouse that overlooks the greens.

HIKING   The sun is hot, and the scant foliage offers little respite, but if you bring water and a wide-brimmed hat, traversing Aruba's hills and coastline is worth the effort. **Arikok National Park** (© 297/ 585-1234) has the best trails. Climb the island's highest hills, explore abandoned gold mines, poke around plantation ruins, trek through caves, and comb limestone cliffs for coral and small-animal bones (leave everything where you found it, please). The network of trails is clearly marked. Hiking boots are nice, but sneakers will do.

HORSEBACK RIDING   Aruba's coastline and outback are just as dramatic when viewed from the saddle. Several ranches offer early-morning and midday excursions, or you can ride off into the sunset. As you wend your way through cacti and random boulders in the outback, watch for iguanas and skittish cottontails. Stop at Alto Vista Chapel and California Lighthouse, and then ride along the shore. Or start at the crashing waves and sand dunes of the northern coast before heading for the Natural Pool. Keep your eyes open for bickering parakeets and hovering hummingbirds. That ominous bird circling over your head? Not to worry: It only looks like a vulture.

JET SKIING Harleys of the sea—just as fast, just as noisy. Put on your black leather swimming trunks and head for Palm Beach, where several vendors have one and two seaters.

KAYAKING The leeward (south) coast's calm waters are ideal for kayaking. Starting near the old fishing village of Savaneta, guided tours hug the coastal mangrove forests before crossing a lagoon to a small island, where you can have a bite to eat and snorkel.

LAND SAILING This relatively new activity, which was developed in Australia, harnesses wind power to propel a lightweight go-kart frame across the flat dunes. Bonaire already has a large track built for this easy-to-learn and completely safe sport. Aruba still uses open dunes, which are sometimes too muddy after it rains. With luck, a track will be created to ensure good sailing conditions year-round.

OFF-ROADING All-terrain vehicles that look like a cross between a dune buggy and a tractor mower let you play road warrior, and can be rented by the hour or the day. For those who want the thrill of the ride without the fear of getting lost, guided tours embark from several tour agencies.

PARASAILING Aruba looks even better from 180m (591 ft.) in the air. Flight time is only 10 minutes, but secure in your boat-towed parachute, you're on top of the world. Several watersports centers along Palm Beach will be happy to put wind in your sails. Take a waterproof camera along to show your friends back home that you've been there, done that.

SAILING Sailing adventures are available day and night. Some include watersports, while others feature drinks, snacks, or a full gourmet dinner. For night owls, dance-and-booze cruises include a midnight dip in the sea. If you have something special to celebrate, charter a private yacht. Catamarans, trimarans, and ketches are available. The calm waters along the southern coast are also ideal for extra-buoyant individual sailboats such as Sunfish. At De Palm Island, the trimaran Windriders come complete with a captain to navigate the waters or give you a crash course in sailing.

SCUBA DIVING Aruba offers enough coral reefs, marine life, and wreck diving to keep most wet suit–wearing folks happy. The water temperature averages 80°F (27°C), but during winter it can dip into the mid-70s. Due to currents and plankton, visibility varies, but at the leeward dive sites it usually ranges from 18 to 36m (59–118 ft.). The bountiful plankton nourishes a dense coral population, especially brain, sheet, finger, and mountainous star coral. Freshwater runoff is minimal. Sunken airplane fuselages and shipwrecks (including the largest in the Caribbean) are among the most popular destinations. In addition to snappers, grunts, angelfish, damselfish, and parrotfish, divers regularly spot less-common species such as frogfish, sea horses, nudibranchs, black crinoids, basket stars, scorpionfish, and eels. Barracudas, tarpons, and jacks also call Aruba's waters home.

SNORKELING Good visibility, several shallow reefs, and a couple of wrecks give snorkelers an array of options. All sites are on the southern, or leeward, coast. Slightly north of Palm Beach, Catalina Bay and Arashi Reef feature brain and star coral, sea fans, parrotfish, angelfish, and an occasional octopus; the 122m (400-ft.) *Antilla* shipwreck is impossible to miss. De Palm Slope, off De Palm Island, features some impressive coral as well.

SNUBA Though not affording you the freedom and excitement of scuba, this technology allows you to breathe while descending up to 6m (20 ft.) by way of a regulator tethered to a floating tank of compressed air. No experience is necessary; most of the catamaran tours allow passengers the option either before or during the trip to sign up and give it a whirl. On De Palm Island, you can also try **Sea Trek,** where you don a diving helmet and weighted boots and explore the seafloor; though you won't see much coral, you will see a submerged bus and plane, and can sit for a photo op at a submerged cafe table.

UNDERWATER TOURING Another way to experience life at the bottom of the sea is aboard a submarine, where you can descend 45m (148 ft.) to observe coral, shipwrecks, and some very curious fish. If you'd rather not have your vessel submerge completely, hop on a glass-bottom boat. The viewing deck is only 1.5m (5 ft.) below the surface, but a scuttled German freighter, encrusted with coral and teeming with other marine life, is just feet away. The sub leaves from a pier in front of the Crystal Casino in Oranjestad; the glass-bottom boat departs from Pelican Pier on Palm Beach.

WINDSURFING & KITEBOARDING Aruba's high-wind season is the longest in the Caribbean. Wind speeds are best in May, June, and July, when they average 20 to 25 knots. From December through April, they slow to 15 to 20 knots, and from September through November they range from 10 to 20 knots. Most launches are on the leeward side of the island, near the hotels and major beaches. The most popular site is off the northwest tip of the island on Malmok Beach, an area known as Fishermen's Huts. Near San Nicolas, Rodgers Beach, and Boca Grandi are alternatives to the hotel area. To avoid collisions, kiteboarders and windsurfers take turns throughout the day.

10 STAYING CONNECTED

While making local calls from your hotel can be outrageously expensive, and even receiving incoming calls is costly to you, long-distance calls are flat-out ridiculous. If you have to make a call, purchase a phone card from a convenience store and use a pay phone. Better yet, send an e-mail from a cybercafe.

To call Aruba from the U.S., dial **011** (the international access code), then **297** (Aruba's country code), then **58** (the area code) and the five-digit local number. When in Aruba, dial only the five-digit local number.

For more information on telephones in Aruba, see "Telephones," p. 192.

CELLPHONES

Cellphone coverage and reception in Aruba is pretty good if a tad pricey. Because Aruba is a small and relatively manageable island, I recommend foregoing the cellphone altogether unless you are part of a scattered group which requires ongoing logistic coordination. Communications with home are cheaper via e-mail, and many hotel lobbies have Wi-Fi and small Internet cafes.

The three letters that define much of the world's wireless capabilities are **GSM** (Global System for Mobile Communications), a big, seamless network that makes for easy cross-border cellphone use throughout dozens of countries worldwide. If your cellphone is on a GSM system and you have a world-capable multiband phone, such as many Sony Ericsson, Motorola, or Samsung models, you can make and receive calls in Aruba. Just call your wireless operator and ask for "international roaming" to be activated on your account.

Most cellphones will work in Aruba, but call your carrier first to be sure. Rates are usually on the order of $2 per minute, even if you're dialing an 800 number.

For many, **renting** a phone is a good idea. At the airport, there is a booth just before you exit the terminal where you can rent a phone for a fair price, depending on how many calls you make. The rental agencies seem to be a bit of a moving target since they are still figuring out how to prevent forgetful tourists from accidentally taking the phones home with them! One company that seems solvent is **Fast Phone** (www.arubafastphones.com), with a booth at the airport and another at Paseo Herencia Mall. For $50 you can rent a phone for a week with 84 minutes included. The two main carriers are **Digicel** (© **297/522-2222;** www.digicelaruba.com) and **SETAR** (© **297/583-4000;** www.setar.aw). Rates with these carriers are $8 per day for

Buying a phone on the island can also be economically attractive, as many nations have cheap prepaid phone systems. Once you arrive at your destination, stop by a local cellphone shop or booth at the airport and get the cheapest package; you'll probably pay less than $100 for a phone and a starter calling card. Local calls may be as low as 10¢ per minute, and in many countries incoming calls are free.

INTERNET & E-MAIL

Most hotels and resorts in Aruba have Internet access, and many places are becoming wireless "hot spots" that offer Wi-Fi access either for free or for a small charge. Some hotels, such as the Radisson Aruba Resort, Casino, and Spa, offer free Wi-Fi for staying guests, while other hotels may charge a daily fee for Internet access. Some resorts may also offer free Wi-Fi access only in the lobby or public spaces. Daily rates can be $10 to $12 per day, so be sure to ask before you start using minutes. There are a number of Internet cafes on the island with rates that are fairly reasonable, with fees averaging about $2 for every 15 minutes. A reliable Internet cafe is **Fast Phone** in the Paseo Herencia Mall (www.arubafastphones.com).

11 TIPS ON ACCOMMODATIONS

HOTELS & RESORTS   Some travelers assume they can't afford the big hotels and resorts. With all the packages and sales, though, this isn't always true. The rates included in this book are "rack rates"—the officially posted rates you'd be given if you walked in off the street. Hardly anyone actually pays these prices. Save yourself a bundle by asking your travel agent or the hotel's reservations agent about packages or discounts.

Some hotels are flexible about rates, and many offer discounts and upgrades whenever they have a big block of rooms to fill and few reservations. Smaller hotels are less likely to be generous with discounts, much less upgrades.

The best deals can be had during off-peak periods, which doesn't always mean from mid-April to mid-December only. Discounts are also available during certain slow periods, called "windows," most often after the New Year's holiday. If you want a winter vacation, choose January rather than February or the Christmas holidays, when prices are at their all-year high.

Several hotels, such as the Divi properties and Renaissance, allow you to access facilities at two or more of their locations on the island at no additional fee. This means you can take advantage of the amenities, such as beaches, water toys, activities, and events at other locations as part of your all-inclusive package. Be sure to ask before you book, since this is not always the case. For example, the Renaissance has an adult-only policy for certain locations, such as their lobby bar and infinity pool, which means that teens and children are not allowed. This can be a problem for families traveling with children, but it can also be a plus for honeymoon couples or seniors who prefer to steer clear of too much youthful exuberance.

ALL-INCLUSIVES   Presumably, everything's paid for upfront at an "all-inclusive" resort, even drinks and watersports. Unfortunately, some packages cover a room and two meals a day only—drinks, sports, and whatever else are extra. Before you book, ask exactly what's included.

Generally speaking, the all-inclusive market is geared to the active traveler who likes lots of organized entertainment and activities, unlimited platters of food, and endless drinks in plastic cups. Some of Aruba's all-inclusive properties, such as the **Holiday Inn SunSpree Aruba–Beach Resort & Casino** (p. 44) and the **Renaissance Ocean Suites** (p. 37), appeal to families (there's so much going on, the kids will never get bored) and young adults (plenty of fun times and other young adults). Other properties such as the **Westin Aruba Resort, Spa & Casino** (p. 43) and the **Renaissance Marina Hotel** (p. 37), are geared more toward the adult couples who want over-the-top luxury, plenty of dining options, and nightlife that includes a casino or show lounge. For the ecoconscious traveler, the **Manchebo Beach Resort & Spa** (p. 52) is Green Globe certified and offers all-inclusive packages. On the other hand, if you want to get out, see the island, and eat at some of the amazing restaurants, or if you're not particularly interested in nonstop organized events, all-inclusive hotels probably aren't for you.

TIMESHARES   Renting an apartment can be one of the least expensive ways to vacation in Aruba. It also offers privacy, independence, and, in most cases, peace and quiet. All of Aruba's timeshare accommodations come with a kitchen, and most have a living room, a dining room, and a guest room or two. Because many tour operators work directly with timeshares that have rentals available, your travel agent may present a suite in a timeshare property as just another accommodations option. In addition, most individual timeshare resorts assist owners in renting their units, so call a property that interests you or visit its website. Some of these include Playa Linda Beach Resort and the Marriott Ocean Club. Some websites have owner bulletin boards with a listing of rentals available. General bulletin boards, such as **Aruba Bulletin Board** (**www.aruba-bb.com**), abound with timeshare rental opportunities.

Where to Stay in Aruba

You'll be hard-pressed to find a lemon among Aruba's hotels and resorts. At the very least, accommodations on the island are above average; in many cases, they're downright amazing. Hotels appreciate your business, and it shows, from the bend-over-backward service to the endless array of amenities.

Lodging is a competitive business on the island. When one hotel introduces a new feature, the others scramble to match or beat it. As a result, all of the upscale resorts have a casino, a fitness center, some kind of spa, an assortment of dining and drinking venues, lush gardens, and magnificent pools. Even modest lodges have amenities you wouldn't expect for the price.

So how do you decide where to stay?

If you'd rather be in the middle of the action than on an expansive beach, stay in Oranjestad. It's not a big town, but it has big-town casinos, restaurants, shopping, and nightlife. And it's no more than a 10-minute drive from the best beaches.

A 15-minute walk northwest from Oranjestad, the Low-Rise area has the feel of an unpretentious beach town. It's a mix of boutique hotels, peaceful timeshares, and large, low-lying resorts. Rooms here are generally a good value. As the lengthy, uncrowded beach extends up the coast, its name changes from Bushiri to Druif to Manchebo to Eagle. Not all the Low-Rise hotels are beachside—a small road separates several from the water—but that keeps the beach tranquil. Drink and snack bars are few and far between, motorized watersports are generally not allowed, piers are nowhere to be seen, and the beach is wide and generally uncrowded, but restaurants and other amenities are just across the road.

A brief limestone outcrop separates Eagle Beach from Palm Beach and the High-Rise area. A mix of Miami Beach and San Juan's Isla Verde, the glamorous High-Rise hotels usually have several stars next to their names in travel-agent brochures. Most front the beach, all boast amenities that go on and on, and some rise as high as 18 stories. Despite the glitz associated with the area, moderately priced options are readily available. The mile-long strand here is as dazzling as Eagle Beach, but it's narrower and there's less room for isolation. Smart bars and beachside restaurants line the strip. Piers projecting into the sea serve diving and fishing boats as well as plentiful motorized equipment.

Hotels and timeshares inland from the Low-Rise and High-Rise areas lack the allure of instant beach access, but most are still within a 10- to 20-minute stroll of the sea. Naturally, their rates are lower.

In general, you'll find more Americans and a more mature crowd during the first 4 months of the year. After April, families, budget-conscious travelers, and Europeans make up an increasing part of the mix. South Americans have a greater presence during their winter (June–Aug). Just a hop, skip, and a jump away from Aruba, Venezuelans and Colombians pop over for holiday weekends year-round. Recent economic and political crises worldwide have hurt Aruba's businesses, and according to reports many hotels and restaurants are empty. A few restaurants, including LeDome—a virtual institution—have closed their doors. It's uncertain if or when it will reopen.

A word about rates: Some hotels have extremely complex rate schedules, with prices varying within certain months and several times a year. I've condensed some of these schedules in the listings below; of course, you'll always want to confirm rates before you book. Also know that the prices quoted are rack rates. Rack rates are the published prices that hotels charge customers who walk in off the street. In most cases, you can get an infinitely more affordable rate by opting for a package, offered by tour operators or the hotels themselves.

In the same vein, although hotels are grouped by price category, think of the groupings as ballpark figures. Hotels change rates at different times during the year and spontaneously to reflect supply and demand, so an "expensive" hotel could be more affordable than a "moderate" resort during a seasonal window of opportunity. Also, lumping traditional hotels and all-inclusives together is like comparing apples to mangos. To determine the relative value of an all-inclusive, you'll have to add the estimated cost of food, drink, and other amenities offered by the all-inclusive to the price of accommodations alone at a traditional hotel.

One last point: Every hotel listed below provides guest-room phones and safes, laundry services, tour and activity desks, and ample free parking unless otherwise stated.

(Value) **Off-Season Savings**

Although occupancy rates during the low season (about mid-Apr to mid-Dec) remain high, prices plummet by up to 50%.

It's for the Birds

Some of the bigger hotels, such as the Westin, Radisson, and Renaissance, insist upon keeping gorgeous wild birds such as macaws, flamingos, cockatoos, and toucans in cages in the lobby or outdoor areas. While spectacular, these birds are increasingly rare, threatened with extinction, and may have been captured from the wild. Oh, and they can bite off your finger. While hotel managements will insist their birds are healthy and happy, the reality is that many of these "friendly" birds are actually young and have not yet reached maturity. When these birds get older, some of them may exhibit such behaviors as screeching, rocking, self-biting, pulling or shedding of feathers, or snapping at fingers. These "unfriendly" birds are often returned to the breeder, sold as pets, set free, or otherwise disposed of. They are then miraculously replaced with a shiny new bird, which may be a baby, fresh from the nest—or worse, possibly fresh from the wild. If you are distressed by this sight, feel free to express your concerns, voice your objection, and suggest alternatives, such as parakeets, which breed well in captivity and are not a draw on wild bird populations.

Some bird attractions will claim to do breeding and conservation work, and one in Curaçao will even show you a breeding facility complete with incubators. While it's true that some birds can be bred in captivity, the reality is that it is much cheaper, faster, and easier to acquire illegally caught birds. In one place, a lone hyacinth macaw sits in a cage since his mate died nearly 10 years ago. Among the rarest macaws in the world, and valued at tens of thousands of dollars, this bird belongs in a legitimate breeding facility, not a roadside menagerie.

Log on to www.bornfree.com to learn more.

1 ORANJESTAD

EXPENSIVE

Renaissance Aruba Resort & Casino ★★★ This resort has two distinct hotel choices: the adults-only **Renaissance Marina Hotel** and the family-friendly **Renaissance Ocean Suites.** The six-story Marina Tower anchors a shopping mall and is popular with business travelers and vacationing couples, since this facility only accommodates guests who are 18 and over. The compact rooms feature thick carpeting, modern colors, stylish furniture, and step-out balconies. The bathrooms are small but have separate sink and bath areas. Overlooking the mall, atrium rooms are quiet, but lack an ocean view. Get a corner room on the sixth floor if you like high ceilings. On the waterfront and favored by groups and families, the five-story Ocean Suites feels more like a resort. It features a small man-made beach, a pool with elaborate slides, and 258 roomy one-bedroom suites with living rooms, large bathrooms, balconies or patios, and stocked wet bars. Carpeted floors, solid pastels, and glass bricks brighten the rooms.

Hop on the free water taxi to Renaissance Island (a 10-min. ride), for a relaxing day on the resort's private beach. Also on the premises are two casinos (including the island's only 24-hr. casino) and a theater that presents a flashy Vegas-style show.

L.G. Smith Blvd. 82, Oranjestad. ⓒ **800/421-8188** in the U.S. and Canada, or 297/583-6000. Fax 297/582-5317. www.marriott.com. 558 units. Mid-Dec to Apr $350–$450 double, $517–$950 suite; May to mid-Dec $215–$305 double, $298–$800 suite. Children 17 and under stay free in parent's room in Ocean Suites. AE, DISC, MC, V. Children 17 and under not permitted in Marina Tower. **Amenities:** 4 restaurants, including L.G. Smith's (see review, p. 58); 4 bars; babysitting; 2 casinos; children's/teen programs; concierge; health club & spa; fitness center on Renaissance Island; 2 outdoor pools; room service; smoke-free rooms; tennis court; watersports equipment/rentals; Wi-Fi in lobby (for a fee); rooms for those w/limited mobility. In room: A/C, TV, minibar, hair dryer, robes.

INEXPENSIVE

Talk of the Town Hotel & Beach Club ⓥⓐⓛⓤⓔ   Between the airport and downtown Oranjestad, this unassuming hotel is Aruba's oldest operating resort. It books mostly Europeans, especially 20-somethings, and Dutch families. An outdoor restaurant and bar border one side of the good-size pool and deck area; palms and rooms line the other three sides. Parallel to a busy road, the standard rooms are the least desirable except during Carnival, when they offer prime parade views. The nicer and quieter superior rooms face the pool, are tropically decorated, and feature a refrigerator, microwave, and coffeemaker. All rooms have two double beds or one king-size bed; superior rooms also have a sofa bed. The "beach club," across the street, features a small strand, towels, chairs, *palapas* (shade huts), a small pool, and a snack bar. This hotel offers Wi-Fi throughout the public areas and in some superior rooms. If you would rather travel light, the hotel also offers complimentary use of an in-house computer.

L.G. Smith Blvd. 2, Oranjestad, Aruba. ⓒ **297/582-3380.** Fax 297/582-0327. www. tottaruba.com. 51 units. Dec to mid-Apr $158 standard, $176 superior, $203 1 bedroom, $294 2 bedroom; mid-Apr to Nov $105 standard, $119 superior, $143 1 bedroom, $199 2 bedroom. Dive package available. AE, MC, V. **Amenities:** Bar and grill; babysitting; nearby health club; outdoor pool; watersports equipment/rentals. *In room:* A/C, TV.

2 HIGH-RISE HOTELS/ PALM BEACH/NOORD

VERY EXPENSIVE

Aruba Marriott Resort & Stellaris Casino ★★★ The Marriott's airy, tastefully subdued rooms are the largest in any of Aruba's luxury High-Rise hotels. Its 9-sq.-m (97-sq.-ft.) balconies are also the most commodious in the area. As the last resort along Palm Beach, the Marriott boasts a beach that's ideal for sunbathers craving space, with ample *palapas* and palm trees to relax under. In 2009, the resort underwent a $50-million renovation, which updated its guest rooms, public spaces, and facade, making the resort feel modern, spacious, and luxurious. The renovation also added the Tradewinds Club, an executive floor that is a type of hotel within a hotel, with a lounge that offers snacks and beverages throughout the day. Guests run the gamut from honeymooners to retirees to corporate-incentive rewardees. There are plenty of families, too, but children here are well-behaved. The eight-story complex forms a U that overlooks a large free-form pool, a waterfall, and lush palm, banana, and jacaranda trees. The beachside seafood restaurant, **Simply Fish** (p. 64), makes for a great sunset meal. The **Mandara Spa** at the Marriott's sister property, the Ocean Club, offers Aruba's most spiritually transformative indoor experience. Shopping arcades and a casino cater to your material needs.

L.G. Smith Blvd. 101, Palm Beach, Aruba. **☎ 800/223-6388** in the U.S. and Canada, or 297/586-9000. Fax 297/586-0649. www.marriott.com. 413 units. Jan–Apr $454–$699 double, from $699 suite; May to mid-Dec $249–$564 double, from $614 suite; Christmas and New Year's $679–$1,189 double, from $1,189 suite. Packages available. Children 11 and under stay free in parent's room. AE, DISC, MC, V. **Amenities:** 5 restaurants; 3 bars; babysitting; casino; children's center/program; concierge; health club & spa; large outdoor pool w/waterfall; room service; smoke-free rooms; 2 tennis courts lit for night play; watersports equipment/rentals; rooms for those w/limited mobility. *In room:* A/C, TV, fridge, hair dryer, Wi-Fi.

Hyatt Regency Aruba Resort & Casino ★★★ This elegant nine-story beachfront resort has stunning public spaces and a stellar reputation. The full-service resort completed a $20-million renovation in 2007, which updated the lobby, public spaces, and guest rooms. Monumental, comfy chairs stud the refined open-air lobby, and just outside, carpets of bougainvillea, moss and ivy-covered boulders, and towering palms spill down to a multilevel pool where exotic macaws and toucans doze. Although attractively furnished with Art Deco–inspired furniture and modern carnival colors, the rooms are significantly smaller than the Marriott's. And the "Parisian" balconies offer just enough room for one person to stand. Overlooking the pool area, standard rooms have no balconies. Other rooms provide vistas of the pool and ocean, while garden units boast views of the lush tropical foliage.

J.E. Irausquin Blvd. 85, Palm Beach, Aruba. ✆ **800/55-HYATT** [554-9288] in the U.S. and Canada, or 297/586-1234. Fax 297/586-1682. www.aruba.hyatt.com. 360 units. Jan–Apr $525–$725 double; May–Nov $335–$485 double. Packages available. Children 17 and under stay free in parent's room. AE, DISC, MC, V. **Amenities:** 6 restaurants, including Café Japengo (see review, p. 65) and Ruinas del Mar (p. 64); 4 bars; babysitting; casino; children's center/program; concierge; concierge-level rooms; health club & spa; high-speed Internet (50¢ per minute); 3-level outdoor pool/lagoon complex; room service; smoke-free rooms; 2 tennis courts lit for night play; watersports equipment/rentals; Wi-Fi ($10 per day for hotel-wide access); rooms for those w/limited mobility. *In room:* A/C, TV, hair dryer, minibar.

Marriott's Aruba Ocean Club ★★★ This is Aruba's poshest timeshare resort featuring modern, comfortable one- and two-bedroom suites. Shaped like a giant U, the six-story building echoes the design of the Aruba Marriott Resort, its sister property next door. The villas at the Ocean Club have a sumptuous look. Hardwoods, dark rattan, and tasteful fabrics create an elegant yet homey feel. All suites hold a full gourmet kitchen. Bar seating separates the kitchen from the semiformal dining room and spacious living room, and an open whirlpool in the king-size bedroom beckons. Vistas from the large balcony take in the ocean and the central rock-and-palm lagoon pool; two-room villas boast two balconies. The pricier oceanfront villas have even larger balconies with spectacular views. Ocean Club guests have full access to the Marriott's impressive array of amenities, including the Mandara Spa, tucked away off the beaten path, which is without peer on the island (see "Spa Retreats," above).

L.G. Smith Blvd. 99, Palm Beach, Aruba. ✆ **297/586-9000.** Fax 297/586-8000. www.timeshares.marriott-vacations.com. 311 units. Dec 22–Jan 5 $825–$875 1 bedroom, $1,250–$1,325 2 bedroom; Jan 6–31 $720–$785 1 bedroom, $900–$1,050 2 bedroom; Feb–Apr $649–$675 1 bedroom, $850–$875 2 bedroom; May–Dec 21 $390–$465 1 bedroom, $490–$625 2 bedroom. AE, DISC, MC, V. **Amenities:** 5 restaurants; bar; babysitting; children's center/program and play area; concierge; health club & spa; Internet kiosks; outdoor Jacuzzis; large outdoor pool; children's pool; room service; smoke-free rooms; 2 tennis courts lit for night play; watersports equipment/rentals; Wi-Fi in lobby; rooms for those w/limited mobility. *In room:* A/C, TV/DVD, portable crib (on request), highchair (on request).

Radisson Aruba Resort & Casino ★★★ This eight-story resort has the most stylish and beautiful rooms in Aruba. Integrating Caribbean plantation and South Beach Art Deco elements, the complex

Amsterdam Manor Aruba
  Beach Resort **16**

Aruba Beach Club **22**

Aruba Bucuti Beach Resort &
  Tara Beach Suites & Spa **20**

Aruba Marriott Resort
  & Stellaris Casino **1**

Aruba Millennium **12**

Aruba Divi Phoenix
  Beach Resort **10**

Palm Beach

PALM BEACH

Old Dutch Windmill

BUBALI BIRD SANCTUARY

NOORD

Santa Ana

SAN MIGUEL

WASHINGTON

Eagle Beach

MALPAIS

BUBALI

Hato

Manchebo Beach

MANCHEBO

Druif Beach

PARADIJS

Area of detail

Oranjestad

A R U B A

Belgie Straat

ORANJESTAD

(i) Information

WHERE TO STAY IN ARUBA

2

HIGH-RISE HOTELS/PALM BEACH/NOORD

Arubiana Inn **15**

Brickell Bay Beach Club Aruba **6**

Caribbean Palm Village Resort **14**

Casa del Mar Beach Resort **23**

Coconut Inn **13**

Costa Linda Beach Resort **19**

Divi Aruba All Inclusive **24**

Holiday Inn SunSpree Aruba
  Resort & Casino **3**

Hyatt Regency Aruba
  Resort & Casino **5**

La Quinta Beach Resort **18**

Manchebo Beach Resort & Spa **21**

Marriott's Aruba Ocean Club **2**

The Mill Resort & Suites **11**

Occidental Grand Aruba **7**

Paradise Beach Villas **17**

Playa Linda Beach Resort **4**

Radisson Aruba Resort & Casino **8**

Tamarijn Aruba All Inclusive **25**

Westin Aruba Resort,
  Spa & Casino **9**

Moments   Spa Retreats

Diamonds may be a girl's best friend, but corporeal indulgence is a close second. The **Mandara Spa** at Marriott's Aruba Ocean Club, L.G. Smith Blvd. 99, Palm Beach (© 297/586-9000), re-creates the tranquillity of a Japanese rainforest with Thai silk wall hangings, soft Balinese gamelan music, and the scents of clove and cinnamon. Personal attention is the hallmark of this meditative retreat, which offers state-of-the-art massages, body wraps, and facials. Programs cater to couples and men, who make up a hefty portion of the clientele. Other upscale spas can be found at **Tierra del Sol** (© 297/586-4861), the **Hyatt** (© 297/586-1234), and the **Okeanos Spa** at the **Renaissance** (© 297/583-6000). For a more rustic pampering experience, try **Spa del Sol at the Manchebo Beach Resort & Spa,** J.E. Irausquin Blvd. 55 (© 297/582-6145), a garden sanctuary by the sea featuring massages, yoga, reflexology, and other treatments in beachside cabanas. The training of masseurs and masseuses on the island varies greatly. Be sure to ask for the most experienced person available.

is both sophisticated and personal. Because the lush gardens, lagoons, and waterfalls ramble over more than 5 hectares (14 acres), the tone is tranquil and the feel is spacious. The guest rooms aren't large, but they're remarkable. West Indian colonial louvered doors, rather than drapes, cover the terrace doors, and intricately carved finials crown the mahogany four-poster beds. The reading chairs' retractable ottomans and floor lamps mix Bauhaus and plantation influences. Elegance stretches out to the balconies, too, where mahogany slatted chairs and flagstone floors enhance the view over the gardens or sea. To create the warmth of a private home, the Radisson adds such touches as frosted drinking glasses, silver ice buckets, and earth-toned pottery. Originally built in 1959 as Aruba's first High-Rise hotel, it's now Radisson's flagship hotel.

J.E. Irausquin Blvd. 81, Palm Beach, Aruba. © 800/333-3333 in the U.S. and Canada, or 297/586-6555. Fax 297/586-3260. www.radisson.com/aruba. 354 units. Christmas to New Year's $549–$700 double, from $920 suite; Jan and Apr $400–$575 double, from $829 suite; Feb–Mar $549–$700 double, from $929 suite; May–Christmas $275–$399 double, from $419 suite. Children 16 and under stay free in parent's room. Discounts for guests 51 and over. Packages available. AE, DISC, MC, V. **Amenities:** 3 restaurants, including Sunset Grille (see review, p. 65); 2 bars; babysitting; casino; children's center/program; concierge-level rooms; health club & spa; 2 outdoor Jacuzzis; outdoor pool; room service; smoke-free rooms; 2 tennis courts lit for night play; watersports equipment/rentals; rooms for those w/limited mobility. *In room:* A/C, TV, hair dryer, minibar, free Wi-Fi.

Westin Aruba Resort, Spa & Casino ★★★   Built in 1975 and most recently renovated in 2006, this hotel attracts couples, honeymooners, and families—and a fair number of business groups. The rooms are spacious, with a decor of olive, beige, and mustard fabrics that accent the cherrywood furniture. Subtle carpeting, flatscreen TVs, and modern rectangular lamps add more Miami style. The trademark Westin "heavenly" beds are indeed a white fluffy retreat from the world. The balconies are cozy, but, with 18 floors, this is Aruba's tallest building; a terrace anywhere near the top means superb ocean views. The kids' program includes scuba lessons in the pool. The free-form pool with a fountain is nice, and the iguanas that patrol the pool area are adorable. You have to wait in line in the morning to reserve a beach hut, and one never gets used to the sad sight of parrots, toucans, and cockatoos squawking in their cages.

J.E. Irausquin Blvd. 77, Palm Beach, Aruba. © **877/822-2222** in the U.S. or Canada, or 297/586-4466. Fax 297/586-0928. www.westinaruba.com. 481 units. Dec–Apr $305–$489 double, from $589 suite; May–Nov $259–$459 double, from $605 suite. Meal plans and packages available. Children 11 and under stay free in parent's room. AE, MC, V. **Amenities:** 6 restaurants, including Pago Pago (see review, p. 62); 4 bars; babysitting; casino; children's center/program; concierge; health club & spa; large outdoor pool; room service; smoke-free rooms; 2 tennis courts lit for night play nearby; watersports equipment/rentals. *In room:* A/C, TV, hair dryer, minibar, Wi-Fi ($12 per day).

EXPENSIVE

Aruba Divi Phoenix Beach Resort ★   A quiet timeshare affiliated with Divi Resorts, the Phoenix has some distinctive features. Its triangular, private balconies offer unobstructed ocean views, and its

 Tips   Freebies for Kids

The One Cool Family Vacation (OCFV) program entices families to visit Aruba during the summer (June–Sept). Here's the deal: Kids 12 and under get an assortment of freebies such as breakfast, daily activities, sightseeing tours, cruises, snorkeling, and scuba lessons; with this package, kids can stay free in their parents' room. In addition, discounts are offered for a submarine ride, horseback riding, car rental, and even film developing. The program covers two children for every paying adult. Contact the **Aruba Tourism Authority** (© **800/TO-ARUBA** [862-7822]; www.aruba.com) for a list of participating resorts.

well-equipped health club is inviting. The 66 tower units feature tile floors, sisal mats, rattan furniture, and kitchenettes or full kitchens; some one-bedroom units have an extra half bathroom and second balcony. Next to the tower, one- and two-bedroom villas boast enormous rooms, balconies that open off the master bedroom and living room, full kitchens, and living/dining areas. Some one bedrooms have two bathrooms. Ask for a villa away from the noisy air-conditioning unit. Guests are independent and 30-plus, with a smattering of kids. The 14-floor Phoenix tower marks the beginning of Palm Beach. Breakwaters protect the resort's large, peaceful oceanfront, but it's windier than farther up the strip.

J.E. Irausquin Blvd. 75, Palm Beach, Aruba. ✆ **800/376-3484** in the U.S. and Canada, or 297/586-6066. Fax 297/586-1165. www.diviphoenix.com. 101 units. Jan–Apr 14 $338 studio, $382 1 bedroom, $528 2 bedroom; Apr 15–Dec $207 studio, $233 1 bedroom, $322 2 bedroom. Children 15 and under stay free in parent's room. Packages available. AE, DISC, MC, V. **Amenities:** Restaurant; bar; children's activities; concierge; health club & spa; 2 outdoor pools; tennis courts nearby; watersports equipment/rentals; Wi-Fi ($10 per day). *In room:* A/C, TV/VCR, hair dryer, kitchen or kitchenette.

Holiday Inn SunSpree Aruba–Beach Resort & Casino ★ (Value)

Holiday Inn reserves SunSpree status for its best resorts. In this one, the inviting open lobby showcases Aruba's signature trade winds, which blow freely through the louvered teak wood walls, past the Southeast Asian furniture, toward the palm trees, bright sand, and turquoise waters outside. While not the ritziest hotel on the strip, it offers value. You'll find lots of families, couples, and honeymooners here, and many South Americans (although North Americans still account for more than 60% of guests). Distributed among three seven-story towers, the rooms feature wall-to-wall carpeting, handsome hardwood furniture, and cheerful colors. Some have sofa beds; all have full, if only average, bathrooms and balconies or patios. Microwaves are available for $5 per day. Essentially identical in layout and furnishings, units are classified by view—garden or ocean. Because it's bounded by development on one side only, the Holiday Inn's beach is the largest in the High-Rise area.

J.E. Irausquin Blvd. 230, Palm Beach, Aruba. ✆ **800/HOLIDAY** [465-4329] in the U.S. and Canada, or 297/586-3600. Fax 297/586-5165. www.sunspreeresorts.com. 600 units. Christmas to New Year's $350–$400 double; Jan–Apr $300–$350 double; May–Christmas $145–$185 double. Children 17 and under stay free in parent's room. Children 11 and under eat free with dining adult. Packages available. AE, MC, V. **Amenities:** 3 restaurants; 2 bars; babysitting; casino; children's center/program and playground; concierge; small exercise room; large outdoor pool; children's pool; room service; smoke-free rooms; spa; 4 tennis courts lit for night play; watersports equipment/rentals; rooms for those w/limited mobility. *In room:* A/C, TV, fridge, hair dryer, Wi-Fi ($10 per day or $35 per week).

Playa Linda Beach Resort ★★   Centrally located on Palm
Beach, this luxurious timeshare overlooks the Caribbean coastline.
Built in the '80s, the resort is undergoing a renovation, which will
update all units and is slated for completion in September 2010.
Accommodations have balconies or decks with impressive views.
Studios feature fully equipped kitchenettes, a queen-size bed, and a
pullout sofa. One-bedrooms have master suites with full kitchens and
living/dining areas. The one-bedroom lanai suites feature patios that
open onto the pool area. Slightly larger than other one-bedroom
units, they have spacious wooden decks and minigardens rather than
balconies. The two-bedroom oceanfront units boast large master
suites with king-size beds and two-sink bathrooms, guest rooms with
two twin beds, kitchens, living and dining rooms, another full bathroom, and wraparound terraces with unbeatable vistas. Rooms facing
away from the pool are generally quieter. During the peak season,
most guests are luxury conscious and older, but as the year progresses,
families and honeymooners begin to predominate.

J.E. Irausquin Blvd. 87, Palm Beach, Aruba. ⓒ **800/992-2015** in the U.S. and Canada, or 297/586-1000. Fax 297/586-3479. www.playalinda.com. 198 units. Early
Dec to Apr $300 studio, $425 1 bedroom, $625 2 bedroom; May to late Dec $200
studio, $280 1 bedroom, $400 2 bedroom. AE, MC, V. **Amenities:** 3 restaurants; 2
bars; babysitting; children's program; concierge; fitness center; outdoor lagoon
pool; children's pool; spa; 3 tennis courts lit for night play; watersports equipment/
rentals nearby. *In room:* A/C, TV, kitchen or kitchenette.

MODERATE

Caribbean Palm Village Resort Close to Santa Anna Church,
the three-story Caribbean Palm Village Resort rests in the town of
Noord, a 15- to 20-minute walk inland from Palm Beach. Because
units in this timeshare are completely sold out, vacation rentals are
limited. The attractive Spanish mission–style buildings, first opened
in 1987, feature white stucco walls, terra-cotta tile roofs, and plenty
of columns and arches. The spacious rooms feature cane and glass
furniture, fabrics in soothing shades, and white tile floors. All units
have roomy full bathrooms and queen- or king-size beds. Each studio
has a kitchenette, and the airy, bright one- and two-bedroom suites
come with full kitchens and sofa beds. Attractive gardens surround
the two pool areas. Because the front pool is the center of activity,
rooms adjacent to the back pool are quieter. The resort's a hike from
the sea, but the beach shuttle is free.

Palm Beach 43E, Noord, Aruba. ⓒ **297/586-2700.** www.cpvr.com. Fax 297/586-
2380. 228 units. Late Dec to Mar $170 studio, $225 1-bedroom suite, $290 2-bed-
room suite; Apr to early Dec $100 studio, $125 1-bedroom suite, $165 2-bedroom
suite. AE, DISC, MC, V. **Amenities:** 2 restaurants; bar; Internet kiosks; 2 outdoor
pools; tennis court; barbecue grills. *In room:* A/C, TV, kitchenette or kitchen.

The Mill Resort & Suites ★ (Finds The only Low-Rise in the High-Rise area, this resort combines Dutch efficiency and Aruban warmth. Originally opened in 1990, the two-story complex lies opposite Palm Beach and the Westin. Its strengths include personal service, easy access to amenities, and reasonable prices. Guests vary from honeymooning couples to singles looking to have a good time. The sunny units feature bamboo furniture and tile floors. Junior rooms have a king-size bed, a full bathroom, a sitting area with sofa bed, a good-size porch or balcony, and a kitchenette. Studios have one king-size bed, a pullout sofa, a shower-only bathroom, a dining/sitting area, and a kitchen. A Jacuzzi is steps away from a king-size bed in the royal rooms, which also boast a sitting area, and a porch or balcony. Garden- and pool-view rooms cost the same; the pool's party atmosphere wanes later in the day, but garden rooms are quieter round-the-clock. Beach access is directly across the street.

J.E. Irausquin Blvd. 330, Palm Beach, Aruba. (℡ **800/992-2015** in the U.S. and Canada, or 297/586-7700. Fax 297/586-7271. www.millresort.com. 200 units. Dec 20–Mar $274 royal room, $287 studio, $314 junior suite, $481 1-bedroom suite, $676 2-bedroom suite; Apr–Dec 19 $140 royal room, $150 studio, $188 junior suite, $295 1-bedroom suite, $436 2-bedroom suite. Children 11 and under stay free in parent's room. Packages available. AE, MC, V. No children in royal rooms. **Amenities:** Restaurant; bar; babysitting; concierge; exercise room & spa; pool; children's pool; smoke-free rooms; 2 tennis courts lit for night play; Wi-Fi around pool and in lobby ($7 per day); 1 room for those w/limited mobility. *In room:* A/C, TV, hair dryer.

Occidental Grand Aruba This resort reinvented itself as an Occidental in 2006. The lobby combines Moroccan- and European-style furnishing and fixtures. Guest rooms include tile and marble floors, and private balconies or terraces. The pool has a bustling feel, so if you're looking for a casual house-party atmosphere with lots of action and organized activities, this place is for you. Most people choose an all-inclusive package or the ultradeluxe Royal Club option. The resort is popular with almost everybody—families, young couples, middle-age folks, and some seniors. About 80% of the guests come from the U.S. and Canada, and most use their rooms for little more than crashing. You have a choice of garden, pool, or ocean view. The ground-floor lanai rooms (next to the pool) have terraces instead of small balconies and are great for families.

J.E. Irausquin Blvd. 83, Palm Beach, Aruba. (℡ **800/858-2258** in the U.S. and Canada, or 297/586-4500. Fax 297/586-3191. www.occidentalhotels.com. 380 units. May 1–Dec 22 from $444 per person; Dec 23–Apr 30 from $538 per person. Rates are all-inclusive. Children 1 and under stay free in parent's room. Children 2–12 half price. Packages available. AE, DISC, MC, V. **Amenities:** 6 restaurants; 5 bars; babysitting; casino; children's center/program and playground; exercise room; 2 outdoor pools; room service; smoke-free rooms; spa; 2 tennis courts lit for night play; watersports equipment/rentals; rooms for those w/limited mobility. *In room:* A/C, TV, fridge (on request), hair dryer.

Aruba Millennium This two-story bright-yellow motel is a 10-minute walk inland from Palm Beach. The studios and one-bedroom units, each with a kitchenette, face either the small pool or one of two cozy courtyards. Ask for a room facing the serene and inviting pool. Each of the courtyards features two minuscule and somewhat dodgy-looking Jacuzzis with small, rickety wooden decks. All rooms boast either a balcony or a raised rustic-wood terrace with patio furniture and a blue-and-white-striped awning. Inside, faded and well-worn blue and yellow floral prints accent the white wicker and bamboo furniture. Ask for a nonsmoking room to avoid the smoke smell, which has permeated the drapes. White tile floors run throughout the compact dining areas and functional bathrooms. Restaurants and other shops are within easy walking distance. The motel's quiet ambience makes it popular with budget-conscious families, locals, and couples looking to zone out by the pool.

Palm Beach 33, Palm Beach, Aruba. ✆ **297/586-3700.** Fax 297/586-2506. www. arubamillenniumresort.com. 20 units. Dec–Apr $130 studio, $175 1 bedroom; May–Nov $60 studio, $95 1 bedroom. Children 11 and under stay free in parent's room. AE, MC, V. **Amenities:** Small outdoor pool. *In room:* A/C, TV, kitchenette.

Brickell Bay Beach Club Aruba ⓥalue This four-story complex is much like an American-style chain motel, but its cleanliness and proximity to the action make it the island's best budget option. This hotel has no beachfront, but the sea is no more than a 5-minute walk away, and the pool is inviting. Although the rooms have cookie-cutter uniformity, and a slightly musty aroma, the walls, carpet, and furnishings are cheerfully colored. All rooms have either two double beds or one king. The bathrooms are bright and functional if not luxuriously spacious. Many guests are here for the nearby casinos, but the hotel also has dive and honeymoon packages. The wide selection of shopping and casual dining venues nearby is a plus, though the Hooters and Benihana, only steps away from the lobby, have removed some of the hotel's former quiet charm.

J.E. Irausquin Blvd. 370, Palm Beach, Aruba. ✆ **800/324-6965** in the U.S. and Canada, or 297/586-0900. Fax 297/586-4957. www.brickellbayaruba.com. 101 units. Jan–Mar $185 double; Apr–Dec $135 double. Packages available. AE, MC, V. **Amenities:** 3 restaurants; 2 bars; babysitting; pool; spa. *In room:* A/C, TV, fridge (on request), hair dryer, Wi-Fi.

Coconut Inn This low-budget bed-and-breakfast is about a 20-minute walk inland from Palm Beach, in a hamlet near Santa Anna Church. Brick pathways lined by coconut palms border the five bright yellow-and-white stucco buildings. The corrugated metal rooftops are painted to look like terra-cotta tile. Wood decks with rustic chairs front the ground-floor rooms; second-floor units have balconies.

The basic accommodations feature white-tile floors and simple furnishings. All rooms have a kitchenette or full kitchen. The bathrooms sport Liliputian sinks and offer only cold running water. The motel serves a complimentary hot breakfast of eggs, sausage, toast, coffee, and juice in its now-defunct restaurant. Shops and restaurants are nearby, but take care walking at night as the winding road to the main street has no sidewalk.

Noord 31, Noord, Aruba. ℂ **297/586-6288.** Fax 297/586-5433. www.coconutinn. com. 40 units. Dec 16–Apr 15 $87 superior studio double, $101 deluxe studio or 1-bedroom apt double; Apr 16–Dec 15 $71 superior studio double, $85 deluxe studio or 1-bedroom apt double; Christmas–Apr $588 superior studio double weekly, $684 deluxe studio or 1-bedroom apt double weekly; May–Christmas $483 superior studio double weekly, $523 deluxe studio or 1-bedroom apt double weekly. Rates include breakfast. Children 11 and under stay free in parent's room. MC, V. **Amenities:** High-speed Internet in lobby; small outdoor pool. *In room:* A/C, TV, kitchen or kitchenette.

3 LOW-RISE HOTELS/EAGLE & MANCHEBO BEACHES

VERY EXPENSIVE

Costa Linda Beach Resort ★★★   On a glorious 183m (600-ft.) stretch of Eagle Beach, this timeshare offers some of Aruba's most impressive accommodations. Its five-story Dutch-Caribbean buildings feature sunny ocher walls with white trim and terra-cotta tile roofs. Inside, tropical colors, split-cane furniture, and light-tile floors brighten the enormous two- and three-bedroom suites. All units have expansive living/dining rooms, kitchens, at least two TVs, a master suite with raised Roman tub and separate shower, a guest bedroom with twin beds and full bathroom, and a large private balcony with an ocean view. The three-bedroom suites boast an adjoining studio with its own kitchenette, TV, and bathroom; and an enormous balcony. Big enough to entertain 20 to 30 cocktail guests, these ocean-facing terraces feature patio furniture for eight, a raised Jacuzzi for four, and a party-size barbecue grill. Built in 1991, the resort undergoes constant refurbishment and promotes environmental consciousness: Recycling bins and posted exhortations to conserve are everywhere.

J.E. Irausquin Blvd. 59, Eagle Beach, Aruba. ℂ **800/992-2015** in the U.S. and Canada, or 297/583-8000. Fax 297/583-6040. www.costalinda-aruba.com. 155 units. Christmas to New Year's $751 2-bedroom suite, $1,467 3-bedroom suite; Jan–Apr $589 2-bedroom suite, $1,305 3-bedroom suite; May to late Dec $378 2-bedroom suite, $751 3-bedroom suite. AE, DISC, MC, V. **Amenities:** 2 restaurants; 2 bars; babysitting; children's program; teen program; concierge; exercise room;

Sustainable Tourism

A kind of environmental *Good Housekeeping* seal of approval, the **Green Globe** certificate recognizes hotels around the world that develop and implement sound, ecofriendly policies. The Amsterdam Manor Aruba Beach Resort was Aruba's first resort to be certified, followed quickly by the Aruba Bucuti Beach Resort and Tara Beach Suites & Spa, Costa Linda Beach Resort, Manchebo Beach Resort & Spa, and Playa Linda Beach Resort. The Aruba Beach Club is the latest hotel to make the list. Bucuti guests and nonguests alike are invited to join in on beach cleanups at 8:30am on the third Wednesday of every month. Volunteers are rewarded for their efforts with a hearty free breakfast and a group photo. Log on to www. greenglobeint.com to learn more.

large outdoor pool; children's pool; 2 tennis courts lit for night play; watersports equipment/rentals nearby; beach wheelchair available; barbecue facilities. *In room:* A/C, TV, hair dryer, kitchen.

EXPENSIVE

Aruba Bucuti Beach Resort and Tara Beach Suites & Spa ★★★ (Finds) This elegant oasis provides Aruba's most adult ambience. Set on one of the Caribbean's best beaches, a serene 5.7-hectare (14-acre) expanse of sand, it's a favored retreat for sophisticated couples of all ages, especially honeymooners. About half are from Europe, and most are independent and well traveled. And though most guests are straight, the Bucuti is both appealing and welcoming to gay couples. Contemporary minimalist design with walnut and linen tones warm the spacious rooms, and the large balconies overlook gardens or the beach. Penthouses and the junior suites have kitchenettes. Because the owner is the driving force behind many environmental initiatives, the hotel is one of Aruba's greenest; recycling bins, water-conservation measures, and beachwide cleanups are part of the effort. Beach lovers appreciate the Bucuti's *palapa*-to-guest ratio—it's the highest on the island. At the breezy, open-air fitness area, nature and exercise go hand in hand.

L.G. Smith Blvd. 55B, Eagle Beach, Aruba. © **888/4BUCUTI** [428-2884] in the U.S. and Canada, or 297/583-1100. Fax 297/582-5272. www.bucuti.com. 104 units. Dec 23–Apr 18 $364–$459 double, $535 suite; Apr 19–Dec 22 $250–$336 double, $416 suite. Rates include full American breakfast buffet. Packages available. AE, DISC, MC, V. **Amenities:** Restaurant; bar; bike rental; concierge; open-air health club; outdoor pool. *In room:* A/C, TV, fridge, hair dryer, microwave, minibar.

Casa del Mar Beach Resort ★★ On Manchebo Beach, across from the Alhambra Casino, this timeshare resort is affiliated with the Aruba Beach Club next door; amenities at both complexes are available to guests of either hotel. Casa del Mar consists of two four-story buildings (each with a pool) separated by a quiet street. The majority of the timeshare owners and rental guests are North American families. Constructed in 1986, the two-bedroom presidential suites feature three TVs and fully equipped kitchens. Both the living rooms and master bedrooms open to the large square balconies. The guest rooms have two twin beds and full bathrooms. Pleasant dark-rattan furniture, muted solid colors, and off-white tile floors decorate the spacious living/dining area. Ocean- and island-view suites cost the same; ocean views are prettier, but the island-view units are quieter. Across the street, the ambassador wing has no beachfront; the tranquil one-bedroom suites here also have two TVs, but the kitchen/dining/living area is more compact.

J.E. Irausquin Blvd. 51, Punta Brabo Beach, Aruba. © **297/582-7000.** Fax 297/582-9044. www.casadelmar-aruba.com. 147 units. Dec 19–Apr 10 $450 presidential double; $225 ambassador double; Apr 11–Dec 18 $325 presidential double, $175 ambassador double. AE, DISC, MC, V. **Amenities:** Restaurant; Internet cafe; pool bar; babysitting; children's program; exercise room; Jacuzzis; 2 outdoor pools; children's pool; 2 tennis courts lit for night play; watersports equipment/rentals; rooms for those w/limited mobility. *In room:* A/C, TV, kitchen or kitchenette.

MODERATE

Amsterdam Manor Aruba Beach Resort ★★ (Finds This cheerful gem is a refreshing alternative to cookie-cutter uniformity. With a strong European accent and couples-friendly slant, the Amsterdam Manor features a quiet atmosphere and boutique size that's perfect for independent travelers. The last Low-Rise resort on the road to the High Rises, the hotel's across the street from Eagle Beach and near the bus stop for easy access to town. Bird lovers enjoy the proximity to the Bubali Bird Sanctuary. The architecture of the three-floor complex is Dutch gingerbread with quaint gabled roofs, and whimsical turrets. Scattered around a series of intimate courtyards, the studios and one- and two-bedroom suites feature oak furniture and stylish wicker sofa sets. All units feature a balcony or terrace and kitchen or kitchenette. Standard studios have shower-only bathrooms, while superior units have a Jacuzzi and an ocean view. Suites on the top floor boast high-barn ceilings. An environmental leader, the resort is Green Globe certified, and the staff organizes a beach cleanup every third Wednesday of the month.

J.E. Irausquin Blvd. 252, Oranjestad, Aruba. © **800/969-2310** in the U.S. and Canada, or 297/527-1100. Fax 297/527-1112. www.amsterdammanor.com. 72 units. Dec 20–Apr 13 $249–$279 studio, $329 1-bedroom suite, $400 2-bedroom suite; Apr 14–Dec 19 $159–$189 studio, $239 1-bedroom suite, $289 2-bedroom suite. Packages available. Children 11 and under stay free in parent's room. MC, V. **Amenities:** 2 restaurants; 2 bars; concierge; outdoor pool; children's pool; smoke-free rooms; watersports equipment/rentals; free Wi-Fi in lobby; rooms for those w/ limited mobility. *In room:* A/C, TV, kitchen or kitchenette.

Aruba Beach Club   Rather than dazzle guests with an array of activities, this intimate, family-friendly resort and timeshare charms with friendliness and service. Each spacious room has two queen-size beds, and most have large balconies or terraces. The good-size bathrooms have a vanity chair and lots of counter space. Each studio has a large, shower-only bathroom and a kitchenette. The units on the second floor have much higher ceilings. Deluxe and royal superb one-bedroom suites boast a dining area, comfortable living room, and a full kitchen; royal superb rooms have two bathrooms. Guests are free to avail themselves of all amenities offered by the adjacent Casa del Mar Beach Resort.

J.E. Irausquin Blvd. 53, Punta Brabo Beach, Aruba. ✆ **297/582-3000.** Fax 297/583-8191. www.arubabeachclub.net. 131 units. Dec–Apr $249 studio double, $328 deluxe suite, $370 royal superb suite; May–Nov $177 studio double, $220 deluxe suite, $244 royal superb suite. AE, DISC, MC, V. **Amenities:** Restaurant; Internet cafe; bar; babysitting; children's program; exercise room; large outdoor pool; children's pool; 2 tennis courts lit for night play; watersports equipment/rentals; Wi-Fi; rooms for those w/limited mobility. *In room:* A/C, TV/VCR, kitchen or kitchenette.

Divi Aruba All Inclusive   This resort on Druif Beach is one of Aruba's top hotels for honeymoon bookings. Stays include unlimited food and beverages at 10 dining outlets and seven bars, unlimited watersports, bicycles, tennis, nightly entertainment, activities, taxes, and service charges, plus access to all the facilities and amenities of the adjacent Tamarijn Aruba All Inclusive. All rooms boast balconies or patios. Garden rooms are less expensive and farther from the beach than oceanview and oceanfront units, but they're quieter. Rooms in the double-story Lanai building open directly onto the wide beach, and casitas/beachside rooms face small patios just steps from the beach. Free golf-cart transport connects guests with the adjacent Tamarijn. How to choose between them? The Divi Aruba is closer to other Low-Rise amenities, such as the Alhambra Casino, while the Tamarijn is closer to the adjacent Divi Links golf course, and all its rooms are oceanfront.

J.E. Irausquin Blvd. 45, Druif Beach, Aruba. ✆ **800/554-2008** in the U.S. and Canada, or 297/525-5200. Fax 297/525-5203. www.diviaruba.com. 203 units. Jan 3–31 $476–$550; Feb $512–$688; Mar $476–$550; Apr 1–17 $438–$512; Apr 18–Dec 18 $412–$488; Dec 19–Jan 2 $550–$626. Rates are all-inclusive. Minimum 3-night stay. Children 1 and under stay free in parent's room. Children 2–18 additional $50 per child per night in room with 2 paying adults. Maximum 2 children per room. Packages available. AE, DISC, MC, V. **Amenities:** 10 restaurants; 7 bars; babysitting; bikes; children's program; concierge; adjacent 9-hole golf course; 18-hole championship golf course nearby; fitness center; Internet lounge (rates start at $2.50 for 10 min.); 3 outdoor pools; spa; sports center w/outdoor climbing wall on the beach; 2 tennis courts lit for night play; watersports equipment; wedding services; rooms for those w/limited mobility. *In room:* A/C, TV, video-on-demand system w/Internet access ($15 per day), minifridge, hair dryer ($2 per day).

Manchebo Beach Resort & Spa ★ (**Value**) Next to the Bucuti Beach Resort on a fabled stretch of Eagle Beach, this little hotel offers good value and friendly, personal service. The glorious 4-hectare (10-acre) beach speaks for itself, and the open-air lobby boasts stylish Indonesian furniture, which is echoed in the serene beachfront spa. Too restrained to be kitschy, both of the two-story wings feature white stucco walls, pink and turquoise accents, and whimsical painted embellishments over the doorways. The rooms have mahogany furniture, and while not spectacular, they're pristine, with gleaming bathrooms, and a patio or balcony with a garden or ocean view. Members of the staff welcome guests—lots of honeymooners and repeat visitors—as family. Built in 1967, the Manchebo is constantly renovated, but it retains its aura of a simpler time.

J.E. Irausquin Blvd. 55, Eagle Beach, Aruba. ⓒ **888/673-8036** in the U.S. and Canada, or 297/582-3444. www.manchebo.com. 71 units. Dec 22–Apr 5 $255–$305 double; Apr 6–Dec 21 $169–$195 double. Packages available. Children 11 and under stay free in parent's room. AE, DISC, MC, V. **Amenities:** 3 restaurants, including the French Steakhouse (see review, p. 70); 2 bars; concierge; 18-hole championship golf course nearby; fitness room; free Internet access in lobby; outdoor pool; smoke-free rooms; outdoor spa on the beach; watersports equipment/rentals. *In room:* A/C, flatscreen TV, fridge, hair dryer, microwave, Wi-Fi.

Paradise Beach Villas ★ Across the street from one of Eagle Beach's nicest sections, this quiet, welcoming timeshare features Spanish mission–style two- and three-story buildings. Because many owners come back yearly, there's an air of family reunion. American couples in their 30s, 40s, and 50s, are often joined by children and grandkids during the high season. Independent rental guests enjoy the laid-back atmosphere. White-tile floors, tropical colors, and wicker furniture brighten every unit. Balconies are large, and bathrooms have a Jacuzzi. Studios have a kitchenette, while suites have a full kitchen. In the two- and three-bedroom suites, guest rooms feature two single beds and adjacent bathrooms. The master bedrooms have a queen- or king-size bed and a bathroom. In town houses, a spiral staircase ascends to the master suite. The more expensive Phase II units are closer to the beach, are roomier overall, and have a larger pool nearby.

J.E. Irausquin Blvd., Eagle Beach, Aruba. ⓒ **297/587-4000.** Fax 297/587-0071. www.paradisebeachvillas-aruba.com. 80 units. Dec 23–Apr 4 $158 studio double, $220–$315 1-bedroom suite, $331–$473 2-bedroom suite, $661 3-bedroom penthouse; Apr 5–Dec 22 $125 studio double, $175–$237 1-bedroom suite, $265–$357 2-bedroom suite, $495 3-bedroom penthouse. Children 1 and under stay free in parent's room. Children 2–12 stay in parent's room for $15 per day. AE, DISC, MC, V. **Amenities:** 2 restaurants; bar; babysitting; exercise room; Jacuzzis; 2 large outdoor pools/lagoons; rooms for those w/limited mobility. *In room:* A/C, TV, VCR (on request), kitchenette or kitchen.

Tamarijn Aruba All Inclusive   This hip yet casual, all-inclusive, oceanfront Druif Beach resort is a perennial favorite for families. All stays include unlimited food and beverages at 10 dining outlets and seven bars, unlimited use of three freshwater pools, all the nonmotorized watersports you can handle, bicycles, tennis, activities, and nightly entertainment plus access to all the facilities, services, and amenities of the adjacent Divi Aruba All Inclusive. Children ages 5 to 12 can enjoy the Kids Camp, offering activities such as T-shirt and face painting, pool and beach games, scavenger hunts, snorkeling, tennis clinics, and more. All rooms are oceanfront with a balcony or patio. The spacious rooms in the two-story buildings feature blue upholstery, rattan furniture, and tile floors. The Tamarijn Aruba is ideal for families but it's still low-key enough to attract older guests. There is also a weekly Latin night and limbo show.

J.E. Irausquin Blvd. 41, Druif Beach, Aruba. © **800/554-2008** in the U.S. and Canada, or 297/525-5200. Fax 297/525-5203. www.tamarijnaruba.com. 236 units. Jan 3–31 $446; Feb $488; Mar $446; Apr 1–17 $414; Apr 18–Dec 18 $362; Dec 19–Jan 2 $514. Rates are all-inclusive. Minimum 3-night stay. Children 17 and under stay, play, and eat free with 2 paying adults. Packages available. AE, DISC, MC, V. **Amenities:** 10 restaurants; 7 bars; babysitting; bikes; children's center/program; concierge; adjacent 9-hole golf course; 18-hole championship golf course nearby; fitness center; Internet lounge (rates start at $2.50 for 10 min.); 3 outdoor pools; spa; sports center w/outdoor climbing wall on the beach; 2 tennis courts lit for night play; nonmotorized watersports equipment; wedding services; rooms for those w/limited mobility. *In room:* A/C, TV, video-on-demand system w/Internet access ($15 per day), minifridge, hair dryer.

INEXPENSIVE

Arubiana Inn (Value)   A 15-minute walk inland from Eagle Beach, this quiet, tidy motel lies in wild, cactus-covered terrain a few hundred feet from a main road. The single-story structure of coral stucco and terra-cotta tile encloses a central pool area that boasts plenty of chairs and tables. Each of the squeaky-clean studio units opens to the palm-lined pool and courtyard. The cozy rooms feature white-tile floors, white wicker furniture, and pastel floral prints. The small bathrooms are blindingly white with salmon accents. A minimart supplies food and other items. Restaurants, a supermarket, and miniature golf are a few minutes away by foot.

Bubali 74, Noord, Aruba. © **297/587-7700.** Fax 297/587-1770. www.arubianainn. com. 16 units. Dec 15–Apr 14 $98 double; Apr 15–Aug 31 $82 double; Sept 1–Dec 14 $75 double. Children 11 and under stay free in parent's room. AE, MC, V. **Amenities:** Small outdoor pool. *In room:* A/C, TV, fridge, microwave.

4 TIERRA DEL SOL

VERY EXPENSIVE

Tierra del Sol Aruba Resort & Country Club ★★ If you think more about sand traps than sand castles, Tierra del Sol tops the board. This resort combines the sun and golf of Scottsdale with the waves and dunes of Aruba's north coast. Tierra del Sol offers a championship 18-hole golf course designed by Robert Trent Jones II and Mediterranean-style condominiums, villas, and homes clustered in intimate neighborhoods, spread over hectares of desert landscaping. Each unit has a golf-course or ocean view, a living room, dining room, kitchen, a master suite with a full bathroom, guest rooms with another bathroom, a covered terrace with patio furniture, and a washer and dryer. Some also feature walk-in closets, a sauna, balcony, outdoor Jacuzzi, private pool, and a garage. You can arrive to a fully stocked kitchen by ordering items online beforehand.

Malmokweg z/n, Noord, Aruba. Ⓒ **800/992-2015** in the U.S. and Canada or 297/586-7800. Fax 297/586-4970. www.tierradelsol.com. 114 units. Jan 3–Apr 11 $350–$425 2-bedroom condo, $500 3-bedroom condo, $495–$575 2-bedroom villa, $700 3-bedroom villa; Apr 12–Dec 18 $300–$375 2-bedroom condo, $400 3-bedroom condo, $400–$475 2-bedroom villa, $575 3-bedroom villa; Dec 19–Jan 2 $525–$625 2-bedroom condo, $675 3-bedroom condo, $625–$675 2-bedroom villa, $875 3-bedroom villa. Golf packages are available. AE, MC, V. **Amenities:** 2 restaurants, including Ventanas del Mar (see review, p. 71); 3 bars; concierge; 18-hole championship golf course; fitness center & spa; outdoor pool; 2 tennis courts lit for night play. *In room:* A/C, TV, kitchen.

3

Where to Dine in Aruba

If you're like lots of folks vacationing in Aruba, you'll spend all day on the beach thinking about where to dine that night. The options are prodigious. Few places as small as Aruba can boast such a variety of quality restaurants. In fact, with the exception of the French islands and Puerto Rico, Aruba leaves most of the Caribbean in the dust.

This is due in large part to fierce competition. Most restaurateurs never stop thinking of new ways to bring you through their doors. And most are loath to leave anyone behind, so there's usually something for vegetarians, kids, and couples celebrating special occasions (how about a romantic private room or a table on the beach?). Because some form of entertainment has become almost de rigueur, expect to be serenaded by live bands, jazz saxophonists, or a pianist. Frequent culinary competitions spur chefs to experiment and hone their skills, constantly raising the quality bar. And while most restaurants offer Continental cuisine, there are plenty of ethnic spots to choose from as well, so when you're not feasting on steak, seafood, or Aruban specialties, you can try something Argentine, French, Caribbean, Swiss, Indonesian, Cuban, Italian, Mexican, or Asian Fusion.

Restaurant prices are a bit steep in Aruba, but with good reason. Almost nothing grows on the arid island, so most edibles, with the exception of some seafood, are imported. That gets to be expensive. Fruits and vegetables come primarily from the United States and Venezuela, but some make the trip from as far away as Europe. Beef is flown in from Argentina and the U.S. Portions are large, if that's any consolation. In fact, most deserts are served on full-size dinner plates, and are more than enough for two to share.

Most restaurants are an $8-to-$16 taxi ride from your hotel, but many are within easy walking distance of the major resorts in the High-Rise area. If you have a car, call for explicit directions: Inadequate street signs and a cabdriver's substandard navigation skills often lead to wrong turns and missed reservations. Another caveat: If you're going into Oranjestad from the hotel areas, allow yourself some time to get there. Traffic into the capital is absurd at times, and parking can be hard to find.

It used to be tough to find a restaurant that was open for lunch on Sunday, but no more. Some—especially hotel restaurants—even do a lavish brunch, but double-check before you set out.

EXPENSIVE

Mathilde ★★★ FRENCH   Opulence and first-rate French cuisine make Mathilde a superb choice for special occasions. In 2007, the restaurant was transformed from a classically elegant ambience to a new sleek, modern, and artistic decor. A classic French fusion menu is served, complete with table-side preparation of salads and crepes. Two things that have not changed are the outstanding array of wines in the perfectly cooled wine cellar, and the outstanding food. Appetizers include escargot and beef carpaccio. The Dover sole, which is sautéed in butter with lemon, baby carrots, grilled zucchini, and almond potato, is filleted at your table. You can also feast on chateaubriand, rack of lamb, Kobe beef, or ostrich. For dessert, the crème brûlée or soufflé are bested only by the crepes. Finish with a Café Mathilde (espresso with Kahlúa and a dash of cognac topped with fresh whipped cream and cinnamon) or some homemade chocolates and a cognac.

Havenstraat 23, downtown Oranjestad. ✆ **297/583-4968.** www.matildearuba. com. Reservations recommended. Proper attire required (no shorts). Main courses $32–$52. AE, DISC, MC, V. Daily 11:30am–2:30pm and 6–11pm.

MODERATE

Cuba's Cookin' ★ (Finds) CUBAN   This fun, informal, and hip eatery is located in an old farmhouse. Original art captures whimsical scenes of Cuban street life while up-tempo music keeps the warm staff smiling each night. Sip a *mojito* (a traditional Cuban cocktail), and start with the plantain chips, great with the *muy picante* (very hot) salsa. Your conga cocktail appetizer should arrive just in time to extinguish the fire in your mouth. Served in a half shell, the cool appetizer features lobster, crab, red onions, and carrots in a light vinaigrette. The seafood boat is a winning main course: Lightly grilled shrimp, calamari, conch, and mussels rise from a flavorful ragout of green and red peppers, onions, garlic, tomatoes, and cucumbers. Other Cuban specialties include *ropa vieja* (shredded skirt steak sautéed in tomatoes, onions, and green peppers) and *picadillo de res* (ground beef with raisins and olives). For dessert, try *tres leches* (three-milk) pound cake then light up a Cuban cigar with your *café con leche.*

Wilhelminastraat 27 (across from the police station), downtown Oranjestad. ✆ **297/588-0627.** www.cubascookin.com. Reservations recommended. Main courses $18–$38. AE, MC, V. Mon–Sat noon–3pm and 5:30–11pm. Closed Sun.

Driftwood ★ ARUBAN/SEAFOOD   Authentic Aruban seafood doesn't get any fresher or better than the fare at this rustic restaurant tucked away on a side street. Keeping with its name, this cozy venue

Dining Details

What to Wear?   Dress is almost always casual. At many places, dinner dress is elegant casual (sundresses for women, long pants for men). A couple of restaurants enforce a "no shorts" policy.

How Much to Tip?   Many, but not all, restaurants add a service charge, ranging from 10% to 15%, to your bill. Most of this money is distributed among all restaurant employees, so your waiter will receive only a portion of this. If you feel your waiter or waitress has earned it, leave about 10% on the table. If no service charge is automatically added, tip 15% or 20% if the service was exceptional.

What About Reservations?   Reservations are universally appreciated. During the high season, or for large groups, they're necessary at the most popular places. Your hotel concierge will be happy to make reservations for you.

What About Sustainability?   Most restaurants in Aruba continue to serve local species that are on the decline, such as conch and Caribbean lobster. If you are concerned about your impact, you may want to steer clear of Caribbean lobster, conch, and reef fish, such as grouper, snapper, and grunt, and opt for equally tasty ecofriendly alternatives, such as wahoo, dorado, and barracuda, caught far off the fragile reef.

is full of gnarled driftwood posts and slats laced with ship lanterns and Captain Nemo underwater helmets. The owner wakes up early every morning, hops on his boat, and stalks the coast for your dinner. In fact, he also charters fishing boats for the day and half-day, and will cook up whatever you catch that day. Depending on what he snags, you might enjoy shrimp, octopus, squid, or mahimahi. The house special drink is white sangria (white wine with fresh melon), which is as refreshing as it is ingenious. The Aruban seafood soup with fish, shrimp, scallops, and vegetables is an authentic taste of the island. Lightly floured wahoo sautéed in garlic and served with cilantro-butter sauce is unfussy and delicious. Just about everything comes with the local corn bread, pan bati. For dessert, it's a tossup between the cheesecake and the crème brûlée.

Klipstraat 12, downtown Oranjestad. ✆ **297/583-2515.** www.driftwoodaruba.com. Reservations recommended. Main courses $21–$46. AE, DISC, MC, V. Wed–Mon 5–10:30pm.

Le Petit Café SEAFOOD/STEAK   When they say the plate's hot here, they mean it. Le Petit Café offers seafood and beef served on stone platters as hot as molten lava. With the "stove" at your table, you determine how much your meal's cooked. A boon on breezy evenings, a hot plate is a mistake during the heat of the day. The pink and turquoise stucco walls fit right in with the confectionery architecture of the surrounding shopping mall. Start things off with a Crazy Monkey; boasting vodka, Bailey's Irish Cream, Kahlúa, crème de banana, and amaretto, it covers three of the major food groups. The crispy conch fritters are a good appetizer. For the main course, jumbo shrimp "on the stone," marinated in olive oil and enough garlic to keep vampires at bay, tastes like it just came off the barbie. The lobster, shrimp, and beef tenderloin combo is just as flavorful.

3 locations: Royal Plaza Mall (downtown Oranjestad; ✆ **297/583-8471**), Playa Linda Beach Resort (Palm Beach; ✆ **297/587-4046**), and Paradise Beach Villas (Eagle Beach; ✆ **297/587-4620**). Reservations recommended. Main courses $18–$33. AE, MC, V. Mon–Sat 11am–midnight; Sun 6–11pm.

L.G. Smith's Chop and Steak House ★★ SEAFOOD/ STEAK   The dining choices at the Renaissance Aruba Resort & Casino are vast, but nothing quite tops this hip and sophisticated venue, with its wood paneling, quartzite-stone columns, black furniture with white-leatherette cushions, and a panoramic view of the Oranjestad marina. Located next to the upper level of the casino entrance, the restaurant doesn't survive on its trendy decor alone, but serves one of the best selections of meat in Aruba, ranging from porterhouse to New York strip. Naturally, you expect surf and turf on the menu, but the chef goes far beyond the routine, offering such dishes as locally caught tuna with a cilantro-laced mango salsa or free-range chicken with a red-pepper laced cranberry sauce. The desserts are not as impressive; the carrot cake is too dense and a bit tame, though the chocolate cake is a bit more daring and considerably more rewarding.

L.G. Smith Blvd. 82, downtown Oranjestad, at the Renaissance Aruba Resort & Casino. ✆ **297/583-6000**. Reservations recommended. Main courses $19–$36. AE, DISC, MC, V. Daily 5:30–11pm.

The Waterfront Crabhouse (Kids) SEAFOOD   Here's a kid-friendly place that won't cause you to regress. Colorful murals of happy dolphins adorn the walls inside. The kids' menu looks like a coloring book page and comes with crayons. Time-honored treats for finicky eaters include grilled-cheese sandwiches cut into fours (with or without the crust) and "psketti." I can't vouch for the deliciousness of these meals, but the more sophisticated adult fare features local and not-so-local seafood. You can pass a death sentence on any crustacean in the lobster tank, but crabs are king here. The tasty snow crabs are

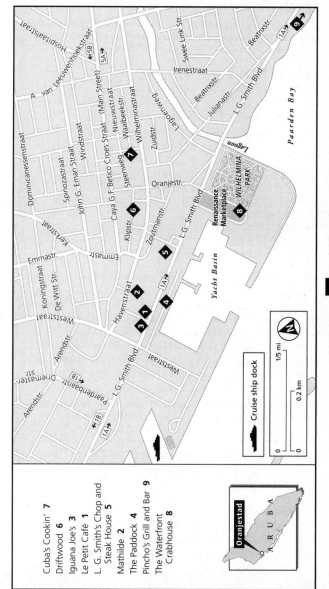

Cuba's Cookin' **7**

Driftwood **6**

Iguana Joe's **3**

Le Petit Café **1**

L. G. Smith's Chop and
Steak House **5**

Mathilde **2**

The Paddock **4**

Pincho's Grill and Bar **9**

The Waterfront
Crabhouse **8**

prepared with herbs, garlic, and butter. In season, soft-shell crabs come lightly fried with fresh tartar sauce. The service is accommodating, and the '80s retro decor is fun.

L.G. Smith Blvd., Renaissance Marketplace, downtown Oranjestad. ✆ **866/978-5043** or 297/583-5858. www.waterfrontaruba.com. Reservations recommended. Main courses $19–$32. AE, DISC, MC, V. Daily 8am–10pm.

INEXPENSIVE

Iguana Joe's GRILL   Disguised as a bar and grill, this colorful open-air venue actually serves more dinners than drinks (though it serves its fair share of the latter) and offers a full and creative menu. The appetizers run the gamut from salads to wings to nachos, but the best and most imaginative is the *keshi yena,* a cheese rind layered with Gouda cheese and ground beef. As a main course, try the coconut shrimp, sautéed in a tasty pink cream curry sauce and served with steamed rice. The aroma of the fajitas is a good omen, and the Caribbean curry chicken is rewarding. For dessert, the fried Oreos are too intriguing to pass up.

Royal Plaza Mall, downtown Oranjestad. ✆ **297/583-9373.** www.iguanajoes aruba.com. Main courses $9–$19. AE, DISC, MC, V. Mon–Thurs 10:30am–10:30pm; Fri–Sat 10:30am–11pm; Sun 5:30–10pm.

The Paddock INTERNATIONAL   In the heart of Oranjestad, this cafe and bistro overlooking the harbor is a short walk from virtually every shop in town. Much of the staff is tall, hip, and European, and the atmosphere is decidedly Dutch. No one minds whether you opt for a drink, a cup of coffee, a snack of sliced sausage and Gouda cheese, or a full-fledged meal. The menu offers everything from Wiener schnitzel to oriental stir-fry and spaghetti Bolognese to mahimahi in white-wine sauce. Happy hours change frequently; when they're offered, a festive crowd packs the place.

L.G. Smith Blvd. 13, Oranjestad. ✆ **297/583-2334.** www.paddock-aruba.com. Main courses $10–$19. MC, V. Mon–Thurs 9am–2am; Fri–Sun 9am–3am.

2 HIGH-RISE HOTELS/ PALM BEACH/NOORD

EXPENSIVE

Amazonia ★ STEAK   If you're a carnivore who dreams of eating roasted meat straight off the spit, Amazonia will make your dreams come true. This is one of several increasingly popular gaucho-style restaurants in Aruba where you can eat unlimited servings of grilled Argentine beef, chicken, pork, and lamb. The setting is rustic casual

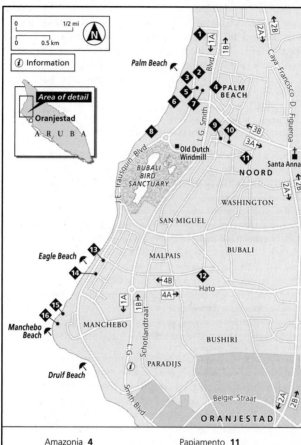

Amazonia **4**

Aqua Grill **4**

Buccaneer **10**

Café Japengo **3**

Chalet Suisse **13**

The French Steakhouse **16**

Gasparito Restaurant
  and Art Gallery **9**

Madame Janette **12**

Pago Pago **8**

Papiamento **11**

Pirates' Nest **15**

Ruinas del Mar **3**

Salt & Pepper **5**

Screaming Eagle **14**

Simply Fish **1**

Smokey Joe's
  Island Grill **2**

Sunset Grille **6**

Tango Argentine Grill **7**

with a definite machismo flair—lots of tanned leather and wood in both the sizeable interior and along the wraparound porch, where you can dine in the warm glow of two Olympic-size torches. The first course is a full-on salad bar complete with soup, sushi, stroganoff, and more. But don't fill up on starters. On your command, a parade of dapper servers show up carrying every imaginable cut of meat stacked on enormous swordlike skewers. They either slide or saw off a chunk for you to sample, and keep returning to deliver new tasty morsels of your favorite cut.

J.E. Irausquin Blvd. 374, Palm Beach, across from the Hyatt Hotel. ✆ 297/586-4444. www.amazonia-aruba.com. Reservations recommended. Complete dinner (not including drinks and dessert) $45. AE, DISC, MC, V. Mon–Sat 6–11pm; Sun 4–11pm.

Aqua Grill SEAFOOD   This cavernous restaurant with dark-wood New England decor lacks the intimacy of a cozier setting, but the outdoor patio provides a breezy alternative to the indoors. The large "raw bar" is an open-air display of raw fish in front of the portrait window through which one can see the large kitchen and extensive wine cellar. However, none of these takes away from the fresh seafood, which is guaranteed fresh, as opposed to frozen (not the case with some other items, spinach included). As long as you order a seafood item, you really can't go wrong. The scallops, tuna, swordfish, and salmon are especially tasty when prepared with Cajun spices. The setting is welcoming of children, who can order fish and chips, burgers, or chicken from the kiddie menu.

J.E. Irausquin Blvd. 374. ✆ 297/586-5900. www.aqua-grill.com. Reservations recommended. Main courses $23–$49. AE, MC, V. Mon–Sat 6–11pm; Sun 5–11pm.

Pago Pago ★★ SEAFOOD/STEAK   The elegant beige-on-beige decor features dark-wood plantation-style window louvers. The framed botanical sketches adorning the walls add sophistication, while the restaurant's multitiered spaciousness whispers luxury. Expectancy and promise hang in the air, fueled by the dramatic first course: jumbo lump crabmeat, served in a martini glass and topped with Russian dressing. The Savannah crab cakes and tropical shrimp cocktail (seasoned with a refreshingly tart mango relish) also score. But they can barely hint at the appeal of the main courses: seafood treasure—scallops, shrimp, and lobster in a creamy Thermidor sauce, and succulent Black Angus steak marinated in garlic and herbs. The climax? Hands down, it's the delectable white chocolate mousse that's served in a delicate nest spun of pecan brittle.

J.E. Irausquin Blvd. 77, Palm Beach, at the Wyndham Aruba Resort, Spa & Casino. ✆ 297/586-4466. Reservations recommended. Main courses $23–$40. AE, DISC, MC, V. Daily 6–10:30pm.

What's Cookin' in the ABC Islands?

Don't go home without sampling the worthwhile local cuisine. Here's some help with the menu:

Bananas hasa   Fried plantains served as a side dish in Curaçao.

Bitterballen   Deep-fried balls of puréed meat, popular in Curaçao.

Empanadas   Similar to *pastechis* but smaller and made with cornmeal rather than flour.

Frickendel   Tiny deep-fried hot dogs popular in Curaçao.

Funchi   Cornmeal polenta.

Giambo   A thick gumbo made with fish filets, salted beef, okra, fresh basil *(yerba di hole)*, and shrimp.

Keshi yena   Edam or Gouda cheese rinds stuffed with beef, chicken, fish, or shrimp, embellished with raisins, grated cheese, bread crumbs, olives, capers, and spices; created by frugal Dutch colonists who had to stretch their provisions to last until the next ship arrived, this recipe ensured that nothing would be wasted.

Kesio   Eggy caramel custard with caramel sauce.

Pan bati   A thick, sweet, corn bread–like pancake cut in thin wedges and served as a side.

Pastechi   Crescent-shaped, deep-fried turnovers filled with spicy meat, shrimp, fish, or cheese; popular for breakfast and as a snack.

Ponche crema   Creamy eggnoglike drink laced with rum and flavored with nutmeg.

Pudin di coco   Coconut pudding made with rum and served with lime sauce.

Salsa creollo   Red, sweet creole sauce made of tomatoes, onions, and peppers and served with fish.

Sopinan   Soups made with salt pork or beef, whole fish, shellfish, greens, potatoes, onions, tomatoes, garlic, peppers, and spices, more common in Curaçao.

Stoba   Hearty stew made with chicken, beef, goat, conch, or fish.

Papiamento ★ ARUBAN/INTERNATIONAL/SEAFOOD
Originally from Holland, the Ellis family has served award-winning
Caribbean food in their 200-year-old *cunucu* (farm) home for almost
2 decades. Over the years, tables have spilled out from the thick-
walled, antiques-filled interiors to the large fairy-lit palm garden. At
twilight, birds serenade outdoor diners around the luminescent pool.
Capers, caviar, basil, passion fruit, and radicchio garnish the smoked
salmon appetizer. The crudités platter features prosciutto, aged
Gouda, and marinated peppers and onions. If you're lucky enough to
be around during the season, order Brazil fish, a luscious, snapperlike
delicacy that's caught only in March and April. Lightly seasoned with
pepper and garlic, it's cooked and served on a stone that's heated in a
600°F (316°C) oven. Mango, onion, and chili-pepper chutney
accompanies *pisca arubiana* (fish Aruban style). Best bets for dessert
are *cocobana,* an ephemeral coconut mousse, and flaky-crusted Dutch
apple pie. Papiamento's espresso may be the island's best.

Washington 61, Noord. ✆ **297/586-4544.** www.papiamentorestaurant.com.
Reservations recommended. Main courses $22–$40. AE, DISC, MC, V. Mon–Sat
6–11pm.

Ruinas del Mar ★★ INTERNATIONAL/SEAFOOD A table
for two in the Garden of Eden? Dining on the crescent-shaped patio
of this romantic restaurant is like spending an hour or two before the
fall. Unperturbed by the muffled waterfalls nearby, serene black swans
and Japanese koi glide through the terrace-side lagoon, while tropical
birds in the luxuriant foliage serenade the setting sun. Start with the
shrimp and mango summer roll, chicken and tuna spring roll, or
lump crab and potato fritters. The seared shrimp and prosciutto-
wrapped sea scallops is a good main course. Other possibilities
include sautéed crispy chicken breast with grain mustard sauce, fork-
smashed potatoes, spinach, and asparagus. Key lime pie or apple pie
is perfect to top it off. The crowded Sunday brunch is a lavish array
of food and includes a carving station, fresh doughnut maker, and
chocolate fondue fountain, as well as fresh bananas Foster, caviar,
oysters, and more—well worth the $40 price tag.

J.E. Irausquin Blvd. 85, Palm Beach, at the Hyatt Regency Aruba Resort & Casino.
✆ **297/586-1234.** Reservations recommended. Main courses $28–$75. AE, DISC,
MC, V. Mon–Sat 5:30–10:30pm; Sun 9am–1pm (brunch).

Simply Fish ★ SEAFOOD Located on Palm beach, this restaurant is the ideal place to take in one of Aruba's spectacular sunsets.
With candlelit tables set up on the beach, the setting feels casual; you
can dig your feet into the sand while dining on the fresh catch of
the day. Serving up fresh seafood nightly, Simply Fish specializes in

serving locally caught fish. Start with the tropical bouillabaisse soup, a type of sweet, creamy fish stew with scallops, mussels, crab, and fresh fish. For a main dish, try the Aruban Triangle: Lobster tail, swordfish, and grilled mahimahi served with chickpeas and avocado in a coconut curry sauce.

L.G. Smith Blvd. 101, Palm Beach, at the Aruba Marriott Resort. ✆ 297/520-6537. Reservations recommended. Main courses $30–$65. MC, V. Daily 6:30–10:30pm.

Sunset Grille ★★★ SEAFOOD/STEAK This chic restaurant's bold Art Deco design palette honors the architectural splendor of Miami's South Beach. Many diners rave about the outside terrace with its view overlooking a garden and lagoon, but the gorgeous interior dining room deserves attention, too. The hammered copper surfaces, glass partitions, and reflective mosaic pillars are richly modern. The stunning decor could overwhelm the food, but the Sunset's prime beef and succulent seafood are outstanding. The generously portioned Maryland lump crab cake is a good start, as is the chophouse martini salad. If it's beef you came for, savor filet mignon or New York sirloin strip. A delicious seafood choice is the pan-seared ruby-red sushi-grade tuna, encrusted with peppercorns and flavored with wasabi soy sauce. To end the evening on a perfect note, moan over the tropical citrus cannoli.

J.E. Irausquin Blvd. 81, Palm Beach, at the Radisson Aruba Resort Casino & Spa. ✆ 297/586-6555. Reservations recommended. Main courses $29–$130. AE, DISC, MC, V. Daily 6–11pm.

MODERATE

Buccaneer (Kids) INTERNATIONAL/SEAFOOD In a rustic stone building in the hamlet of Noord, Buccaneer is one of Aruba's most popular seafood restaurants. The nautical decor, which features hanging fishnets, portholes, and 12 bubbling aquariums chock-full of colorful fish, creates the watery atmosphere of a sunken ship. Another dining area has the feel of an underwater cave and boasts a 7,500-gallon seawater tank. Menu items include shrimp cocktail, escargots in herb-garlic-butter sauce, shrimp in Pernod sauce, and a land-and-sea platter with fish, shrimp, and beef tenderloin. The food is hearty and delicious. The spacious bar area is a great place to linger over a drink or two.

Gasparito 11C, Noord. ✆ 297/586-6172. www.buccaneeraruba.com. Main courses $15–$26. AE, DISC, MC, V. Mon–Sat 5:30–10pm.

Café Japengo ★ ASIAN FUSION Located in the Hyatt, this minimalist cafe serves innovative Pan-Asian cuisine and specializes in fresh seafood and sushi. Red, white, and black Japanese kites adorn the simple walls, providing only temporary distraction from the busy sushi chefs, who command attention in the cozy space. Start with Asian marinated duck salad or Okinawa soup with shrimp, shitake mushrooms, and sake. For the main event, try the Marco Polo: udon noodles with filet mignon, lobster, shrimp, and mushrooms in a ginger lemon-grass broth. There's also fried rice, Hunan beef, and basil chicken, and more than enough green tea to slake any thirst.

J.E. Irausquin Blvd. 85, Palm Beach, at the Hyatt Regency Aruba Resort & Casino. ⓒ 297/586-1234. Reservations recommended. Main courses $19–$44. AE, DISC, MC, V. Wed–Mon 6–10:30pm.

Gasparito Restaurant and Art Gallery ★★ ARUBAN/SEA-FOOD Here's a favorite with people in love. Located in a restored *cunucu* (farm) home, Gasparito features intimate dining rooms inside and a breezy outdoor patio and bar. The tinkling of a fountain, comfortable patio chairs, and candlelight enhance the courtyard's warmth. Inside, vaulted ceilings embrace cozy rooms. Local art, much of it for sale, graces the interior walls. The keri keri ravioli, a favorite appetizer, features shredded fish (dry like *bacalāo*) in a creamy tomato and basil sauce. Main courses focus on seafood and Aruban dishes, but the menu makes a special nod to vegetarians, and the filet mignon has vocal fans. How about shrimp in coconut milk and brandy sprinkled with seasoned coconut flakes? Or try the seafood *keshi yena,* a casserole of scallops, shrimp, squid, and fish in Newburg sauce topped with melted Gouda cheese. For dessert you can't go wrong with *banana na forno,* a whole banana baked with cinnamon.

Gasparito 3, Noord. ⓒ 297/586-7044. www.gasparito.com. Reservations recommended. Main courses $15–$33. AE, DISC, MC, V. Mon–Sat 5:30–11pm.

Pincho's Grill and Bar ★ GRILL Hovering over the water at the end of a short pier, this open-air restaurant is little more than a circular bar surrounded by a ring of dining tables and low-profile sofas nestled dangerously close to the calm water below. Yet two things make this family-run venue remarkable. One is the spectacular setting, with unrestricted views of nearby Oranjestad, passing cruise ships, and incoming flights. The other is the fact that they dish up a full menu from the small grill behind the bar—they prep much of the food off-site, but always grill the crab cakes and the marinated, tender steak and shrimp *pinchos* (skewers) to order. While the salads are uninspiring and the portions are a bit small, the desserts more than make up for it, and the atmosphere is as romantic as it gets.

L.G. Smith Blvd. 7, at Aruba Surfside Marina Hotel. ⓒ 297/583-2666. Reservations recommended. Main courses $19–$32. AE, DISC, MC, V. Daily 5–11pm. Bar Mon–Fri 5pm–midnight, Sat–Sun 5pm–1am.

Epicurean & Eclectic

The **Aruba Gastronomic Association,** or AGA, Salina Serca 39E, Noord (© **800/793-6028** in the U.S., or 297/586-1266 in Aruba; www.arubadining.com), a group of nearly 30 of the island's restaurants—including such recommended spots as the French Steakhouse and Gasparito—offers a Dine-Around program with three options. For $117, you get coupons good for three dinners; $190 gets you five dinners; and for $263, you can have one dinner every day of the week. Children 4 to 12 eat for half price; it is not recommended for children 3 and under. The five-course Wine-Around dinner costs $85 per person and includes perfectly paired wines. The coupons are good at any of AGA's member restaurants and never expire, so you can always turn in old coupons for current ones on your return trip. Each dinner includes an appetizer, main course, dessert, coffee or tea, and service charges. Lunch and dinner plans as well as custom plans are available, and $50 gift certificates can be purchased for only $45. Coupons can be purchased from AGA, or at any De Palm tour desk. You can also fill out the online fax order form at www.arubadining.com or www. aruba.com.

Tango Argentine Grill (Value) ARGENTINE/SEAFOOD/STEAK
Tango features sexy Argentine dance inside, live music outside, and decent food all around. The flavor here is South American, from the *churrasco* beef to the Chilean wines. The large interior dining room features splayed cowhides and views of the open grill. On the stage near the entrance, live tango dancers smolder before a backdrop painted to resemble a Buenos Aires street. The pleasant outside terrace overlooks a brick plaza, where live music fills the air from 8 to 11pm. For a light start, try the tasty Caesar salad or seafood marinated in lime vinegar. The enormous barbecued beef dishes get mixed reviews, but all are better with *chimichurri* sauce, a savory blend of garlic, parsley, and olive oil. Shrimp in garlic and olive oil is a hit and comes with rice, fried plantains, and corn on the cob. Ice cream crowns the Tango dessert crepe, filled with *dulce de leche,* a heavenly caramel confection. From 5 to 7pm a $25 three-course meal special is offered.

J.E. Irausquin Blvd. 370, Palm Beach, across from the Allegro Resort. ✆ 297/586-8600. www.tangoaruba.com. Reservations recommended. Main courses $24–$36. AE, MC, V. Daily 5–11pm.

INEXPENSIVE

Salt & Pepper ★ ⟨Finds⟩ SPANISH/TAPAS   This fresh, appealing spot serves light meals such as salads (don't pass on the salt-and-pepper salad with salty bacon and peppery shrimp), burgers, and sandwiches, but tapas are its specialty. Most of the 30 appetizer-size dishes have a Spanish accent, but others speak Cantonese, Italian, French, or Dutch. What sounds good to you? Pan-fried shrimp in mango sauce? Sautéed mushrooms with Parmesan cheese? Fried calamari? Beef spiced up for the islands? Fried brie? Black-olive spread? Spinach dip? Nothing's too fancy or complicated, but better snacks are hard to find. With prices ranging from $4 to $6 per item, you can have a feast for less than the price of a simple entree at most restaurants in the neighborhood. Live entertainment in the outdoor courtyard begins at 8pm. Show up with salt and pepper shakers to add to their collection and get a free glass of sangria.

J.E. Irausquin Blvd. 368A, Palm Beach, across from the Allegro Resort. ✆ 297/586-3280. www.saltandpepperaruba.com. Main courses $8–$20. AE, DISC, MC, V. Daily 11am–11:45pm. Bar daily until 1am.

Smokey Joe's Island Grill   CARIBBEAN/AMERICAN   This casual outdoor eatery features burgers, wings, and salads, but the ribs are its signature dish and they can be prepared several different ways. Tuesday is ribs night so you may have to wait for a table, but a *mojito* or margarita will help pass the time. Try the dry-rubbed variety, or go whole hog and order all three types. Hungry couples should consider the ultimate combo for two: a full rack of ribs, half rotisserie chicken, and BBQ-pulled pork, served with four sides. Just save room for their signature dessert: fried Oreos.

J.E. Irausquin Blvd. 87, Palm Beach, across from Playa Linda. ✆ 297/586-2896. www.smokeyjoesaruba.com. Main courses $12–$19. AE, DISC, MC, V. Daily 5–11pm. Bar daily until 1am.

3 LOW-RISE HOTELS/EAGLE & MANCHEBO BEACHES

EXPENSIVE

Madame Janette ★ CARIBBEAN/INTERNATIONAL   Especially popular with Aruba's Dutch residents, Madame Janette weds an unlikely pair: the cuisines of northern Europe and the Caribbean. The restaurant's outdoor dining areas spill down steps and around corners, some areas protected by reed-mat awnings, others open to the stars, and all within earshot of the live acoustic music. Rustic potato-and-leek soup with garlic croutons is a nice starter. Madame's hot shrimps show the chefs' ingenuity—juicy prawns baked in a flavorful marinara sauce topped with melted Gouda and Gorgonzola. In fact, nearly every dish features a healthy dose of cheese—the au gratin potatoes are perfect. The pan-seared mahimahi filet with tropical fruit salsa and the Caribbean stuffed shrimp with crabmeat and bacon are new on the menu. For dessert, try the chocolate soufflé with pumpkinseed ice cream, or traditional Austrian Kaiserschmarren, a thick and hearty pancake served with black cherries and ice cream.

Cunucu Abao 37, Bubali, inland from La Cabana, next to the Blue Village Villas. ✆ 297/587-0184. www.madamejanette.com. Reservations recommended. Main courses $26–$68. AE, MC, V. Mon–Sat 5:30–10pm.

Pirates' Nest SEAFOOD/INTERNATIONAL   Open-air, beachside dining is the allure of this breezy restaurant at the Aruba Bucuti Beach Resort. Built to resemble a 16th-century Dutch galleon, the structure contrasts sharply with the elegant beach surroundings. Ask for a table on the recently renovated deck with views of the beach. The extensive menu ranges from inexpensive soups, salads, and sandwiches to more substantial fare (mostly seafood). Start with oak-smoked Scottish salmon with onions and capers, or the flavorful bouillabaisse. Sautéed jumbo shrimp in creamy chili, garlic, and cognac sauce is a zesty main course; other marine options include mahimahi and sea bass. There's also beef stroganoff, rib-eye steak, and grilled chicken in mango and pink peppercorn sauce, and several vegetarian dishes round out the menu. Call in advance for a private table on the beach.

L.G. Smith Blvd. 55B, Manchebo Beach, at the Aruba Bucuti Beach Resort. ✆ 297/583-1100. Dinner reservations recommended. Main courses $19–$49. AE, DISC, MC, V. Daily 7am–10:30pm.

Screaming Eagle ★★ FRENCH FUSION   If the idea of fine dining while luxuriating on white beds and intimate tables shrouded in gauzy drapes sounds romantic, then make a pilgrimage to this sleek new restaurant, with the same owner as Flying Fishbone. Start with a drink at the bar where the award-winning bartender will whip you up something from his list of 110 cocktails, or just order something from their list of 150 wines. Appetizers that stand out are the carpaccio of artichoke with goat cheese and the ahi tuna tartare with soft-shelled crab and spicy papaya mayonnaise. As a main course, the chef recommends the fresh wahoo with shrimp ginger risotto, asparagus, and creamy Cajun sauce, or the Black Angus tenderloin with shitake pine nut sauce. For a dessert almost too beautiful to eat try *la tazza famosa:* a cup and saucer made of chocolate filled with *tia maria,* orange sherbet and chocolate mousse.

J.E. Irausquin Blvd. 228, Eagle Beach. ✆ **297/587-8021.** www.screaming-eagle. net. Reservations recommended. Main courses $26–$45. AE, DISC, MC, V. Daily 6–11pm.

MODERATE

Chalet Suisse SWISS/INTERNATIONAL   Along the road that borders Eagle Beach, a short stroll from La Cabana resort, this alpine chalet restaurant has the feel of an old-fashioned Swiss dining room. In deliberate contrast to the arid scrublands that surround it, the institution is an air-conditioned refuge of thick plaster walls, pine-wood panels, and good old Teutonic *gemütlichkeit* (well-being). Appetizers include avocado filled with crabmeat and shrimp, escargots in herbal garlic butter with shallots, and Dutch pea soup. Main courses include beef stroganoff, pasta, Wiener schnitzel, and roast duck with orange sauce. The array of high-calorie desserts includes Swiss and German standards, such as apple strudel and Toblerone chocolate fondue. The hearty Swiss fare is a nice change for Arubans and expatriates; tourists may find it a bit heavy.

J.E. Irausquin Blvd. 246, Eagle Beach. ✆ **297/587-5054.** www.chaletsuisse-aruba. com. Reservations recommended. Main courses $19–$34. AE, MC, V. Mon–Sat 5:30–10pm.

The French Steakhouse ★ Ⓥⓐⓛⓤⓔ INTERNATIONAL/STEAK/ SEAFOOD   The dining room feels like a 1950s French country bistro—cafe curtains and brick accents decorate the windows, hand-painted tiles border the walls, and gold wrought iron gives the Louis XV–inspired chairs a rustic flavor. The live piano music is mellow, the lighting dim. Start with the Caribbean seafood cocktail with marinated shrimp, scallops, mussels, and grilled salmon in a tequila fruit salsa, or mushroom caps stuffed with herb-flavored crab and grated Gouda. For the main event, carnivores can't resist the beef tenderloin *churrasco* with crispy fried onions, sautéed mushrooms, *chimichurri* sauce, and au-jus. The chef's favorite is the Punta Brabo sampler featuring a crab cake with pineapple mango salsa, chicken breast, and filet mignon with jalapeño Hollandaise and sage Pinot Grigio sauce. Ice cream crowns the apple strudel, a real treat with the strong and flavorful coffee. Value-conscious diners love the $35 Ambassador's Five-Course Dinner, or the early-bird three-course special for $23 before 7pm.

J.E. Irausquin Blvd. 55, Eagle Beach, at the Manchebo Beach Resort & Spa. ℭ 297/ **582-3444.** www.manchebo.com/steakhouse. Reservations recommended. Main courses $19–$32. AE, DISC, MC, V. Daily 5:30–11pm.

71

4 CALIFORNIA LIGHTHOUSE/ TIERRA DEL SOL

EXPENSIVE TO MODERATE

La Trattoria El Faro Blanco ITALIAN Isolated at the top of a hill on the island's northernmost tip, this popular restaurant affords unbeatable vistas. A 360-degree scan takes in the expansive sea, windswept sand dunes, an emerald golf course, and the California Lighthouse. Just steps from the much-photographed beacon, the restaurant's original structure (which has since expanded) once housed the local lighthouse keeper, and the interior dining rooms retain a residential coziness. Seating on the terrace features unobstructed views of the sea. The fare covers a full range of Italian cuisine, with a good helping of Neapolitan specialties. Baby octopus, cooked with garlic, tomato, olive oil, and parsley, is a good way to kick things off. For a main course, try the excellent *osso buco* or filet mignon with porcini mushrooms. Desserts include tiramisu and pears poached in red wine. The outdoor bar is a favorite stop for golfers. Pizza is served between 3 and 5:30pm.

At the California Lighthouse, North Aruba. ℭ **297/586-0786.** www.aruba-latrattoria. com. Reservations recommended. Main courses $22–$48; pizza from $16. AE, DISC, MC, V. Daily 8:30am–11pm (pizza served until 5:30pm). Bar daily 11am–11pm.

Ventanas del Mar ★★ INTERNATIONAL/SEAFOOD When you've got it, you don't have to flaunt it. Flavor combinations at this stylish restaurant are masterful and sophisticated. Each ingredient contributes subtly, never overwhelming the star attraction. The interior dining rooms feature ocher walls and vaulted wooden ceilings, but the outside views dominate. Curved windows overlook the cacti and fairways of the adjacent golf course. The outdoor terrace, bordered by lush bougainvillea, palm trees, and a gentle colonnade, is steps above poolside tables. Sweet lump crab cakes are a good start; served with baby greens and tomatoes, they're accented with a caper and dill vinaigrette. The turbot filet main course is seasoned with braised leeks, white wine, and walnuts. Because the portion sizes have humans, not bears, in mind, you'll have room for dessert. Mango-scented coconut mousse dances to a medley of fresh melons. *Ponche crema* ice cream tastes like creamy, rum-infused eggnog.

WHERE TO DINE IN ARUBA

3

CALIFORNIA LIGHTHOUSE/TIERRA DEL SOL

At the Tierra del Sol Resort & Country Club, Malmokweg, Noord. ✆ **297/586-7800.** Reservations recommended. Main courses $24–$37. AE, DISC, MC, V. Mon 11am–3pm; Tues–Sun 11am–3pm and 6:30–11pm.

5 SAVANETA

EXPENSIVE

Flying Fishbone ★★ INTERNATIONAL   This intimate beachside restaurant is perfect for a moonlit dinner in the old fishing village of Savaneta. Many tables line the rustic wooden deck and serene beach, and are so close to the sea that your feet may get wet. Swaying palm trees and starlight glittering in the sea are the stage for the restaurant's dramatically presented nouvelle cuisine. Carpaccio of artichoke with goat cheese and honey walnut dressing is not to be missed, and the lobster bisque is also a winner. Shrimp roti and smoked duck with apples are other good appetizers. Main courses include Bouillabaisse à la Marseille, and *osso buco* Milanese. The Savaneta Seafood History dish is a rich mélange of seafood in a creamy traditional curry sauce. Save room for champagne mousse or caramel parfait with homemade ice cream.

Savaneta 344, btw. Oranjestad and San Nicolas. ✆ **297/584-2506.** www.flying fishbone.com. Reservations recommended. Main courses $30–$48. DISC, MC, V. Daily 5–10pm.

6 SAN NICOLAS

MODERATE

Charlie's Bar and Restaurant ARUBAN/SEAFOOD   Opened in 1941 by a crusty but lovable Dutchman and his saintly wife, Charlie's has survived several economic recessions as well as Nazi torpedoes (next to Aruba's oil refinery, it was vulnerable to attacks during World War II). A sailor and oil-worker dive for 35 years, the place metamorphosed into a literary and tourist haunt. The decor is early American attic, and every inch of wall and ceiling is encrusted with some kind of memorabilia. Charlie's is a watering hole, but the clientele is on the discreet side of rowdy, and the staff can be downright gentle. The tasty food's just what you'd expect at a seaside bar—fresh shrimp, fish, and squid. Typical main courses come smothered in garlic, stewed peppers, and celery. Beef tenderloin, or *pasapalo*, spiced with tangy brown sauce, comes with hearty steak fries. Don't pass on the Honeymoon Sauce, a three-alarm blend of scotch bonnet peppers, onions, carrots, sweet peppers, coriander, and vinegar. Prices on the menu are listed in Aruban florins, but dollars are readily accepted.

Zeppenveldstraat 56 (Main St.), San Nicolas (follow the signs). © **297/584-5086.** www.charliesbararuba.com. Main courses $19–$31. AE, DISC, MC, V. Mon–Sat 11:30am–9:30pm. Bar until 10:30pm or later. Closed holidays.

Fun in the Aruban Surf & Sun

Warm sunshine and beautiful beaches are Aruba's major attractions. The seemingly endless strips of white, sugary sand along the southwestern coast rank among the Caribbean's widest and most beautiful, and the shallow aqua surf is ideal for swimming. Toys such as jet skis, WaveRunners, parasails, and banana boats are plentiful. Near the island's western tip, steady winds draw windsurfers, while the shallow waters and abundant marine life attract snorkelers. Shipwrecks, sunken planes, and coral reefs dot the entire leeward coast, keeping scuba divers happy, and along the south-central coast, mangrove forests, barrier islands, and calm seas combine for favorable kayaking conditions. For those who prefer to see the wonders of the sea without getting wet, submarines and glass-bottom boats make daily excursions. Anglers can struggle with barracuda, wahoo, marlin, and tuna in the deep waters not far from the coast.

Although dramatically beautiful, the northern coast of the island is pounded with waves. The stunning vistas and craggy limestone bluffs are great for hikes and picnics, but playing in the current is treacherous and strongly discouraged.

Land-based activities include bicycling, golf, hiking, horseback riding, birding, ATVing, and tennis.

1 BEACHES

All of Aruba's beaches are public, but chairs and *palapas* (shade huts) provided by resorts are the property of the hotels and for guest use only. If you use them at a hotel other than your own, expect to be charged. Few of the smaller beaches have facilities other than a shade hut or two, so if you venture afar for privacy, bring your own food, water, and gear. Beer cans and charcoal ash litter a few remote areas, but Aruba's beaches are expansive, and trash is easily avoided. The following beach tour starts at the island's northwest tip, near the California Lighthouse, and moves counterclockwise.

The calm surf and sandy bottom make **Arashi Beach,** near the California Lighthouse at the island's northwestern tip, one of Aruba's

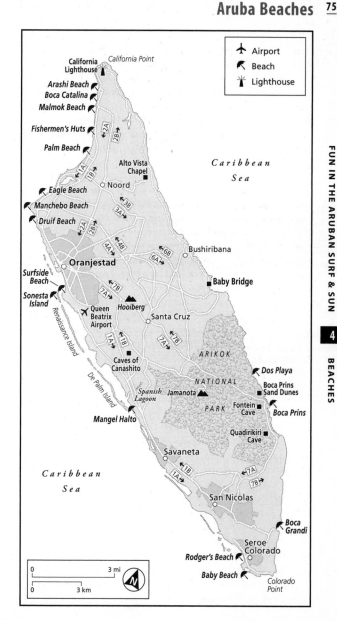

Legend:
- ✈ Airport
- ⚑ Beach
- ⚑ Lighthouse

California Point

California Lighthouse

Arashi Beach
Boca Catalina
Malmok Beach

Fishermen's Huts

Palm Beach

Alto Vista Chapel

Noord

Caribbean Sea

Eagle Beach
Manchebo Beach
Druif Beach

Bushiribana

Oranjestad

Surfside Beach

Sonesta Island

Queen Beatrix Airport

Hooiberg

Santa Cruz

Baby Bridge

Renaissance Island

De Palm Island

Caves of Canashito

ARIKOK

Dos Playa

Boca Prins Sand Dunes

NATIONAL

Spanish Lagoon

Jamanota

Fontein Cave

Boca Prins

Mangel Halto

PARK

Quadirikiri Cave

Savaneta

Caribbean Sea

San Nicolas

Boca Grandi

Seroe Colorado

Rodger's Beach

Baby Beach

Colorado Point

0   3 mi
0   3 km

N

FUN IN THE ARUBAN SURF & SUN

4

BEACHES

best swimming sites. Snorkelers like it for the elkhorn coral, while sunbathers spend lazy minutes watching pelicans fish. The white sand is soft, but look out for pebbles and stones. Although there are no facilities in the immediate area, a few beach huts provide shade.

Just a few minutes south, **Boca Catalina,** with its gentle, shallow water and plentiful fish, is another good spot for snorkeling. The sand is white, with some pebbles and shells, but the real hazard is horse manure left behind by some horseback-riding tours. This small pocket beach has no facilities, but it offers seclusion and tranquillity. Boca Catalina is the beach that you see from every snorkel sail excursion; likewise, from the beach itself, you see the mob of catamarans and sailboats clustered around the nearby reef.

A bit farther south, **Malmok Beach** is another popular swimming and snorkeling spot with tiny coves, white sand, vast shallow waters, and abundant fish. This strand has no facilities, but you can fantasize about the accommodations in the nearby mansions. A scuttled German freighter on the seabed not far from the coast attracts divers. The steady winds make the beach extremely popular with windsurfers.

The island's mecca of windsurfing, though, is just minutes south at **Hadicurari** beach, or **Fishermen's Huts.** Every July, this site hosts the Hi-Winds World Challenge, an important pro-am windsurfing competition, but on any day, you can watch the brilliantly colored boards and sails dance along the waves. The shallow water is also excellent for swimming. A sunken wreck resurfaced in a recent storm and sits frozen and upright, like a rusted ghost ship that ran ashore. Facilities include picnic tables and shade huts, but the white-powder-sand beach is flecked with pebbles and shells at the water's edge.

Home of the High-Rise hotels, **Palm Beach ★★** is Aruba's best spot for people-watching. This stretch of white sand, adjacent to Hadicurari beach, is also great for swimming, sunbathing, sailing, fishing, and snorkeling. The resorts sift the sand daily to get rid of pebbles and sharp shells, ensuring a beach as soft as talcum powder. Located smack-dab in the heart of things, it can get crowded, though, and hotel guests stake out the scores of *palapas* sprouting from the sand early in the morning. With two piers and numerous watersports operators, Palm Beach is also busier and noisier than Aruba's other beaches. The least-crowded areas are to the north, between the Holiday Inn and the Marriott, and to the south, between the Wyndham and the Divi Phoenix. As you walk along the shore, you can wander through the splendid gardens of the beachfront resorts, watch the thriving bird and iguana life, and stop for a cold tropical drink at one of the many open-air bars. The eponymous trees, coconut and date palms, were planted in 1917.

Separated from Palm Beach by a brief outcrop of limestone that's home to a splendid green flock of parakeets, **Eagle Beach ★★★** is across a small road from several timeshare resorts. The wide beach here stretches as far as the eye can see. The sugar-white sand and gentle surf are ideal for swimming. The ambience is relaxed and quiet. A couple of bars, as well as numerous *palapas* and chairs maintained by the hotels, punctuate the expansive strand. Shaded picnic areas are provided for the public, and the beach is popular with tourists and locals alike on weekends. Prime sand conditions are directly in front of the Amsterdam Manor. The famous divi divi tree pictured on many an Aruba souvenir can also be found here, but a sabotage incident in 2005 necessitated heavy-duty pruning and removal of its main graceful branch that leaned longingly windward. Look for the unusually symmetrical lone tree with a visible stump about eye high.

For sheer tranquillity and open space, **Manchebo Beach ★★★**, also known as Punto Brabo, is top-notch. Because the sand here stretches 110m (361 ft.) from the shore to the hotels, congestion is never a problem. The handful of smaller resorts that occupy this coveted location, next to Eagle Beach, offer beverages and food, and the discreet atmosphere makes Manchebo one of Aruba's only tops-optional beaches. The white-powder sand is spectacular, but the surf is steady and brisk. With no watersports in the area, serenity is guaranteed. The premier spots are in front of the Bucuti Beach and Manchebo Beach resorts.

Druif Beach meets Manchebo Beach farther east along the coast. The sand remains white but the strand narrows considerably, and the surf becomes more restless. Rocks and pebbles come out in profusion here. The beach between the Divi Aruba and the Tamarijn Aruba resorts is the widest stretch in the area; the strip south of the Tamarijn is also nice.

South of Oranjestad and across the street from the Talk of the Town Hotel & Beach Club, **Surfside Beach** is sleepy and intimate. Although the hotel operates a bar and provides towels and beach chairs for guests, the small strip is also popular with Arubans, especially residents of nearby Oranjestad. The calm waters are great for swimming, but there are prettier beaches; Surfside's proximity to the capital is its major selling point.

The beaches of **Renaissance Island** are restricted to guests of the Renaissance resort, who board a skiff in the hotel's lobby in downtown Oranjestad for the 10-minute trip to the private island. The 40-acre tropical retreat features cozy white-sand beaches, intimate coves, and protected swimming areas. One secluded area is tops optional. Hammocks span the palm trees, and beach chairs are also provided.

In the hamlet of Pos Chiquito between Oranjestad and Savaneta, **Mangel Halto** is a favorite picnic spot. Its white-powder sand and shallow water are additional enticements for Aruban families, especially on weekends.

The charm of **Rodger's Beach,** south of San Nicolas, is initially overwhelmed by the gigantic oil refinery looming on the western horizon. Like something out of Orwell's *1984* or Dr. Frankenstein's lab, the smoke-belching towers contrast bizarrely with the idyllically beautiful Caribbean waters. The refinery is harmless (they say)—no obvious water pollution, no stench (if the wind's blowing in the right direction)—and the gentle, protected waters are ideal for swimming. The narrow strip of soft, white-powder sand is popular with locals, but tourists who want to get away from the more familiar sites show up as well. *Palapas* and giant sea grape bushes provide shade. There's also a small bar and grill, an array of colorful fishing boats, and shower facilities. Equipment, including snorkeling gear, can be rented nearby at an easy-to-spot shop called **Jada.** The water is shallow for almost 15m (49 ft.) out, and multicolored fish and coral formations are easy to spot.

Baby Beach ★★, near Aruba's easternmost tip, is a prime destination for families with young children. Like a great big bathtub, this shallow bowl of warm turquoise water is perfect for inexperienced swimmers, thanks to the protection of rock breakwaters. The water is never deeper than 1.5m (5 ft.), and the powdery sand is friendly to bare feet. Be on the lookout for gnarled driftwood and sharp shells, though. Giant sea grape bushes and *palapas* offer protection from the sun. Facilities are restricted to a refreshment stand and washrooms. On weekends, the beach is very popular with Arubans, who party with music and barbecues. Coral reefs farther out used to be popular with snorkelers, but a recent storm did a lot of damage and the surf is rough outside the protected lagoon; keep an eye on the kids if they tend to stray. Bring your own towels and snorkeling gear.

If you find yourself sometimes snarling at children, avoid Baby Beach and drive north a few minutes to **Boca Grandi** ★★, a virtually deserted expanse of dramatic sand dunes and sea grasses. The salt air and terrain are reminiscent of Cape Cod, but the aqua, azure, and sapphire waters are unmistakably Caribbean. A penitentiary crowns limestone bluffs rising behind the dunes, and the inmates suffer the ultimate punishment: viewing the ocean and beach and knowing they can't enjoy it. The low-lying sea grapes provide next to no protection from the sun, and pockets of trash and jetsam mar some of the intimate coves. The sand has pebbles, too, but the steady breeze and rolling surf are excellent for advanced windsurfing and kiteboarding. Because the surf is riled up most of the time, Boca Grandi is appropriate for strong swimmers only.

Boca Prins ★, in Arikok National Park on the north coast, also boasts dunes and hardy seaside vegetation, but the rough-and-tumble waters here make swimming out of the question. You'll need a car, preferably an all-terrain vehicle, to get here on the rutted dirt roads. Plan a picnic lunch, or eat at the nearby cafe, also called Boca Prins, walk along the limestone cliffs, and slide down the dunes instead of risking the water.

Dos Playa, a 15-minute walk west along the coast from Boca Prins, is an even more popular picnic spot. With crashing waves and a rugged coast, it too is picturesque but unsuitable for swimming.

De Palm Island (𝄢 297/582-4404; www.depalm.com) has several tiny beaches and a tanning area with trucked-in sand. The newly added Blue Parrotfish Water Park (see De Palm Island, above) is a small area where young children can splash, slide, and frolic in a safe and contained area. The cacophony of squeals from the hoards of giddy tots adds to the crowded and somewhat frenetic atmosphere. However, it's great for parents with young children since it's easy to supervise your children from a shaded area with lounge chairs. The nearby pocket beaches with protective jetties are also great for kids.

For a water park back on the mainland that will thrill parents and children, Morgan's Island, J.E. Irausquin Blvd. 262 (𝄢 297/587-8788; www.arubamorgansisland.com) is the new game in town. This place has slides so high they need warning lights for incoming airplanes. Okay, not quite, but at 21m (70 ft.) tall, these rainbow-hued serpentine chutes dominate the landscape as one drives past. While the high-speed slides and wave pool might be too scary for the tiny tots, the smaller slides, snacks, and shows are sure to keep the whole family entertained and cooled off for at least a few hours. The park is open daily from 10am to 6pm. Admission is $39 for adults, $34 for children 3 to 12, and free for children 2 and under.

2 HITTING THE WATER

BOATING

Aruba offers sailing adventures on yachts, pirate ships, and catamarans day and night. Some include snorkeling, swimming, and lunch; others feature sunset vistas. For night owls, dinner-dance-and-booze cruises include a midnight dip in the sea (see chapter 7). If you have something special to celebrate, you may want to charter a private yacht (about $175–$200 per hour).

De Palm Tours (𝄢 297/582-4400; www.depalm.com) offers more sailing options than anyone else—six different snorkel sails on catamarans and trimarans, and several sail-only cruises. Some cruises offer SNUBA, a cross between scuba and snorkeling. Ranging from 2 to 5 hours in length, the trips depart daily in the morning and afternoon and at sunset. Prices start at $49 and climb to $69.

Boarding at the Hadicurari Pier at Moomba Beach between the Holiday Inn and Marriott, **Jolly Pirates** (📞 297/586-8107; www. jolly-pirates.com) features unique 4^1/$_2$-hour sail, snorkel, lunch, and rope-swing excursions. Friendly and athletic deckhands will astound you with their mast-climbing antics followed by an acrobatic swing into the sea—think Tarzan meets "marine boy." While challenging to follow this act, grab hold and let loose with your best cannonball. Just remember to release the rope and grab hold of your swimsuit before you hit the water! Lucky ladies can double up with Tarzan-deckhand for a **tandem piggyback swing** that would make Jane jealous. Morning cruises embark daily at 9:30am, and return at 2pm ($55, including a tasty, full-service barbecue lunch). Two-hour sunset trips are offered Monday and Friday ($27) and 3-hour afternoon sail and snorkel tours are offered daily ($33). Snorkeling tours include life jacket, mask, fins, and snorkel. All three options include an open bar, and unlike on any of the catamaran tours, the bartender circulates, takes your order, and brings your drinks to you while you relax and enjoy the ride. Don't forget to stop by their shop located at the pier for a souvenir T-shirt, bandanna, or eye patch.

Mi Dushi Sailing Adventures (📞 297/586-2010; www.aruba adventures.com) offers three cruises on a 75-foot sailing vessel built in 1925. The 5-hour morning cruise combines sailing, snorkeling, swimming, and a rope swing, with continental breakfast, barbecue lunch, and an open bar. The boat departs from the De Palm Pier daily at 9:30am. The price is $59 for adults, $20 for children 6 to 14, and free for children 5 and under. (Children 5 and under get no lunch, and parents of children 3 and under are strongly discouraged from subjecting their young children to 5 hr. of confinement in an area full of slippery decks and ledges lacking safety railings.) Also featuring shallow reef snorkeling, swimming, and a rope swing, the 3-hour sundown cruise sets sail at 3:30pm from the same pier on Tuesday and Thursday, and costs $35 for adults and $20 for children 6 to 14; the price includes snacks and an open bar for adults. On Monday, Wednesday, and Friday, the boat leaves at 5pm for a 2-hour all-you-can-drink sunset sail with light snacks. This party is $30 for adults and $20 for children 11 and under.

Pelican Adventures (📞 297/587-2302; www.pelican-aruba.com) offers cruises on four different catamarans. The 2^1/$_2$-hour snorkel cruise departs daily at 2:30pm and includes snacks and an open bar ($48 for adults, $28 for children 4–12). The 3^1/$_2$-hour brunch cruise departs at 9:30am on Wednesday, Friday, and Sunday and features continental breakfast (okay, really just some pastries and juice), champagne lunch, snorkeling, and an open bar ($75 for adults, $50 children 4–12). The 2-hour sunset booze cruise departs at 5pm Tuesday to Monday and includes snacks and drinks ($45 for adults, $25 for children 4–12). The starlight dinner cruise leaves Thurs–Tues at 5pm and includes a three-course meal at the informal Pelican's Nest restaurant at the end of the Pelican pier and unlimited drinks aboard the catamaran ($76 for adults, $46 for children 4–12, and free for children 3 and under). All trips leave from the Pelican Pier near the Holiday Inn, and private charters can be arranged.

Red Sail Sports (© **877/RED-SAIL** [733-5245] in the U.S. and Canada, or 297/586-1603 in Aruba; www.redsailaruba.com) boasts three large catamarans and several sailing options. The 4-hour luncheon snorkel sail departs at 9:15am daily, visits three snorkeling sites, and includes a deli-style lunch and an open bar (no beer however; $69 for adults, $39 for children 3–11). The 2¹/₂-hour afternoon snorkel sail departs at 2:30pm daily and includes snacks and beverages ($49 for adults, $29 for children 3–11). The 2-hour sunset cruise departs at 5:30pm Monday, Tuesday, Thursday, Saturday, and Sunday and features snacks and an open bar, including wine and beer ($45 for adults, $29 for children 3–11). All trips leave from Hyatt Pier, and group charters are available.

(Tips) Savvy Sailing

When deciding which sailing excursion to select, take a walk down the beach and check out the goods. All piers are lined up along Palm Beach and the boats are moored close to land. Go for the operator with the prettiest and newest boat (De Palm is top dog at the moment). If you prefer a wooden hull to a fiberglass catamaran, Jolly Pirates is your best option. But if you want a more traditional catamaran experience (and a roomier deck), be sure to kick the tires before plunking your money down as older boats can be run-down and may have structural damage on the sunbathing nets, which limits access. Be sure to bring a towel since there are none to be had once on board. *A final warning:* Several tour operators offer champagne brunch, which usually consists only of a few pastries and maybe some fruit, but don't expect a full buffet or coffee. The open bar is a bit of a misnomer because beer and wine are generally not included, and drink options are limited to hard liquor, soft drinks, juice, and champagne. That being said, there are several tour operators, such as Red Sail Sports, that do offer wine and beer.

Operated by the same folks who own Mi Dushi, **Tattoo** (© 297/
586-2010; www.arubaadventures.com) conducts nocturnal booze-
and-dance cruises on Wednesday and Friday from 8pm to midnight
with a dinner buffet and $1 to $3 drinks ($49 for adults 18 and over
only). Also on Wednesday and Friday, it offers a 4-hour snorkeling
and swimming cruise that departs from De Palm Pier at 11:30am.
The prices ($35 for adults, $20 for children 12 and under) include a
barbecue lunch, but alcoholic drinks are extra ($2–$3 per drink). All
Tattoo cruises feature a rope swing and a three-level water slide.

DEEP-SEA FISHING

In the deep waters off the coast of Aruba you can test your skill and wits
against barracuda, amberjack, sailfish, wahoo, blue and white marlin
(all marlins are strictly catch and release), kingfish, bonito, and black-
and yellow-fin tuna. Chartered boats, with captain, crew, advice, tackle,
bait, lunch, and soft drinks, usually accommodate four to six anglers.
De Palm Tours (© 297/582-4400; www.depalm.com) books half-day
tours beginning at $300 per boat. The price for full-day trips goes as
high as $700. **Pelican Adventures** (© 297/587-2302; www.pelican-
aruba.com) half-day rates are about $300; full-day excursions cost
$600. **Red Sail Sports** (© 877/RED-SAIL [733-5245] in the U.S.
and Canada, or 297/586-1603 in Aruba; www.redsailaruba.com) offers
half-day expeditions for $350 and full-day trips for $700 for a maximum of four. You can also try your luck with any of the other individually owned boats docked at the **Renaissance Marina,** Seaport
Marketplace 204, Oranjestad (© 297/588-0260); their captains offer
similar prices but may have more flexibility.

PLAYING WITH WATER TOYS

How many different toys will you try out this vacation? Choose from
jet skis ($60 single, $70 double per half-hour), banana boat or tube
rides (both towed behind a speedboat; $15), Hobie Cat sailboats ($20
per hour), water skis ($45 per 15 min.), paddle boats ($15 per hour),
and floatbeds (sturdier than a raft; $5 per day). Check out any of the
watersports operators along Palm Beach such as **Frank's Place Watersports** (© 297/586-0106) under the green-and-yellow striped tent, or
contact **De Palm Tours** (© 297/582-4400; www.depalm.com),
Pelican Adventures (© 297/587-2302; www.pelican-aruba.com), **Red
Sail Sports** (© 877/RED-SAIL [733-5245] in the U.S. and Canada,
or 297/586-1603 in Aruba; www.redsailaruba.com), or **Unique Sports
of Aruba** (© 297/586-0096; www.visitaruba.com/uniquesports).

Available exclusively on De Palm Island through De Palm Tours,
small one- to three-person trimaran sailboats called Waveriders can be
rented with or without a captain, depending on your sailing ability.

Captained tours include a trip across the channel to a **mountain of**
snow-white sand.

KAYAKING

Aruba Kayak Adventures, Ponton 90 (© **297/582-5520;** www.
arubawavedancer.com/arubakayak), offers a 4-hour kayak tour along
the southern coast. Boats launch not far from Savaneta daily at
9:30am, then hug the coastal mangroves, past Pos Chiquito, Mangel
Halto, and Spanish Lagoon, formerly a pirate hide-out. After crossing
the calm lagoon to De Palm Island, paddlers can snorkel, sunbathe,
and lunch at the island's restaurant before kayaking the final leg to
Barcadera Beach. The $99 price includes hotel pickup and drop-off,
training, boat and snorkeling equipment, and lunch.

KITEBOARDING

With the help of large inflatable kites, about 27m (89 ft.) of flying
line, and small surfboards with foot straps, kiteboarders at Malmok
Beach and Fisherman's Hut skim across the water at 48kmph (30
mph) and launch themselves 3 to 10m (10–33 ft.) in the air. Kiteboarding has many of the same elements and thrills as snowboarding
and windsurfing, but with a relatively steeper learning curve. Aruba's
calm, shallow waters and steady winds make the island ideal for giving
it a whirl. **Kite Surfing Aruba Active Vacations** (© **297/586-0989**
or 741-2991; www.aruba-active-vacations.com) has 2-hour introductory lessons for $100. For the beginner, these lessons normally start
with mastering a smaller kite on land before entering the water with
a full-size kite, then finally moving to the board in subsequent lessons.
Dare2Fly Aruba (© **297/586-3735;** www.dare2flyaruba.com) offers
a 6-hour beginner package, in three sessions, including a kite-control
lesson, a body-drag lesson, and a board lesson for $375.

PARASAILING

You can ascend 180m (591 ft.) above the sea in a boat-towed parachute
after making arrangements with one of the watersports centers along
Palm Beach or by calling **Caribbean Aquatics** (© **297/586-0505**) or
De Palm Tours (© **297/582-4400;** www.depalm.com). Although
flight time is only 10 minutes, the exhilaration lasts all day. Expect to
pay about $55 for a single-seater, or about $100 for a parachute built
for two. Some operators restrict flights to persons 7 and over years of
age weighing between 41 and 109 kilograms (90–240 lb.). If under-
weight, an option is to pair up. Bring a waterproof camera.

SCUBA DIVING & SNORKELING

Aruba offers enough coral reefs, marine life, and wreck diving to keep
scuba divers and snorkelers busy for days. The coastal waters have an

4

A Diver's Dilemma

While all major dive certification groups do a fantastic job of training divers in all aspects of safety and responsible diving, they are unable to track graduates to make sure they practice what they learned. Even dive masters and dive instructors, who undergo extensive and rigorous training, sometimes forget the very lessons they are trained to teach and convey to students. I observed a prime example of forgetting to practice what you preach while diving in Curaçao, when a 60-year-old PADI dive instructor and dive shop owner brought a cohort of students to the Caribbean and pet a moray eel in front of the group. When I later grilled him about how he could violate the most fundamental safety rule for both divers and the delicate marine creatures, his response was that he'd done no harm because he was wearing diving gloves. This seemingly harmless act put both the diver and the eel in danger: Diving gloves certainly would not protect the diver from a toothy chomp from a 1.5m (5-ft.) eel, and the touch subjected the eel to acute stress and skin infection. None of the above could compare, however, to the standard of deplorable conduct he conveyed to his disciples, who will no doubt venture forth to pet, stroke, and disturb countless other creatures, and set equally bad examples for countless other divers.

average temperature of 80°F (27°C), and visibility ranges from 18 to 30m (59–98 ft.). Snorkelers: Be forewarned that waves can be choppy at times in some locations. Divers should wear wet suits, especially for deeper dives (the water doesn't always feel like 80°F). The best snorkeling sites are around Malmok Beach and Boca Catalina, where the water is calm and shallow, and marine life is plentiful. Dive sites stretch along the entire southern, leeward coast. Whatever you do, don't miss a visit to the *Antilla* wreck, the best shipwreck in the Caribbean. The easiest dive wreck you'll ever see, its mast is so close to the surface that curious pelicans actually used it as a perch up until January 2009, when the wreck shifted.

Besides snorkeling, SNUBA is another nonscuba underwater option. SNUBA divers breathe compressed air through a regulator on a hose attached to a tank floating at the surface. Though entertaining, interference with the line, guide, other SNUBA divers attached to the same tank, and unintended encounters with the razor-sharp reef make the experience at times frustrating and potentially painful.

The Operators

Unique Sports of Aruba (© 297/5-UNIQUE [586-4783] or 586-0096; www.visitaruba.com/uniquesports), on Palm Beach at the Radisson, is another popular operation that took over Pelican Adventures dive operations in 2008. Its four boats can accommodate 25 divers comfortably. Packages start at $125 for three dives (assuming you have your own equipment), $320 for six, including equipment. The full-service, five-star, PADI-certified Gold Palm operator has an array of diving options. Two-tank morning boat dives are $81, one-tank morning or afternoon boat dives are $54, and one-tank night dives are $63. Nondiving boat passengers pay $25, or $30 to snorkel, space permitting. Snorkeling cruises include instructions, equipment, stops at three sites, snacks, and an open bar for $43. **Pelican** (© 297/587-2302; www.pelican-aruba.com) also conducts 1-day introductory scuba courses ($96) and full-fledged PADI open-water certification instructions ($438).

Red Sail Sports ★ (© 877/RED-SAIL [733-5245] in the U.S. and Canada, or 297/586-1603 in Aruba; www.redsailaruba.com), another full-service, five-star, PADI-certified Gold Palm operator, has locations at the Hyatt, Marriott, and Renaissance. Its dive prices are slightly lower than Unique Sports': Two-tank morning boat dives are $79, one-tank morning or afternoon boat dives are $49, and one-tank night dives are $49. Packages include a five-tank package for $188, an eight-tank package for $285, and a 10-tank package for $356. Nondiving boat passengers pay $20, space permitting. Snorkelers are charged $30, including equipment, but Unique Sports, Pelican, Red Sail, and other operators offer an array of snorkeling-only excursions that visit multiple sites. Red Sail also offers 1-day introductory scuba and refresher courses that include instructions, a morning pool session, a one-tank boat dive, and all equipment for $89. The PADI open-water certification course is $425 or you can do the classroom portion online and bring the price down to $325. Introductory courses are available for children 10 and over.

Two other dive schools operate in the resort area. **S.E. Aruba Fly 'n Dive** (© 297/588-1150; www.se-aruba.com) operates out of Oranjestad harbor and Surfside Beach. It specializes in dives along the island's southeast coast. As the only PADI five-star National Geographic Center, they offer all courses from beginner to instructor. **Mermaid Sports Divers** (© 297/587-4103 or 587-4106; www.scubadivers-aruba.com) is located between the Low-Rise and the High-Rise hotels on the sasaki highway and offers a free dive to anyone who spots a sea horse.

See "Boating," earlier in this chapter, for a comprehensive list of snorkeling operators.

(Tips) **Take the Plunge**

If you weren't born with gills, you'll have to learn certain skills and gain an understanding of your equipment before you scuba dive. Contact the Professional Association of Diving Instructors (PADI), the National Association of Underwater Instructors (NAUI), or Scuba Schools International (SSI) for instruction. Certifying 70% of U.S. divers and 55% of divers worldwide, **PADI**, 30151 Tomas St., Rancho Santa Margarita, CA 92688 (© **800/729-7234;** www.padi.com), is the world's largest diving organization. Equally respected but less of a marketing powerhouse, **NAUI**, 1232 Tech Blvd., Tampa, FL 33619 (© **800/553-6284;** www.nauiww.org), is a not-for-profit association that's been around for 40 years. The last of the big three is **SSI**, 2619 Canton Court, Ft. Collins, CO 80525 (© **970/482-0883;** www.divessi.com), which certifies its divers exclusively through retail dive shops.

The Sites

At the island's extreme northeast point, the *California* **wreck** has haunted the ocean floor for almost 100 years. While traveling from Liverpool to Central America, the wooden passenger ship ran aground, its merchandise, clothing, and furniture eventually washing ashore. Tour guides often circulate the romantic notion that the ship was the only vessel to have heard the *Titanic's* distress signal. It's a nice story but a bunch of malarkey. The ship that ignored the *Titanic's* flares was the *Californian,* which was torpedoed by a German submarine off the coast of Greece in 1915. About 14m (46 ft.) beneath the ocean's surface, what's left of Aruba's *California* is difficult to see and rarely visited by dive boats. Due to strong currents and choppy seas, this dive is strictly for advanced divers, and only when the water is unusually calm.

At **Arashi Reef ★**, around the island's northern tip from the *California,* pieces of a Lockheed Lodestar litter the silty bottom of tranquil Arashi Bay. The wings, cockpit, and front half of the fuselage sit upright in a frozen takeoff position. Maybe the neighborhood angelfish, parrotfish, sergeant majors, yellowtail snappers, Caesar grunts, gray chromis, and blue tangs are contemplating how to reassemble all the pieces. Just south of the plane parts, brain coral, star coral, and sea rods dot the strip before dropping off to a ledge painted with sea fans and multicolored encrusting sponges. The plane's depth of 11 to 12m (36–39 ft.) is ideal for novice divers and snorkelers.

Just south of Arashi Reef, the 394-foot-long ***Antilla* wreck ★★** is the Caribbean's largest shipwreck. Once a German freighter, the ship was scuttled in 1941 when threatened by Allied forces. In January 2009 part of the hull caved in due to strong currents, and the crow's nest, which once jutted from the water, is now submerged. Even so, its proximity to the surface means even snorkelers can peer into the abyss of its fractured hull and imagine (or try not to) what creatures of the depths may lurk within. It's one of the island's most popular dives. Covered by giant tube sponges and coral formations, the 18m-deep (59-ft.) ghost ship is swarmed by angelfish, silversides, moray eels, and the occasional lobster. Octopus, sergeant majors, and puffers can also be spotted.

Leaf and brain coral await you at **Malmok Reef,** just south of the *Antilla.* This 21m-deep (69-ft.) bottom reef's dozing lobsters and stingrays are popular with underwater paparazzi, and the giant purple, orange, and green barrel sponges pose for the camera as well. The *Debbie II,* a 118-foot fuel barge sunk in 1992, attracts schools of fish, including barracudas.

Southwest of Malmok Reef, the mangled midsection is all that remains of the ***Pedernales,*** an American flat-bottomed oil tanker torpedoed by a German submarine in 1942. Cabins, washbasins, lavatories, toilets, and pipelines are scattered about for easy viewing. The bow and stern were hauled back to the United States, refitted with a new hull, and used to transport troops for the Normandy invasion. Chunks of the hull, supports, and crossbeams litter the sandy bottom. The wreckage attracts Caesar grunts, green moray eels, frogfish, trumpet fish, groupers, parrotfish, angelfish, silversides, and yellowtail snappers. Keep an eye open for snake eels and spotted eagle rays, too. White tunicates and orange cup corals coat the metal undersides. At a depth of only 6 to 9m (20–30 ft.), the *Pedernales* is popular with novice divers and snorkelers.

Off the coast of Oranjestad, **Harbor Reef** features an abundance of hard and soft coral formations, including giant brain coral and orange, black, and blue sponges. Nearby, the aging **pilot boat wreck** is encrusted with sponges and brain, star, and sheet coral. The queen angels, parrotfish, and Spanish hogfish bathe the 36-foot vessel in fiesta colors, while a barracuda and a pair of green morays keep divers alert. You may also spot the occasional stingray or spotted eagle ray.

An artificial reef 46m (151 ft.) from **Renaissance Island's** main beach is being helped along by a vintage 1970s Aruba Airlines passenger jet that was sunk 26m (85 ft.) down. The plane sits in takeoff position; the airline logo on the outer hull is still legible. In only 4m (13 ft.) of water and a bit farther off Renaissance Island's main beach, a sunken barge with crowds of swarming fish is also perfect for snorkeling.

Nearby, **Sponge Reef** is the home of a remarkable array of sponges, including orange elephant ears, purple and yellow tubes, vases, and small baskets. Interesting leaf and plate coral formations are also found in the area.

Farther east but still only 6.4km (4 miles) southwest of Oranjestad, **Barcadera Reef** stretches from depths of 6 to 27m (20–89 ft.), accommodating both divers and snorkelers. Dense clusters of elkhorn, staghorn, and finger corals populate the reef, and along the sandy bottom, brain corals and huge sea fans hold sway. Wrasses, scorpionfish, blue and stoplight parrotfish, damselfish, and pink-tipped anemones also set up housekeeping in the area.

West of Barcadera Reef at a depth of 27m (89 ft.), the *Jane Sea* wreck rests in a thick grove of star, boulder, plate, and brain coral. This 246-foot Venezuelan cement freighter was sunk in 1988 to form an artificial reef after it was caught with a cargo of cocaine. Blanketed with hydroids, fire coral, and encrusting sponge, the anchor chain is completely rigid. The ship's sides are orange with cup corals and home to French and queen angels. Keep your eyes peeled for barracudas, green morays, tropicals, and gorgonians, and watch your head when entering the radio room and mess hall.

Even before snorkelers leave the dock of **De Palm Island** (east of the *Jane Sea* wreck), overfed fluorescent blue parrotfish looking for a snack greet them. Though it's tempting to feed them, don't do it. Their powerful beaks and digestive tracts are designed to munch on rock-hard corals, and if they eat what people feel them instead of the coral, it is unhealthy for both the fish and the reef—not to mention somewhat risky for your delicate fingers. Water depths start at 1.2m (4 ft.) at the dock but drop off to 36m (118 ft.) by the time you're 364m (1,194 ft.) out. Divers, who usually reach the reef by boat, are likely to spot a barracuda or two, but snorkelers, who will be underwhelmed by the fish found milling about the damaged reef boulders, will find better diversity elsewhere.

Off the central coast of De Palm Island, **Mike's Reef ★★** offers one of Aruba's best reef dives. Enormous clusters of gorgonians, brain coral, flower coral, and star coral dominate the environment, while brilliant purple and orange sponges direct the procession of rainbow runners and barracuda. This reef is especially popular with macro photographers (underwater photographers who specialize in close-up shots).

Just east of Mike's Reef and 110m (361 ft.) out from Mangel Halto Beach, **Mangel Halto Reef ★★** slopes from 4.5m (15 ft.) to ledges and ridges that plunge to depths of 33m (108 ft.). The area boasts an array of deepwater gorgonians, anemones, and sponges. Mobile marine life includes copper sweepers, grunts, sergeant majors, lobsters, blue tangs, butterfly fish, stingrays, yellow tails, and jacks. You may even spot a sea horse. At the greater depths, octopuses, green morays, nurse sharks, tarpons, and large barracuda inhabit small caves and overhangs. In early spring, graceful sea turtles appear on their way to lay eggs on the nearby beaches.

Continuing east along the coast, **Isla de Oro Reef** rests off the old fishing village of Savaneta. Close to the mangrove-lined shore, the reef is usually swept by a running current, and visibility is excellent. Beginning at 6m (20 ft.), yellow stingrays, lobster, and Spanish hogfish dart along the walls of staghorn, star, brain, and plate corals. Toward the ultimate depth of 36m (118 ft.), sheet and leaf corals form ledges and caves—home to large morays and parrotfish.

A bit farther east, **Commandeurs Reef** slopes from 12 to 27m (39–89 ft.) below the surface. Sheet and leaf coral here attract extensive marine life such as snappers, grunts, and French and queen angels. On occasion, runners and barracuda patrol the area.

UNDERWATER TOURING

If you loved Captain Nemo and *20,000 Leagues Under the Sea,* don't miss your chance to cruise 45m (148 ft.) below the sea in a submarine. **Atlantis Adventures** (© 866/546-7820 in the United States, or 297/588-6881; www.atlantisadventures.com) operates a spacious, modern ship with large portholes for maximum ogling. After a comprehensive orientation on shore, you board a catamaran for the 30-minute sail to deeper water, then transfer to the *Atlantis VI,* a 66-foot-long, fully pressurized and air-conditioned submarine. During the gentle descent, you'll pass scuba divers, coral reefs, shipwrecks, and hundreds of curious sergeant majors, blue chromis, creole wrasse, parrotfish, and angelfish. Brain and sheet coral, sea whips, and tube and barrel sponges are just as easy to spot during the 50 minutes you're submerged. The crew's commentary is expert, informative, and very wry. Depending on the season, trips depart two to three times each day. Each excursion takes 1$^3/_4$ hours, though you are only underwater for 50 minutes. The cost is $99 for adults, $79 for children 13 to 17, and $49 for children 12 and under. All passengers must be at least 91 centimeters (36 in.) tall. It's worth the splurge, but for a cheaper option consider Atlantis's other ship, the *Seaworld Explorer.* This glass-bottom semisubmarine remains above sea level, but its observatory is 1.5m (5 ft.) below the surface. The narrated tour covers Arashi Reef and features an up-close encounter with a scuttled World War II German freighter, encrusted with coral and teeming with other marine life. The daily voyages are $44 for adults, $24 for children 11 and under, and gratis for toddlers 1 and under. The *Atlantis VI* trip leaves from a pier in front of the Crystal Casino in Oranjestad; the *Seaworld Explorer* excursion departs from Pelican Pier on Palm Beach.

If you don't mind getting a little wet but have no desire to learn to scuba dive, consider the Sea Trek helmet dive offered by **De Palm Tours** (© **297/582-4400;** www.depalm.com). Donning a wet suit and a Teletubbies-inspired helmet that supplies a continuous flow of air, you'll descend 6m (20 ft.) beneath the sea to a 105m (344-ft.) walkway, where you can feed the fish, view a sunken Cessna, and generally experience life underwater. If you can walk and breathe, don't deprive yourself of the fun. The 40- to 45-minute stroll is $55 plus the $79 cost of passage to the island. The CD-ROM featuring you in full regalia seated at an underwater cafe is another $35, but worth it. *A word to the wise:* Although Sea Trek and other fun activities are on De Palm Island, don't let anyone convince you to spend all day there. Its beaches are rocky and generally dismal compared to those of the main island, and the snorkeling is unimpressive except for those enormous overfed blue parrotfish.

WINDSURFING

Aruba's world-class windsurfing conditions attract competitors from around the world every July for the Hi-Winds World Challenge, one of the region's most popular windsurfing competitions and the only Professional Windsurfing Association Grand Prix event in the Caribbean. Wind speeds on the island are best in May, June, and July, when they average 20 to 25 knots, and calmest from September through November, when they range from 10 to 20 knots.

The area around **Malmok Beach** and **Fishermen's Huts** is the most popular windsurfing spot on the island. Sailed by novices and pros alike, it features slightly gusty offshore winds, minimal current, and moderate chop. The water is shallow more than 60m (197 ft.) out from the shore. **Boca Grandi,** on the extreme eastern coast, is for advanced and expert wave sailors only. The very strong current here moves out to sea, and on-shore waves rise from 30 centimeters (1 ft.) to mast high on the outer reefs. This is definitely the place to learn—beginners are issued a board the size of a banquet table (read: *stable*) with a sail the size of a cocktail napkin (read: *slow*), meaning you will be up and cruising in no time.

Most windsurfing operations cluster around Malmok Beach, where equipment rental averages $30 to $40 for 2 hours, $45 for half a day, and $55 to $60 for a full day. Two-hour beginner lessons with equipment are about $50; 6-hour introductory courses are $135. Operators include **Aruba Active Vacations,** L.G. Smith Blvd. 486 (© **297/586-0989** or 741-2991; www.aruba-active-vacations.com); and **Vela Windsurf,** at the Aruba Marriott Resort & Stellaris Casino (© **800/223-5443;** www.velawindsurf.com). Like any good college, Vela has prodigious course listings; its offerings include Intro to Harness

Use—Da Cool Stance and Modern Science of Body Drags. Aruba **91**
Active Vacations, Aruba Sailboard Vacations, and Vela are windsurf
specialists—a good bet for novices.

3 HITTING THE LINKS

Tierra del Sol Golf Course (© **297/586-0978;** www.tierradelsol.
com), designed by Robert Trent Jones II, is Aruba's only championship course. With its desert terrain, ocean vistas, and challenging
winds, it's an interesting one, located on the island's northwest tip
near the California Lighthouse. Aruba's persistent winds are a factor
during most approach shots, when club selection can be decisive, but
gusts can affect putts, too. The arid links are flat for the most part, the
Aruba grass fairways are fairly wide for desert links, and the greens are
accommodating. Although there are no hidden breaks, most putts are
fast. Obstacles include sand bunkers, cacti, coral rock formations, and
water hazards (referred to locally as salinas). The par-5, 534-yard 14th
hole, with its crosswinds, narrow greens, and sand bunkers, may be
the course's most challenging hole; play it cautiously. Views of the
ocean and the California Lighthouse make hole 3 one of the most
picturesque. For high-tech geeks, each golf cart is equipped with a
GPS satellite dish and a color video screen that provides graphic hole
and green overviews, and many other options. A morning tee time
from December through March is $159; afternoon rounds drop to
$124. During the summer, mornings are $112, afternoons $92. Pack-
ages are available. Guests renting Tierra del Sol villas (see chapter 2)
can opt for unlimited golfing privileges. The course also offers a 1³/₄-
hour No Embarrassment clinic for golfers of all levels. The $45 fee
includes lunch at the clubhouse. A pro shop, driving range, putting
green, chipping green, locker rooms, spa, and restaurants are on-site.

Opened in 2005, **Divi Links,** near Druif Beach, across the street
from the Divi Aruba resort (© **297/581-4653;** www.divigolf.com),
offers a less-pricey yet elegant alternative. Although it has only 9
holes, the course allows a second pass to simulate an 18-hole round.
The course has two par-5 holes, two par-3s, and five par-4 holes. Six
holes play either over or alongside the numerous man-made lagoons,
and each hole has three tees for different level players. Fees are $104
to $124 for 18 holes, $75 to $85 for 9 holes. The course is open daily
from 7:30am to 5pm. Start before 1pm to complete 18 holes. Golf
carts can be rented at the on-site pro shop, and clubs can be rented
for $25; however, caddies are not available. Weekly tournaments offer
cheaper greens fees and throw in rental clubs and shoes as well as a

few drinks for $75. For all but the die-hard golfer, this is a great way to save a few bucks and have a good time.

Mulligan's restaurant at the clubhouse offers 360-degree views of the greens as well as an extensive menu. While eating lunch there I counted nearly a dozen flatscreen televisions, including one in the ladies' room (presumably there is at least one in the men's too). While the screens were originally intended to allow golfers to review their last shot on the 9th hole, the technology was not in place as of press time, and the annoying visual cacophony of various sports and news programs can be obtrusive.

If putt-putt's more your style, **Adventure Golf,** on L.G. Smith Boulevard (✆ **297/587-6625**), has two 18-hole miniature courses surrounded by a moat, where you can float in paddle boats. Video and table games, a batting cage, a go-kart racetrack, and a restaurant and saloon also provide diversion. During the week, the center's open from 5 to 11pm; on weekends the fun starts at noon. An 18-hole round is $8.25. Paddle-boat rides are $5.25, and go-karts are $8 for a single to $11 per double.

4 OTHER ACTIVE PURSUITS

BICYCLING

Aruba is small—maybe too small for cyclists who think nothing of biking 97km (60 miles) a day. The exotic terrain is flat for the most part, but heading into the wind is a challenge, and the sun is intense at midday. You know to bring plenty of water, a hat, and sunscreen. The most scenic roads trace the northern coast. They're not paved, so think mountain bike. Bring a bandanna, too, to cover your mouth against the dust. To rent a bike, stop by **Pablito's Bike Rental,** L.G. Smith Blvd. 234 (✆ **297/587-8655**). Prices start as low as $15 per half-day. **Rancho Notorious,** Borancana 8E, Noord (✆ **297/586-0508;** www.ranchonotorious.com), offers a couple of guided mountain bike tours that visit Alto Vista Chapel and the California Lighthouse. One's $2^1/_2$ hours long ($47); the other tacks on a bit of snorkeling ($55, snorkeling gear included). Bikers must be at least 8 years old to take the tours.

BIRDING

Although no organized tours are offered, ardent birders have the opportunity to spy 170 different species in Aruba. In early winter, migratory birds swell the number to about 300. In the High-Rise area, the Bubali Bird Sanctuary's ponds and wetlands attract more than 80 species, including brown pelicans, black olivaceous cormorants, herons, and egrets. Arikok National Park, which makes up much of the island's north-central region, is home to hummingbirds (common emerald and ruby-topaz), rufous-collared sparrows, ospreys, yellow orioles, American kestrels, black-faced grassquits, yellow warblers, Caribbean parakeets, long-tongued bats, common ground doves, troupials, crested caracaras, and Aruban burrowing owls. For more information, see chapter 5.

BOWLING

Eagle Bowling Palace, Pos Abao z/n, inland from the Low-Rise hotels (© **297/583-5038;** www.eaglebowling.com), has 16 lanes, a cocktail lounge, and a snack bar. It's open Friday and Saturday from 10am to 2am; Wednesday, Thursday, and Sunday from 10am to 1am; and Monday and Tuesday from 5pm to 1am. Children 11 and under must clear out before 7pm. Depending on the time of day, lanes rent for $11 to $16 per hour. Shoes are another $1.25. Reservations are recommended.

HIKING

The sun is hot, and shade is scarce, but if you bring water and a wide-brimmed hat, traipsing around Aruba's hills and coastline is full of rewards: otherworldly rock formations, bizarre cactus groves, fluorescent parakeets, and dewlapped lizards. Hiking boots are nice, but sneakers are fine. There are no organized tours; Arikok National Park has many clearly marked trails. Scale the island's highest hills, explore abandoned gold mines, tiptoe around plantation ruins, trek through caves, and comb sea bluffs for coral and bones.

HORSEBACK RIDING

Time to get back in the saddle or just saddling up for the first time? Several ranches offer morning and midday excursions, and, if you're hopelessly romantic, rides off into the sunset. The horses are good-natured and calm (although the ranch hands have been known to get a bit frisky). Long sleeves, long pants, closed shoes, sunglasses, and sunblock are strongly recommended. *Tip:* Since helmets are required, despite being a bit musty, don a baseball cap before strapping on one of these well-worn numbers for a better (and no doubt cleaner) fit. The protruding bill will also afford you an extra inch or two of shade.

Based at a 17th-century coconut plantation on the northern coast, **Rancho Daimari,** Tanki Leendert 249 (© **297/586-6285;** www. visitaruba.com/ranchodaimari), offers 2-hour trips through Arikok National Park and to the Natural Pool, where snorkeling and swimming in the restorative waters are encouraged. The price is $75, and for an extra $40 per person you can have a private honeymoon sunset or sunrise ride.

Rancho Notorious, Borancana 8E, Noord (© **297/586-0508;** www.ranchonotorious.com), offers several options. The 1-hour tour passes through the countryside for $45. The 2-hour tour covers more countryside, Tierra del Sol, the California Lighthouse, and Malmok Beach for $70. Finally, the beach and snorkeling tour includes a trot along Malmok Beach and snorkeling for $120. The **Gold Mine Ranch** (© **297/594-1317;** www.thegoldmineranch.com) offers 2-hour tours starting at $55 and offers free transportation.

OFF-ROADING

For those who want a rough-and-ready (if noisy and treacherous) island adventure, several places rent all-terrain vehicles. **Georges,** L.G. Smith Blvd. 124 (© **297/593-2202**), next to the Harley-Davidson store in Oranjestad, rents ATVs and scooters for $20 per hour or $50 and up per day. For an organized tour, check in with **De Palm Tours,** L.G. Smith Blvd. 142 (© **297/582-4400;** www.depalm. com); **Rancho Daimari,** Plantage Damairi (© **297/586-6284** or 586-6285; www.visitaruba.com/ranchodaimari); or **Rancho Notorious** (© **297/586-0508;** www.ranchonotorious.com). *Tip:* As with horseback riding, safety helmets are a must and work well over your own baseball cap, providing a more comfortable fit and feel. Select a helmet with the word "Bell" on the back—these are actual safety helmets. It's best to avoid the ones with a message inside that reads, WARNING, THIS IS A NOVELTY ITEM AND NOT INTENDED TO BE USED AS A SAFETY DEVICE.

If a jeep tour is too slow and an ATV is too fast, then a TomCar is juuuust right. These dune buggies drive like a car, have four-point seat belts, and are so stable, you can't flip them if you try (yes, we tried). Feel free to play Mad Max as your convoy snakes along gravel slopes, dirt roads, and sand dunes on one of two routes. **Aruba Off-Road** (© **297/585-0027**) is based at the Aruba Ostrich Farm and offers two daily tours. The morning drive costs $109 and takes you to Seroe Colorado, Baby Beach, and Quadirikiri caves and includes a tasty lunch at Boca Prins. The afternoon expedition is $89 and wends its way through Ayo Rock Formation, Bushiribana Gold Mine, Baby Natural Bridge, Alto Vista Chappel, California Lighthouse, and Boca Catalina Beach.

TENNIS

Most of the island's beachside hotels have tennis courts, many of them lit for night play. Some also boast pros on hand to give clinics or individual instruction. Nonguests can make arrangements to play at hotel courts, but guests have priority. The island's best facilities are at the **Aruba Racket Club,** Rooi Santo 21, Palm Beach (© **297/586-0215;** www.arc.aw/tennis/tennisschool.html), which features eight lighted courts, a swimming pool, a fitness center, and a bar and restaurant. The club is open Monday through Friday from 6am to 11pm, Saturday 7am to 10pm, and Sunday from 9am to 8pm. Rates are $10 per hour per court, and lessons are $30 for a half-hour. The club is near the Tierra del Sol complex on the northwest coast.

Exploring Aruba

Spend every day on the beach if you want—but you'll miss Aruba's wilder charms. With stark wind-swept hills, towering cacti, and rough and rocky coasts, the outback is completely different from the posh resort areas, and worthy of exploration. The island's small enough to cover in a day or two. For a complete adventure, rent a four-wheel-drive vehicle: The most picturesque routes are rubble-strewn dirt roads; ordinary cars will do, but rugged Jeeps are better, and in Arikok National Park they are highly recommended. The circuit around the island's northern tip—to California Lighthouse, Alto Vista Chapel, Bushiribana Gold Smelter Ruins, and Ayo and Casibari rock formations—is the most popular. Although less frequented, Arikok National Park, with its flora, fauna, caves, dunes, and history, is just as worthwhile. If you're not the outdoorsy type, visit Oranjestad's small museums or drive down to San Nicolas on your way to Rodger's Beach or Boca Grandi.

1 GUIDED TOURS

Major tour operators conduct guided tours through the outback or around Arikok National Park. Several incorporate sightseeing with swimming and snorkeling. **De Palm Tours** (© 297/582-4400; www. depalm.com) dominates the field, with half-day and full-day excursions in air-conditioned motorcoaches, four-wheel-drive vehicles, or all-terrain buggies. On the four-wheel-drive trips, you drive your own Jeep as part of a caravan led by a guide who broadcasts commentary over the radio. Competitors include **ABC Aruba Tours** (© 297/582-5600), and **Pelican Adventures** (© 297/587-2302; www.pelican-aruba.com). Three-hour excursions start at $39; for 4¹/₂-hour trips with refreshments and snorkeling the price climbs to $77. For a more natural experience your best bet is **Aruba Nature Sensitive Hiking and Jeep Tours** (© 297/594-5017 or 585-1594; www.sensitive hikers.com) where you can take an easy or challenging hike in Arikok National Park, or a moonlight hike, complete with transportation in an open-sided transport. The company is owned by one of the founding members of Aruba's natural parks, Eddy Croes, who is a driving force of conservation on the island and a wealth of knowledge.

For a bird's-eye view of the island, take a helicopter tour with **Heli-Tours** (© **297/731-9999;** www.arubahelitours.com), located at the Heli-Pad near the Renaissance Marketplace in downtown Oranjestad. A 15-minute Beach Safari to the lighthouse is $85 per person; a 30-minute tour of the entire island will set you back $130 per person.

2 ON YOUR OWN

If you'd like to explore at your own pace, rent a Jeep. Prices for a roof-less four-wheel-drive with standard transmission start at $48 per day. Air-conditioned automatics are $60 and up. Driving around on your own is fun, but be forewarned that road signs are often small, hand-made, and unnoticeable. Ask for a map: Even if it's hopelessly inaccu-rate—which it will be—a bad map's better than no map at all. If you plan to take a popular route, discreetly join a caravan or ask directions along the way. Even if you find yourself in the middle of nowhere, the island's too small to truly lose your bearings (the wind always blows from east to west). Some car rental agencies will also rent you a cell-phone along with the car for a nominal fee. This may be a good option if you are worried about getting lost or breaking down. If you're more interested in sites along paved roads and don't feel like getting lost, hire a cab. The going rate is $40 per hour for a maximum of five people. See "Getting Around," in chapter 1.

3 WHAT TO SEE

ORANJESTAD

Aruba's capital attracts more shoppers than sightseers; it's also a popular cruise port. The town has a sunny Caribbean demeanor, with **Dutch colonial-style buildings** painted in vivid colors. While the gingerbread architecture proliferates along the main streets in town, the vast major-ity is not original; the modern buildings were designed to replicate the ornate gingerbread architecture of the colonial era. The main thorough-fare, L.G. Smith Boulevard, runs along the **waterfront** and abounds with marinas, shopping malls, restaurants, and bars. Caya G.F. Betico Croes, or Main Street, runs roughly parallel to the waterfront several blocks inland; it's another major shopping venue. The harbor is packed with fishing boats and schooners docked next to stalls, where vendors hawk fruits, vegetables, and fish. On the other side of the Seaport Mar-ketplace shopping mall, **Queen Wilhelmina Park,** named after one of Holland's longest-reigning monarchs, features manicured lawns, views of colorful fishing boats, and luxuriant tropical vegetation. If you're looking for a little culture, Oranjestad has a handful of museums and houses of worship.

Archaeological Museum of Aruba   Recently relocated to more convenient and roomier digs at Schelpstraat z/n, and scheduled to reopen in July 2009, this museum highlights the island's Amerindian heritage. Pottery vessels, shell and stone tools, burial urns, and skulls and bones are among the artifacts in its collection. The museum is a must for archaeology and history buffs.

J.E. Irausquinplein 2A. ℂ **297/582-8979.** Free admission. Mon–Fri 8am–noon and 1–4pm.

Beth Israel Synagogue   Jews, mostly merchants, arrived in Aruba at the beginning of the 20th century, when the oil refinery drew people from the Caribbean and Europe. The Jewish population today is small, but this synagogue endures, with a membership of about 35 families. Most congregants at Friday night services are visitors on vacation.

Adriaan Lacle Blvd. 2. ℂ **297/582-3272.** Fri service 7:30pm.

Fort Zoutman, Willem III Tower, and Museo Arubano ★
During the 18th century, pirates menaced Oranjestad's harbor, raiding for horses and anything else of value. To defend the island, the Dutch erected Fort Zoutman in 1796. Aruba's oldest example of Dutch architecture, the bastion stands on what was once the shore (landfill construction in 1930 altered the coastline). In 1867, it gained Willem III Tower, named after the then-reigning Dutch monarch. Over the years, the site has served as an aloe garden, jail, courthouse, junk room, and tax office. The fort was restored in 1974, the tower in 1983. The Museo Arubano, which displays a few prehistoric Caiquetio artifacts and numerous remnants from the Dutch colonial period, underwent a major renovation in 2004. On Tuesday from 7 to 9pm, the museum hosts the Bon Bini Festival, a small touristy fair with some local arts and crafts, homemade food, local music on traditional instruments, and dance, such as tumba and the Aruban waltz. There is a $3 admission fee for the fair.

Zoutmanstraat 1. ℂ **297/582-6099.** Admission $8. Mon–Fri 8:30am–3:30pm.

Aruba Numismatic Museum ★   This small museum is housed in a modern building in order to accommodate its rather impressive collection of coin exhibits. Dedicated numismatists can spend the better part of a morning perusing the 40,000 specimens from more than 400 countries, but anyone with a passing interest in coins or history will appreciate this labor of love. The amazing collection is the work of three generations of a single Aruban family, who research and

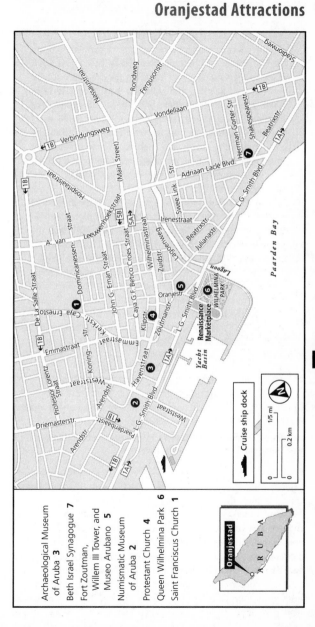

Archaeological Museum
of Aruba **3**

Beth Israel Synagogue **7**

Fort Zoutman,
Willem III Tower, and
Museo Arubano **5**

Numismatic Museum
of Aruba **2**

Protestant Church **4**

Queen Wilhelmina Park **6**

Saint Franciscus Church **1**

(Fun Facts) Aruban History 101

The first Arubans came from Venezuela by boat about 4,500 years ago. Living in small nomadic groups, they fished, hunted small animals, and collected fruit. They also fashioned crude tools from shells and stones and buried their dead in well-organized family groups. About 3,500 years later, the **Caiquetios** arrived, also from Venezuela and also by boat. Cultivating maize and manioc, this peaceful, more advanced group established villages near freshwater gullies.

In 1499, Alonso de Ojeda, a cohort of Christopher Columbus, became the first European to set foot on the island. Finding nothing of immediate value, the **Spanish** ignored Aruba until 1515, when they forcibly moved the entire Caiquetio population to Santo Domingo (now Haiti and the Dominican Republic) to work as slaves. Amerindians returned to Aruba in 1526, when Spain set up ranches on the island.

The Spanish left in 1636, when the **Dutch** gained control, but the first Dutch settlers arrived more than 100 years later, in 1754. For brief stints in the early 19th century, the English occupied the land, but Dutch sovereignty prevailed. Aruba remained a largely **ranch economy** with Amerindians and Dutch landowners herding horses and goats and cultivating millet, coconut, mango, and aloe.

write the detailed historical notes for each item as well as give tours of the museum and create excellent changing exhibits.

Weststraat 15 A-Zn 1 ⓒ **297/582-8831.** www.museumaruba.org. Admission $5. Mon–Thurs 9am–4pm; Fri 9am–1pm; Sat 9am–noon.

Protestant Church Built in 1846, Oranjestad's Protestant Church is Aruba's oldest house of worship. Looming above a terracotta tile roof, the square tower, decorated with stars, hearts, and wooden shutters, looks like something out of Pennsylvania Dutch country. The church is usually locked, but its tiny Bible Museum is open Monday through Friday from 10am to noon.

Wilhelminastraat 1 (behind the Renaissance). ⓒ **297/582-1435.** Mon–Fri 10am–noon. Services (in Dutch and English) Sat 8:30 and 10:30am.

Saint Franciscus Church The largest Roman Catholic Church in Aruba, modern St. Franciscus boasts several architectural details

In 1824, **gold** was discovered on the north coast, and a small gold rush ensued. Very little of the metal was actually found, though, and the industry petered out as the first shots of World War I rang out. Production of phosphate waned at about the same time.

The island entered the modern era in 1924, when Standard Oil of New Jersey built an **oil refinery** at San Nicolas. To supplement Aruba's labor force, thousands of workers arrived from North America, Europe, and other islands of the Caribbean, bringing the first people of African descent to the island. In 1942, U.S. troops landed to protect the highly valuable refinery which was instrumental in fueling Allied war efforts. The complex closed in 1985, temporarily devastating the economy but prodding Aruba to develop its now successful tourism industry. (The refinery has since reopened.)

Although the island gained independence from the Netherlands Antilles in 1986, it remains an autonomous unit of the Kingdom of the Netherlands. Today, Aruba's multicultural population boasts more than 60 nationalities.

that make it worth a visit. The barnlike ceiling soars heavenward, and a series of arches frame the altar, where the central crucifix stands in front of simple but elegant *trompe l'oeil* clouds and sky.

Irausquinplein 3, Oranjestad. © **297/582-1434.** Daily 24 hr. Sun Mass (in Papiamento and English) 6:30, 8, and 10am, and 7pm.

ALONG THE NORTHWEST COAST

If you can lift yourself from the sand, rent a four-wheel-drive vehicle and venture into the island's outback. Follow the dirt roads as they toil through alien landscapes of oddly balanced boulders, jagged cliffs, and furious seascapes. The terrain may seem harsh, but the cacti and divi divi trees love it. The tall organ-pipe cacti are known locally as cadushi, the prickly-pear variety is called tuna, and the barrel species is Bushi. Start from the resort area, head toward the California Lighthouse, and then follow the dirt road as it traces the island's perimeter.

Ready for something completely different? At the south end of the High-Rise area, the tropical gardens of the **Butterfly Farm** ★, on J.E. Irausquin Boulevard, across the street from the Divi Phoenix Beach Resort (© **297/586-3656;** www.thebutterflyfarm.com), you can dance with a thousand beautiful butterflies. The 40 species bred at the facility hail from every corner of the tropical world. It's fun to marvel at the colors of the ethereal flutterers, and guides provide amusing explanations of the short but sweet life of the average lepidopteran. Did you know that caterpillars double in size every 24 hours? That butterfly sex lasts for up to 48 hours? Visit as early in the day as possible—that's when the wing flapping is maximal. Admission is $15 for adults and $8 for children 4 to 16, and is good for unlimited return trips for the duration of your vacation. The farm is open daily from 8:30am to 4:30pm.

Aruba's most distinctive landmark is the **Old Dutch Windmill,** J.E. Irausquin Blvd. 330, around the corner from the Butterfly Farm, near Palm Beach. It's an anomaly in the Caribbean, but it's authentic. Built in Friesland, Holland, in 1804, it originally drained water from low-lying land. Damaged by a storm in 1878, it was later rebuilt at another site in the Netherlands to mill grain. In 1929, another storm hit the windmill, which stood idle until 1960, when a Dutch merchant shipped it to Aruba. It reopened in 1974 and has at various times over the years housed a series of restaurants and late-night bars, which seem to open then shut down depending on the direction of the wind, perhaps.

Although Aruba is as arid as the desert, the lush **Bubali Bird Sanctuary,** on J.E. Irausquin Boulevard, serves as a resting and breeding area for more than 80 species of local and migratory birds. Across the street from the Old Dutch Windmill, the poorly marked but worthwhile sanctuary was once a salt pan. Today the two interconnected man-made lakes are flooded by overflow from a nearby water-treatment facility and surrounded by lush vegetation. The fish in the nutrient-rich ponds attract brown pelicans and black olivaceous cormorants. In the constantly undulating marsh grasses (like something out of a van Gogh painting), black-crowned night herons, Louisiana herons, great blue herons, common egrets, and snowy egrets abound. Gulls, skimmers, coots, and numerous species of ducks also make appearances. The rickety **observation tower** has fallen into disrepair and is now unsafe to climb, but if it gets the restoration it deserves, it will provide avian enthusiasts a bird's-eye view of the oasis—though nonbirders and romantics alike will enjoy the spectacular view of the entire area. Dawn and dusk, when the birds are most active, are the best times to visit. The sanctuary is always open, and there's never an admission fee.

Go north from the bird sanctuary, past half of the High-Rise hotels, and turn right at the first traffic light. Proceed a mile or two to the next traffic light. Originally built in 1776 and last renovated in 1916, **Santa Anna Church** boasts a soaring ceiling and an intricately carved altar, communion rail, and pulpit. The neo-Gothic oak altar, carved in 1870 for a parish in the Dutch province of Noord-Brabent by Hendrik van der Geld, came to Aruba in 1928. The two stained-glass windows, dating from 1932 and 1965, honor four former lay priests of Alto Vista Chapel (described below). The adjacent cemetery contains a hodgepodge of crypts painted in tropical pastel colors and festooned with a verdant garden of plastic flower wreaths that are both bright and meditative. The quiet observer may catch a glimpse of a resident burrowing owl staring down from a perch at uninvited intruders. The church, which is usually locked, is on Caya F.D. Figaroa at its intersection of Palm Beach in Noord (© **297/586-1409** or 587-4747). Sunday Mass is celebrated at 7:30am and 6pm in Papiamento. Mass in English is at 11am.

From the church, drive north for about 5 minutes. The **California Lighthouse** ★ sits on a hilltop perch at Aruba's northernmost tip, but its active days are over. Part of the adjacent restaurant once served as the lighthouse keeper's home. The beacon itself has been closed to the public for a number of years, ever since someone committed suicide by jumping from its summit. The surrounding area features some of the island's most spectacular scenery—gentle sand dunes, rocky coral shoreline, and turbulent waves. The picturesque structure gets its name from the *California,* a passenger ship that sank off the nearby coast before the lighthouse was completed in 1916.

Now it's time to leave paved roads behind. Turn right at the lighthouse and follow the dirt trail along the dramatic northern coast. The road's rough state precludes speeding, but within 15 minutes you'll reach another man-made attraction. Built in 1750, abandoned in the 1800s and rebuilt 200 years later, the picturesque **Alto Vista Chapel** ★ radiates serenity from its cactus-studded perch overlooking the sea. The chapel, Aruba's first, was built by Caiquetio Indians and Spanish settlers before the island had its own priest. The church's ancient Spanish cross is one of the oldest European artworks in the Dutch Caribbean, and the altar's statue has a devoted local following. Secluded near the island's northwestern corner, just off the road hugging the northeast coast, the bright yellow structure, little more than a hut, rests at the end of a winding road lined with white crosses marking the Stations of the Cross.

Five minutes farther down the coast, you'll come to the **Bushiribana Ruins.** According to local legend, in 1824 a 12-year-old boy came across gold in one of the dry creek beds on Aruba's north coast.

Naturally, the discovery set off a gold frenzy. For 30 years, Arubans were allowed to collect the precious metal, provided they sold it at a set price. In 1854, a gold-mining concession was granted to the Aruba Island Goldmining Company, which built this smelter on the north coast in 1872. Although the facility operated for only 10 years, its hulking ruins still dominate the area. Climb the multitiered interior for impressive sea views. Too bad the walls have been marred with artless graffiti.

From the ruins, you'll be able to see a line of cars heading for the next site, just minutes away. Once the island's most photographed attraction, the **Natural Bridge** ★★ rose 7.5m (25 ft.) above the sea and spanned 30m (98 ft.) of rock-strewn waters. Centuries of relentless pounding by the surf carved the arch out of the limestone coast and no doubt led to its unfortunate collapse in September 2005. Luckily, the appropriately named **Baby Bridge** stands only a few feet away. While it lacks the dramatic arch of its namesake, it's still pretty cool and is sturdy enough (so far) to stand on, where you can view the rugged sea below. The nearby thirst-aid station supplies refreshments and souvenirs.

Retrace the dirt road back to the first intersection and turn left. The road soon becomes paved, and within 5 minutes, take a right. (Signage is nonexistent here, so don't be shy about asking for directions.) Looking like something out of the *Flintstones,* the eerie **Ayo Rock Formations** served Aruba's early inhabitants as a dwelling or religious site. The reddish-brown petroglyphs on the boulders suggest magical significance, and the strange stones look as though they were stacked by giants. The site is open daily from 9am to 5pm, and admission is free.

If you like the Ayo rocks, continue on the main road to its end. Turn right, then take another right at the sign for the **Casibari Rock Formations.** These alien rocks rise from the cacti- and lizard-infested hills. Although the boulders weigh several tons each, they look freshly scattered by some cyclopean dice roller. Look for the formations that resemble birds and dragons, or climb the trail to the top of the highest rock mound for a panorama of the area. Watch your head on the path to the top, though; the tunnels have low clearance. The rock garden is open daily from 9am to 5pm, with no admission charge. The nearby stands sell souvenirs, snacks, soft drinks, and beer.

If you have children, or just like animals, stop by the **Donkey Sanctuary** (© **297/965-6986** or 568-4091; www.arubandonkey. org), .8km (¹/₂ mile) from the Ayo Rock Formations, where dozens of these feral yet gentle animals are corralled, fed, and cared for. The staff will eagerly share their knowledge with you about the history and ecology of Aruba's donkeys, many of which still roam the countryside.

A small refreshment stand serves drinks and snacks. Hours are from 9am to 12:30pm weekdays and 10am to 3pm Saturday and Sunday. Even if the sanctuary is closed, you can still pet and ogle the friendly donkeys over the fence. For VIP treatment from the resident inmates, be sure to bring an apple or some carrots.

Another opportunity for animal encounters is the **Ostrich Farm** (*©* **297/585-9630;** www.arubaostrichfarm.com), on the road between the Baby Bridge and the Bushiribana Gold Smelter Ruins. Here you can tour the grounds and meet the resident ostriches and emus; the 20-minute tour is sadly lacking in any valuable information about these amazing birds, which stand over 1.8m (6 ft.) tall and can weigh close to 136 kilograms (300 lb.). The tired tour guides seem more interested in getting the tour over with than bestowing pearls of wisdom about the ecology of the birds themselves. Visitors can, nonetheless, feed a hungry harem of females; compare and contrast the ostriches with their close kin, emus; test the incredible strength of an egg at the hatchery; then head back to the pavilion to browse the impressive gift shop full of carved wood and textiles shipped in from Africa. One can also sample ostrich meat at the African-themed restaurant. While the idea is disturbing, the dark meat is surprisingly tasty and bears a striking resemblance not to chicken, but rather to steak. The ostrich farm and restaurant are open daily from 9am to 5pm. The last tour is at 4pm.

ARIKOK NATIONAL PARK

Arikok National Park ★★★ (*©* **297/585-1234**), Aruba's showcase ecological preserve, sprawls across nearly 20% of the island. Rock outcrops, boulders, and crevices create microclimates that support animal species found only in Aruba, including the Aruban rattlesnake, Aruban whiptail lizard, Aruban burrowing owl, and Aruban parakeet. Iguanas and many species of migratory birds live in the park as well, and goats and donkeys graze on the hills. Examples of early Amerindian art, abandoned mines from Aruba's gold-rush past, and remains of early farms dot the park. Sand dunes and limestone cliffs ornament the coast. It's easy to explore the preserve, but bring water, sunscreen, and food, and wear a hat and comfortable walking shoes. Birds and animals are most active in the morning, so go as early in the day as you can.

The government has plans to develop the area responsibly, but for now the sites can be reached by dirt road and hiking trail only. Routes are clearly marked, and signs are becoming more frequent and informative. If you're really into it, though, stop by the park's new office at San Fuego z/n, on the main road between the Low-Rise area and Santa Cruz, to pick up a map. The office is open Monday through Friday from 7:30am to 3:30pm.

Miralamar, a complex of gold mines and trenches, was active during the first decade of the 20th century. The hills along the path here are overgrown with yellow poui and white gum trees, and derelict buildings at the site include the foundations of an ore-testing lab, sleeping quarters, and a forge. Due to transportation problems and low-quality ore, the mines were abandoned in 1916, and many of the shafts collapsed. Century plants have now reclaimed the area.

Masiduri served as an experimental garden in the 1950s; the convergence of several creek beds makes the location reasonably moist. The eucalyptus trees and *cunucu* (farm) house date from the same era. The site now features an aloe-cultivation exhibit. In the early 1900s, Aruba was a major exporter of this plant known for its medicinal and healing properties. Today the sheltered location and comparatively moist conditions draw a variety of reptiles, including Aruban cat-eyed snakes. Feral donkeys, descendants of animals domesticated for transportation, come at night to rest.

The partially restored farm known as **Cunucu Arikok ★** recalls Aruba's agricultural past. It takes 45 minutes to complete the circular hiking trail through boulders, vegetation, and wildlife; shaded benches provide relief along the way. Beans, corn, millet, peanuts, and cucumbers were once cultivated at the site, and to protect the crops from goats, sheep, and donkeys, cactus hedges and stone walls were built. The restored adobe farmhouse has the typical small windows and a sloping roof. Dried cactus stems were used to make roof beams, and mud and grass form the walls. A barn, threshing floor, pigpen, and outhouse surround the house. Before Europeans arrived, Amerindians left drawings of birds and marine animals on overhanging rocks just off the trail near the parking lot. At dawn and dusk, the area is alive with parakeets, doves, troupials, mockingbirds, hummingbirds, lizards, and cottontail rabbits.

At the seacoast, the terrain and vegetation change dramatically from hills covered with cacti and divi divi trees to sand dune and limestone bluffs studded with sea grapes and sea lavender. Soldier crab and lizard trails crisscross the morning sand of **Boca Prins ★**, and in the early spring, baby sea turtles hatch and wobble frantically toward the sea. A 20-minute walk farther west along the coast, **Dos Playa ★** features two coves carved out of the limestone bluff. With its wide, sandy beach, the first cove attracts sunbathers and is perfect for picnics, but its strong current makes swimming too dangerous. Stop by the nearby restaurant for some tasty local fare; it's the only restaurant in the park so it's a good thing the view and food are both decent.

Tucked away on the coast northwest of Dos Playa, the **Natural Pool ★** or *conchi* known as Cura di Tortuga is protected from the rough sea by surrounding rocks. It's said that the pool was once used

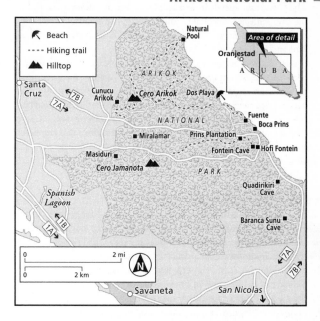

to hold sea turtles before they were sold (*tortuga* means turtle in Papiamento). On quiet days, the pool is great for a swim, but bathing is risky when waves leap the rock barrier. It's a considerable hike to the pool from the parking lot at Boca Prins; take a **horseback or ATV tour** to the site on another day to fully enjoy the unforgettable experience of taking a refreshing dip in this anything-but-placid pool.

A 15-minute walk from Boca Prins, **Fontein Cave ★** is the most popular of several small limestone hollows along the north coast (you'll pass the park's only restaurant on the way to the cave). Brownish-red drawings left by Amerindians and graffiti etched by early European settlers ornament the walls and ceilings. Calcareous-rich water dripping through the limestone has caused stalagmites and stalactites to form, some in the shape of bison or human heads (park rangers stationed at the cave will point them out). The hole is an important roosting place for long-tongued bats. Early in the evening, the flying mammals leave the cave for nectar and pollen.

The **Quadirikiri Cave** features two large chambers with roof openings that allow sunlight in, making flashlights unnecessary. Hundreds of small bats use the 30m-long (98-ft.) tunnel as a passageway to their

EXPLORING ARUBA

5

WHAT TO SEE

nests deeper in the cave. A tale associated with Quadirikiri is dubious: The fiercely independent daughter of an Indian chief was trapped in the cave with her "unsuitable" suitor and left to perish. Defiant even in death, the spirits of the star-crossed lovers burst through the cave's roof and up to heaven.

Also known as the Tunnel of Love because of its heart-shaped entrance, the **Baranca Sunu** cave is home to a colony of bats sensitive to disturbance. As a result the cave is temporarily closed and may become permanently closed if studies of the colony indicate the bats require protection. Stories of pirates using the cave to hide treasure have circulated for generations, but there's no evidence to confirm the rumors. Rather than return to the park entrance, follow the road along the coast. It eventually becomes a paved route that leads to San Nicolas.

SAN NICOLAS & SAVANETA

Roughly 80% of Arubans are Roman Catholic, and parish churches dot the island. In Seroe Pretoe, near San Nicolas on the way from Arikok National Park, the **Lourdes Grotto,** a shrine to Our Lady of Lourdes, was built in the limestone rocks in 1958 to celebrate the 150th anniversary of the Virgin Mary's purported appearance to a peasant girl, St. Bernadette, in the south of France. Another grotto lies directly across the road. Neither is particularly noteworthy, probably because the local parish prohibits anyone from leaving candles, statues, pictures, or testimonials. Chartreuse parakeets inhabit the area.

Farther along the same road, the outback suddenly gives way to Aruba's second-largest town, **San Nicolas.** A phosphate-exporting port from 1879 until 1915, this town landed Esso's Lago oil refinery in 1924. Once the world's largest, the refinery attracted workers from other Caribbean islands, South America, and Europe. In 1942, U.S. troops landed to protect the complex, which supplied much of the Allies' aircraft fuel during the war. By 1951, the town had a population of 20,000, far more than Oranjestad at the time. The refinery closed in 1985, devastating the town and the island. It reopened in 1990 with a new owner, Texas-based Coastal Oil. It was then sold to Valero in 2004. Now that tourism has replaced oil as the island's major business, San Nicolas has waned in importance. One remnant of the town's "port atmosphere" remains: Prostitution is actually legal in San Nicolas.

The center of Aruba's fishing industry, **Savaneta** is the island's oldest town and original capital. During the early Dutch period, its harbor was the safest place for ships, and in the mid-1800s, the area was known for breeding cochineals, insects that were crushed to produce the dye carmine. Retaining its salty tang, the town boasts a couple of good restaurants and a beachside spa.

On your way back home, you'll pass **Hooiberg.** At 162m (531 ft.), it may not be Aruba's highest hill, but it's the island's favorite landmark. If you have the stamina, climb the hundreds of steps (15–20 min.) to the summit; on a clear day, you can see Venezuela.

6

Shopping in Aruba

Although Aruba boasts a veritable plethora of shopping opportunities, the days of Caribbean bargains are waning. A 3% sales tax has been introduced recently, and it may be absorbed directly into the price of merchandise or show up as a government tax on your bill. Nevertheless, the island's low 3.3% duty can make prices on certain items such as jewelry and fragrances attractive.

Dutch goods such as Delft porcelain, chocolate, and Gouda cheese are especially good buys. Items from Indonesia, another former Dutch colony, are reasonably priced, too. Although Aruban souvenirs tend toward cheesy resin casts of *cunucu* (farm) houses or divi divi trees, some impressive works by Aruban artists can be viewed or purchased at the local art galleries. Skin- and hair-care products made from locally produced aloe are also popular and practical. If you're looking for big-ticket items, Aruba offers the usual array of Swiss watches; German and Japanese cameras; gold and diamond jewelry; Cuban cigars; premium liquor; English and German china; Spanish porcelain; French, Swedish, and Danish crystal; and French and American fragrances. If you plan to make a major purchase, do a little research at home so you know you're getting a good deal.

1 THE SHOPPING SCENE

Stores accept American dollars, credit cards, and traveler's checks. They do not, however, accept currency from the Netherlands Antilles. So, if you plan to go to Bonaire or Curaçao, only exchange what you think you will spend there—better yet, stick with U.S. dollars, which are accepted on all three islands. Shopkeepers, like most Arubans, are pleasant, but haggling is considered rude, so don't push your luck.

Most stores are open Monday through Saturday from 9am to 6pm; a few close for an hour at noon or 1pm. Stores in Oranjestad's malls tend to open on Sunday as well, especially if cruise ships are in port.

Parking can be a hassle in downtown Oranjestad. If the lots along the waterfront are packed, try for a space behind the Renaissance

2 GREAT SHOPPING AREAS

Although the major resort hotels boast shopping arcades, Aruba's retail activity centers on Oranjestad. Half-mile-long **Caya G.F. Betico Croes,** better known as Main Street, is the city's major shopping venue, attracting tourists, young and fashionable Arubans, office workers, and families. Downtown also teems with contiguous shopping malls that stretch for several blocks along the harborfront. The gingerbread pastel-colored buildings are impossible to miss. **Renaissance Mall** (L.G. Smith Blvd. 82, Oranjestad; www.shoprenaissancearuba.com/mall) is adjacent to the Renaissance Hotel and marked by a distinctive clock tower that also indicates the presence of the Crystal Casino. On the other side of L.G. Smith Boulevard and just past the marina is the **Renaissance Marketplace;** both the Renaissance Mall and Renaissance Marketplace feature more than 130 stores, 2 casinos, 20 restaurants and cafes, and a movie theater. Just up the road, adjacent to the Renaissance Mall, the bright pink-and-white fanciful-looking **Royal Plaza Mall** on L.G. Smith Boulevard is chock-full of popular restaurants and generally midscale boutiques. **Port of Call Marketplace,** also on L.G. Smith Boulevard, is the first complex that cruise-ship passengers encounter on their way downtown and is directly across the street from the main bus terminal. An adjacent mall stands complete but empty, awaiting resolution of final legal matters before stores can fill the vacancies and open for business.

An enormous shopping center called **Paseo Herencia (Aruba's Pride)** opened in 2008 on the High-Rise district's main street (J.E. Irausquin Blvd.). Located right across the street from the Holiday Inn SunSpree, it contains a multiplex cinema, a fountain with water shows every evening, an indoor parking garage, and dozens of shops and restaurants.

A new shopping mall called the **Village,** across the street from the Radisson and also on J.E. Irausquin Boulevard, opened in 2009, but at press time was still filling its rafters with stores. In place at press time was a large branch of **Red Sail Sport** (© 297/586-1603) and a few new restaurants such as Chino-Latino and Papillion.

Merchandise stands clutter Oranjestad's waterfront, most selling garden-variety T-shirts and souvenirs at bargain prices. Fruit and vegetables brought daily by boat from Venezuela add color to the hubbub.

3 SHOPPING A TO Z

ART/FOLK ART/CRAFTS

Art & Tradition   The most impressive items at this folk-art and handicrafts shop are mopa mopa boxes and figures made by the Quillasinga Indians of Colombia. Although the figures look hand painted, they're actually inlaid with layers of mopa mopa, a tree bud that's boiled until reduced to resin, stretched like gum, and cut into bits of color. Caya G.F. Betico Croes 30, Oranjestad. ✆ 297/583-6534. www.mopamopa.com. Additional locations at Paseo Herencia Mall (the store's name is the Mask; ✆ 297/586-2900) and Royal Plaza Mall (the store's name is INTI; ✆ 297/582-7862).

Artistic   This store specializes in Spanish porcelain, Asian antiques, handmade dhurries and rugs, hand-embroidered linens, organdy tablecloths, and Indonesian woodcarvings. L.G. Smith Blvd. 90, Oranjestad. ✆ 297/582-3142.

Gasparito Restaurant and Art Gallery   This is one of the best places to buy paintings by local artists. Styles ranging from folk to abstract cover the restaurant's walls. Gasparito 3, Noord. ✆ 297/586-7044.

Mopa Mopa   This shop carries the island's largest selection of mopa mopa art (see "Art & Tradition," above), with prices starting at $10. Renaissance Marketplace, Oranjestad. ✆ 297/583-7125. Second location at Renaissance Mall, Oranjestad. ✆ 297/588-7297.

Qué Pasa?   This restaurant and gallery displays and sells eclectic contemporary Aruban paintings. Wilhelminastraat 18, Oranjestad. ✆ 297/583-4888.

BOOKS

If reading on the beach is one of your favorite pastimes, bring books from home; the selection in Aruba is limited and the prices are steep.

Plaza Bookstore   Primarily a stationery store, this shop has a reasonable selection of English-language titles, including cookbooks, self-help guides, and two rotating racks of paperbacks. Ave. Milo Croes 8, Oranjestad. ✆ 297/582-1821.

Van Dorp Aruba   This shop stocks some English-language titles, including books on Aruban history, birds, and plants. Ave. Milo Croes 21, Oranjestad. ✆ 297/582-3076.

CHINA, SILVER & GLASS

Champagne Linens & Gifts   This store boasts Royal Albert bone china, Limoges Castel glassware, and Belleek china. Renaissance Marketplace, Oranjestad. ✆ 297/582-2621.

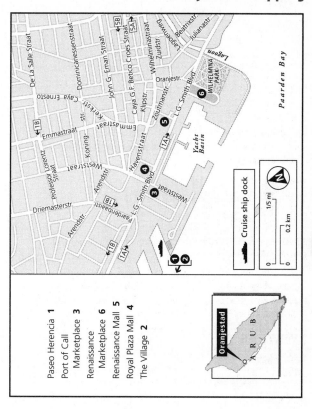

Paseo Herencia **1**
Port of Call
Marketplace **3**
Renaissance
Marketplace **6**
Renaissance Mall **5**
Royal Plaza Mall **4**
The Village **2**

Colombian Emeralds International This shop carries Waterford crystal and Lenox china, not to mention emeralds and every other gemstone known to man or woman. Renaissance Mall, Oranjestad. ✆ **297/583-6238.** Second location at the Marriott. ✆ **297/586-0400.**

Gandelman Jewelers This shop offers Lladró porcelain and Swarovski crystal. Royal Plaza Mall, Oranjestad. ✆ **297/588-6159.** Additional locations at the Hyatt and Radisson resorts, and at Renaissance Mall (✆ **297/588-6159** to reach any store).

Little Switzerland Jewelers For china, crystal, and figurines from Baccarat, Waterford, Kosta Boda, Lalique, Swarovski, Lladró, and others, visit this store. They even have a Tiffany & Co. department. Royal Plaza Mall, Oranjestad. ✆ **297/583-4057.** Additional locations at the Holiday Inn (📞 297/586-3506), Occidental (📞 297/586-1166), and Westin (📞 297/586-9151).

CIGARS

Cigar Emporium   This store features cigars from Cuba, with labels including Cohiba, Montecristo, Romeo y Julieta, Partagas, H. Upmann, and Bolivar. Renaissance Mall, Oranjestad. 📞 297/582-5479.

International Cigars   This smoke shop is centrally located, and sells a wide selection of cigars and accessories. Port of Call Marketplace, Oranjestad. 📞 297/583-6895.

La Casa del Habano   Here you'll find Cohibas, Romeo y Julietas, and Montecristos in walk-in humidors. Royal Plaza Mall, Oranjestad. 📞 297/583-8509.

DEPARTMENT STORES

The Aruba Trading Company   This department store offers one of the island's best moderately priced selections of fragrances, cosmetics, shoes, leather goods, clothing for men and women, liquor, and cigarettes. Caya G.F. Betico Croes 12, Oranjestad. 📞 297/582-2602.

Boolchand's   This store sells watches (Seiko, Swiss, Citizens), cameras (Canon, Minolta, Nikon, Olympus, and Pentax), and electronics (Bose, Braun, JVC, Kenwood, Nintendo, Sony, and Pioneer). Havenstraat 25, Oranjestad. 📞 297/583-0147. www.boolchand.com/phototour-aruba.htm.

EYEWEAR

Kok Optica   Located in a charming, Dutch colonial-style building, Kok carries eyeglass frames, sunglasses, and contact lenses. Whileminastraat 11, Oranjestad. 📞 297/583-7237. www.kokoptica.com.

Sun Specs   This store sells designer sunglasses, but nothing prescription. Aventura Mall, Oranjestad. 📞 297/583-9690.

FASHION

BCBG MAXAZRIA   This designer boutique sells women's shoes, dresses, and tops, as well as accessories such as bags, bangles, and chic shades. Renaissance Mall, Oranjestad. 📞 297/583-8984. www.bcbg.com.

Benetton   The sleek, teen-targeted offerings here range from understated formal to very casual. Havenstraat 2, Oranjestad. 📞 297/583-0312.

Caperucita Roja   The name means "Little Red Riding Hood" in Spanish. The store once sold only baby and children's clothes and shoes, but has now branched out to retail women's clothing. Wilhelminastraat 17, Oranjestad. 📞 297/583-6166.

Carolina Herrera This designer store just opened in early 2009 and is stocked with a rich supply of leather purses, totes, wallets, and high-end accessories. Renaissance Mall, Oranjestad. ✆ **297/585-6906.**

CoCo Sol This sleepy shop at the Tamarijn Aruba (p. 53) is filled with a frantic selection of colorful jewelry, scarves, clothes, glassware, and tropical-colored kitchenware. J.E. Irausquin Blvd. 41, Druif Beach. ✆ **297/858-4133.**

Confetti on the Beach This store has a wide selection of European and American beachwear for women, including swimsuits, coverups, and hats. Renaissance Mall, Oranjestad. ✆ **297/733-8614.**

Custom Style This shop merges biker cool with big-city couture by offering studded blazers, tattoo-style tees, and designer jeans. The zebra-striped chairs and gilded gold mirrors that adorn the shop aren't for sale, but they should be. Weststraat 2, Oranjestad. ✆ **297/588-6992.**

Del Sol This chain store touts T-shirts, tanks, totes, and tchotchkes that all change color when exposed to the sun. The line has expanded to include color-morphing sunglasses, yo-yos, key chains, hair clips, and even nail polish. Royal Plaza Mall, Oranjestad. ✆ **297/583-8448.**

EVA This boutique carries an elegant selection of designer swimsuits, beach coverups, and accessories. Renaissance Mall, Oranjestad. ✆ **297/587-3910.** Additional locations at the Radisson Resort (✆ **297/586-6555**) and Casa del Mar (✆ **297/582-7000**). www.crdgroup.com/retail.

Guess This chic and sparse store carries all the latest Guess fashion musts for women. Renaissance Mall, Oranjestad. ✆ **297/583-6781.** www.guess.com.

Hugo Boss This shop offers men's and women's fashion by Germany's premier designer. Emmastraat 2, Oranjestad. ✆ **297/588-5406.** www.hugoboss.com.

Kenneth Cole This store carries the same goods as its stateside counterparts for men and women. Plaza Daniel Leo 1, Oranjestad. ✆ **297/583-8955.** www.kennethcole.com.

Lacoste This store sells the brand's signature polo shirts plus pants, dresses, skirts, and accessories. Renaissance Mall, Oranjestad. ✆ **297/582-5315.** www.lacoste.com.

Louis Vuitton This glitzy store, opened in the spring of 2007, is as high-profile as the designer's clothing and accessories for men and women. Renaissance Mall, Oranjestad. ✆ **297/588-0209.** www.louisvuitton.com.

Mango Part of an international chain of more than 500 stores, Mango offers casual but fashionable women's clothing. Caya G.F. Betico Croes 9, Oranjestad. ✆ **297/582-9700.** www.mango.com.

Pinko This store offers chic, fashion-forward designs for women. Strada Mall III (near Caya G.F. Betico Croes and Plaza Daniel Leo), Oranjestad. ✆ 297/588-3680.

Ralph Lauren Ralph Lauren's classic line of clothing and accessories are all readily available. Renaissance Mall, Oranjestad. ✆ 297/582-3674. www.ralphlauren.com.

Red Sail Sports This shop stocks European, South American, and U.S. sportswear, scuba and snorkeling equipment, souvenirs, sun-care products, and beachwear. Port of Call Marketplace, Oranjestad. ✆ 297/733-1087. www.aruba-redsail.com/shopping.shtml.

Tommy Hilfiger Boutique This shop stocks fashionable casual wear for the style-conscious man, woman, and child by the renowned American designer. Royal Plaza Mall, Oranjestad. ✆ 297/583-8548. www.tommy.com.

Women's Secret Supplying lingerie, massage oils, and lotions, Secret caters to those looking to add a little spice to their love life. Renaissance Mall, Oranjestad. ✆ 297/583-3413.

Wulfsen & Wulfsen This shop offers classic and casual clothing for both men and women. Operating in the Netherlands Antilles for 30 years and in Holland for more than a century, the store features designs by Betty Barclay, Bianca, Verse, Cerruti, and Zegna. Caya G.F. Betico Croes 52, Oranjestad. ✆ 297/582-3823.

GIFTS & SOUVENIRS

The Butterfly Farm The Butterfly Farm's (p. 102) gift shop has a large, quality collection of notecards, postcards, books, jewelry, and gifts focused on butterflies, including dried, framed, and behind glass specimens. J.E. Irausquin Blvd., Palm Beach. ✆ 297/586-3656. www.thebutterflyfarm.com.

Coconut Trading Co. This shop offers a good selection of gifts and handcrafted jewelry. L.G. Smith Blvd. 99, Palm Beach, in the Marriott Ocean Club. ✆ 297/586-3696.

Ecco This shop offers an eclectic inventory of tablecloths, Delft blue porcelain, handicrafts, T-shirts, beachwear, and men's sportswear. Caya G.F. Betico Croes 22, Oranjestad. ✆ 297/582-4726. www.visitaruba.com/ecco.

Juggling Fish Owned and operated by a transplanted New Englander, this shop supplies beachwear, casual clothing, and quirky souvenirs. Divi Tamarijn. ✆ 297/583-8196. Additional locations at the Aruba Beach Club (✆ 297/582-4598) and the Playa Linda (✆ 297/586-4999).

Tips **Hello, Aloe—So Long, Sunburn**

Aruba has cultivated aloe for more than 150 years. The plant—pronounced "*ah*-loh-weh" locally—serves as a moisturizer and sunburn healer. My brother swears by the sunburn gel. Aruba Aloe, a local company, manufactures a wide assortment of shampoos, facial masks, creams, and gels that soothe after a day in the sun. The products are cheapest at a pharmacy or supermarket, but you can also get them at souvenir stands and the factory itself (where you also get a factory tour, showing the history of this industry on the island).

T.H. Palm   This fun and funky store next to the Playa Linda Beach Resort sells whimsical housewares that include leaded glass and tasseled lampshades, shell-encrusted pillows, and scented soaps and candles. Its clothing line includes vacation wear for women and men, as well as jewelry, hats, and shoes. J.E. Irausquin Blvd. 87, Palm Beach. *(C)* 297/586-6898.

HOUSEWARES

Décor Home Fashions   This shop sells sheets, towels, and place mats from Italy, Germany, Holland, Portugal, and the United States. Steenweg 14, Oranjestad. *(C)* 297/582-6620.

Little Holland   This store also offers a good collection of linens, napkins, and embroidered tablecloths from Spain, Belgium, and Portugal, as well as Blue Delft china and Nao by Lladró figurines. Royal Plaza Mall, Oranjestad. *(C)* 297/583-8494.

JEWELRY & WATCHES

Boolchand's   Boolchand's boasts jewelry and watches from Movado, Concord, and Bulgari. L.G. Smith Blvd. 90–92, Oranjestad. *(C)* 297/583-0147. www.boolchand.com.

Colombian Emeralds International   This shop stocks emeralds, diamonds, sapphires, and semiprecious jewelry, as well as watches by TAG Heuer, Baume & Mercier, and Seiko. Renaissance Mall, Oranjestad. *(C)* 297/583-6238. Second location at the Marriott. J.E. Irausquin Blvd. 101. *(C)* 297/583-6238.

Diamonds International   This shop features 60 showcases of jewelry and watches. Choose loose diamonds and mountings to custom design your own piece. Port of Call Marketplace, Oranjestad. *(C)* 297/588-0443. www.shopdi.com.

Effy   Effy boasts a selection of diamond, emerald, ruby, and sapphire earrings, pins, rings, bracelets, and necklaces. L.G. Smith Blvd. 90–92, Oranjestad. ✆ **297/588-9812.**

Gandelman Jewelers   This jeweler offers an extensive collection of diamond, gemstone, and fine gold jewelry, as well as timepieces and writing instruments. Brands include David Yurman, Gucci, Rolex, and Montblanc. Royal Plaza Mall, Oranjestad. ✆ **297/529-9980.** Additional locations at the Hyatt (✆ **297/529-9920**) and Renaissance Mall (✆ **297/588-6717**). www.gandelman.net.

Jeweler's Warehouse   This shop stocks a complete line of jewelry with diamonds, rubies, emeralds, sapphires, and pearls. Watches from Seiko, Citizen, Raymond Weil, and Pulsar abound. Renaissance Mall, Oranjestad. ✆ **297/583-6045.** www.jewelerswarehouse.com.

Kenro Jewelers   This shop features pearls, gemstones, gold, and watches. Renaissance Mall, Oranjestad. ✆ **297/583-4847.**

Little Switzerland   Little Switzerland offers 14- and 18-karat gold jewelry and designer watches. Locations at the Holiday Inn SunSpree (✆ **297/586-3506**), Occidental Grand (✆ **297/586-1166**), Westin (✆ **297/586-9151**), Tamarijn Aruba (✆ **297/583-2284**), and in Royal Plaza Mall (✆ **297/583-4057**). www.littleswitzerland.com.

Noble Jewelers   This shop sells yellow and white diamonds, emeralds, rubies, sapphires, and platinum jewelry. Watch brands include Bulova and Festina. Weststraat 4, Oranjestad. ✆ **297/583-8780.**

Pearl Gems   Create your own strand from an extensive collection of unstrung pearls, including black specimens from Tahiti. Prestrung strands are also available. L.G. Smith Blvd. 90–92, Oranjestad. ✆ **297/588-4927.**

Rage Silver   This shop specializes in sterling silver with a Southwestern U.S. theme; it carries Danish, German, Greek, and Italian designs as well. Renaissance Marketplace, Oranjestad. ✆ **297/588-6262.** www.ragejewelry.com.

Shiva's Gold and Gems   This store boasts a large loose-diamond inventory and a collection of emerald, tanzanite, ruby, and sapphire jewelry. Watch brands include Franck Muller, Audemars Piguet, Bucherer, Citizen, and Girard-Perregaux. Royal Plaza Mall, Oranjestad. ✆ **297/583-4077.** www.trident-shivas.com.

Touch of Gold   This shop features platinum and gold jewelry set with diamonds, tanzanite, emeralds, rubies, and sapphires. Havenstraat 32D, Oranjestad. ✆ **297/588-9587.** www.touchofgold.com.

PERFUMES & COSMETICS

Many of the island's jewelry stores also carry fragrances and cosmetics from the United States and France.

Aruba Aloe Balm   Direct from the factory, here you'll find soothing moisturizer, sunscreen, and shampoo made from Aruba's famous aloe. Pitastraat 115, Oranjestad. ✆ **297/588-3222.** Second location at the Renaissance Mall. ✆ **297/582-9301.** www.arubaaloe.com.

Aruba Trading Company   This shop offers a good, reasonably priced selection of perfumes and cosmetics. Caya G.F. Betico Croes 12, Oranjestad. ✆ **297/582-2602.**

Dufry Aruba   This shop sells only cosmetics and a wide selection of fragrances. Royal Plaza Mall, Oranjestad. ✆ **297/582-2790.**

L'Occitane   L'Occitane is a fine purveyor of Euro-chic fragrances, lotions, room sprays, powders, and soaps. L.G. Smith Boulevard, Oranjestad. ✆ **297/583-5277.** www.loccitane.com.

Penha   This shop boasts a large selection of top-name perfumes and cosmetics, including such brands as Boucheron, Dior, Cartier, and Givenchy. Caya G.F. Betico Croes 11, Oranjestad. ✆ **297/582-4160.** www.jlpenha.com.

PHARMACIES
D.A. Drugstore   This Dutch chain carries all the basic necessities and has a larger selection of toiletries and everyday cosmetics than most hotel gift shops. L.G. Smith Blvd. 134, Oranjestad. ✆ **297/588-2700.**

Hacienda Drug Store   This well-stocked chain store sells the basics from sunblock to shampoo. J.E. Irausquin Blvd. 382, Oranjestad. ✆ **297/586-4704.**

SHOES & ACCESSORIES
ALDO   This brand is known for its urban chick footwear for both men and women. Renaissance Mall, Oranjestad. ✆ **297/583-3427.** www.aldoshoes.com.

The Athlete's Foot   This chain store is your best bet in Aruba for Nike, Adidas, New Balance, and Asics. Caya G.F. Betico Croes 14, Oranjestad. ✆ **297/582-6162.** www.theathletesfoot.com.

Gucci   Boasts everything you expect from the Italian luxury store, including handbags, luggage, wallets, shoes, watches, belts, and ties. Don't expect bargains unless there's a sale going on. Renaissance Mall, Oranjestad. ✆ **297/583-3900.** www.gucci.com.

The Nike Shop   This athletic shop stocks a range of Nike merchandise, including shoes, clothes, watches, and sunglasses. Emmastraat 1, Oranjestad. ✆ **297/588-0103.**

Salvatore Ferragamo   Shoes and handbags from the fabled Italian designer. Renaissance Mall, Oranjestad. ✆ **297/582-8218.** www.ferragamo.com.

SUPERMARKETS

Kong Hing Supermarket This is a massive, modern, American suburban-style supermarket with wide aisles. In addition to familiar items such as Oreos and Coca-Cola, the store stocks Dutch cheeses, South American fruits and vegetables, liquor, fresh baked breads, and over-the-counter pharmacy items. L.G. Smith Blvd. 152, Oranjestad. ✆ **297/582-5545.** Second location at Havenstraat 16, Oranjestad. ✆ **297/582-1219.**

Ling & Sons IGA Super Center This island institution's superstore carries a large assortment of American and European foods as well as a wide selection of South American and Asian items. It also has a deli, a liquor department, a bakery, and over-the-counter drugs and personal care items. Ling & Sons takes grocery orders online for delivery to your hotel the day you arrive. Italiestraat 26, Oranjestad (behind Kong Hing Supermarket). ✆ **297/583-2370.** www.lingandsons.com.

WINE & LIQUOR

The supermarkets on the road connecting Oranjestad with the Low-Rise area—Kong Hing Supermarket and Ling & Sons IGA Super Center, listed above—boast sizable liquor departments and the best prices.

Aruba Trading Company This store carries an array of liquors and wines and operates a duty-free shop at Queen Beatrix International Airport. A variety of fragrances, cosmetics, watches, cigars, and chocolates are also available. Caya G.F. Betico Croes 12, Oranjestad. ✆ **297/582-3950.**

Bacchus Liquortique The selection of wines here is not as expansive as the liquor selections. Bacchus also carries a wide array of local and imported beers. L.G. Smith 82, Renaissance Mall, Oranjestad. ✆ **297/583-1381.**

La Bodega Wine Store This wine shop sells vintages from Australia, Argentina, Chile, Italy, France, Spain, New Zealand, Portugal, the United States, and South Africa. Gutenbergstraat 4, Oranjestad. ✆ **297/588-5330.**

7

Aruba After Dark

Another "busy" day on the beach, another great day of shopping, diving, and exploring. So, what's next? On an island with so many elegant, romantic, sumptuous, and exotic dining options it's worth noting that dinner should never be rushed and is often an event in and of itself. If your reservations are for 7pm, you are likely to be wrapping up by around 9:30 or 10pm, after which you may be ready to hit the sack. On the other hand, if after a good meal and a couple of drinks, you're ready for some gambling, dancing, or a little carousing, you've definitely come to the right island.

Aruba's casinos are a surefire after-dinner diversion, attracting both serious players and dabblers who've saved a few dollars for the slot machines. Even if risk makes you nervous, the sensory overload is an irresistible spectacle—bells ringing, lights flashing, people groaning and screaming. Better yet, watching's free.

Striving to keep you and your wallet in the neighborhood, several hotels have theaters with Las Vegas–style shows, most of them spectacles with beautiful dancers in outrageous outfits. Unfortunately, while the singing is good, the choreography and talent can be eclipsed by the dizzying number of costumes, feathers, and sequins. Still, if an over-the-top, 1950s-esque show is your thing, book the hottest tickets in advance—especially during the high season, or book a dinner-and-show special. Ask your hotel's concierge or activities desk for help.

Luckily, the bar and club scene is surprisingly robust. You can start early with a beachside-bar happy hour, move on to dinner and cocktails, and then progress to a little jazz and cigars, or maybe board a booze cruise for some shenanigans at sea. Expect live entertainment or a DJ at most bars. If you're still not sated, head for one of the dance clubs, but don't show up before midnight or 1am—that's when the party really starts. To find out what's happening, check any of the free local magazines: *Aruba Nights, Island Temptations, Aruba Experience, Menu, Aruba Events, Destination Aruba,* and *Aruba Food & Wine.* For daily and weekly entertainment listings, consult the three English-language dailies—*Aruba Today, Aruba Daily,* and the *News*—and the weekly pamphlet *K-Pasa.* All of these publications are free and available at hotels and restaurants. Check with your hotel's activities and tour desks, too. The free flyers that you'll find on every public countertop are also a good source of information; many have coupons for discounts or freebies such as free drinks and casino chips.

The dress code in Aruba is clean and casual, but a touch of elegance or trendiness never hurts.

1 CASINOS

For many years after Aruba's first casino opened in 1959, gambling was the island's major attraction (next to the beaches, of course). Today, Aruba boasts a dozen gambling venues, most of them casually elegant. Table games such as baccarat, blackjack, poker, roulette, and craps usually start in the afternoon or early evening; slot machines can usually be played in the morning. Bingo, another diversion, starts in the afternoon at some places, in the evening at others. The action goes on as long as there's a crowd, usually until 2, 3, or 4am. The Crystal Casino in downtown Oranjestad is open 24 hours a day, 7 days a week.

ORANJESTAD

Located in downtown Oranjestad at the Renaissance Aruba Resort, the **Crystal Casino,** L.G. Smith Blvd. 82 (© **297/523-6318**), is Aruba's only 24-hour casino. More elegant than most gaming venues on the island, the Crystal boasts Austrian crystal chandeliers, gold-leaf columns, ornate moldings, Spanish mirrors, and Italian marble and brass. The 1,393-sq.-m (14,994-sq.-ft.) parlor features 373 slot machines, bingo, and tables for roulette, craps, baccarat, blackjack, Caribbean stud poker, and Texas hold 'em. The adjacent Crystal Theatre is home to Aruba's hottest show, *Havana Dance!* an extravaganza with impressive performers, costumes, and choreography.

The **Seaport Casino,** L.G. Smith Blvd. 9 (© **297/523-6318**), also part of the Renaissance in downtown Oranjestad, is Aruba's only waterfront casino. The casual 743-sq.-m (7,998-sq.-ft.) emporium fits in well with the surrounding shopping mall; you might think it's just another store. Besides more than 400 slot machines, the casino features tables for blackjack, roulette, and Caribbean stud poker. In a sequestered area, the race and sports book boasts a satellite linkup and wagering based on Las Vegas odds. Most major sporting events are covered. The Sunday bingo games are especially popular. Slot machines are available from 10am to 4am; tables are open from 4pm to 4am.

LOW-RISE AREA

The **Alhambra Casino,** J.E. Irausquin Blvd. 47, Manchebo Beach (© **297/583-5000;** www.casinoalhambra.com), is a busy complex in the Low-Rise area near the Divi and the Casa del Mar. The theme at this 20-year-old facility is pure kismet. Dressed like a jovial genie, the doorman greets every guest with a robust handshake. Inside, the casino's leaded glass, serpentine mahogany columns, arches, and domes have a pronounced Moorish flavor. The atmosphere is casual. The 929-sq.-m (10,000-sq.-ft.) casino features 300-plus slots and tables for Caribbean stud poker, three-card poker, craps, blackjack, Let It Ride, and roulette, with a range of wagering minimums. Slots open at 10am; tables start business at 6pm. Year-round, you can play into the early morning, usually 4am. Bingo starts at 1pm on Thursday and Saturday.

HIGH-RISE AREA

The **Occidental Grand Casino** at the Occidental Grand Aruba, J.E. Irausquin Blvd. 83, Palm Beach (© **297/586-4500**), opens daily at noon for slot action; table games are available after 5pm. As long as folks are making wagers, the casino stays open until 4am. You can feed one of the 300-plus slot machines (with as little as a penny) or play craps, blackjack, roulette, poker, or Texas hold 'em at the tables. Bingo takes center stage at 10:30pm and 11:15pm every night. There's live entertainment most nights as well.

Casablanca Casino at the Westin, J.E. Irausquin Blvd. 77, Palm Beach (© **297/586-2283**), is buzzing with action in the evening, especially after the hotel's show lets out. The 1,114-sq.-m (11,991-sq.-ft.) facility features no fewer than 300 slot machines, nine tables for blackjack, three roulette wheels, as well as craps tables, and Caribbean stud, three card, and Let It Ride poker tables. The theme has something of a Bogart twist, complete with a Moroccan-style Rick's Café. There's also a bar and live entertainment. The room in back caters to higher rollers. At the adjacent bar, exotic cocktails are on hand. The casino is open daily from noon to 4am; table games start at noon.

The **Casino** at the Radisson, J.E. Irausquin Blvd. 81, Palm Beach (© **297/586-4045;** www.thecasinoaruba.com), twinkles with thousands of lights and looms over 1,300 sq. m (13,993 sq. ft.) of space. The 235 slots open at noon, while tables for blackjack, roulette, and craps, as well as the live poker room, featuring Caribbean stud, three card, Texas hold 'em, seven-card stud, and Let It Ride, open at 4pm in the high season, at 5pm otherwise. The action lasts until 4am daily. The bar features big-screen TVs tuned to sporting events, and there's live music Wednesday through Saturday.

The Hyatt's **Copacabana Casino,** J.E. Irausquin Blvd. 85, Palm Beach (© **297/586-1234,** ext. 4583; www.hyattcasinoaruba.com), has a tropical palm theme and works to evoke the glamour of Monaco. With the many columns, murals, and stone walls, it's certainly one of Aruba's more elegant gambling venues. The 21 tables feature craps, roulette, blackjack, baccarat, and Caribbean stud poker.

The 1,115-sq.-m (12,000-sq.-ft.) facility also has more than 260 slot machines. Live bands play Latin or popular American music every evening. Slots and tables open at noon and the action lasts until 4am.

The Holiday Inn's busy **Excelsior Casino,** J.E. Irausquin Blvd. 230, Palm Beach (© **866/358-6518** or 297/586-7777; www.excelsior casino.com), has plenty of slots, plus tables for blackjack, craps, roulette, Let It Ride, and Caribbean stud poker (this popular game originated at the Excelsior in 1988). It's the only Aruban casino besides the Seaport Casino to offer a horse race and sports book with live simulcasts. Slots are available at 8am, sports book from noon to 8pm, and tables are ready for play from noon to 3 or 4am. Daily bingo games fill the house at 3:30pm on weekdays and 12:30pm on weekends. There's an ATM next to the cashier, a bar, and live entertainment.

The **Stellaris Casino,** at the Marriott, L.G. Smith Blvd. 101, Palm Beach (© **297/586-9000**), hums with the sound of slot machines from 10am, but the real buzz begins after noon, when the tables open and the crowd thickens. The 500 slots range from a nickel to $50. The 32 game tables include blackjack, craps, Caribbean stud poker, roulette, and Let It Ride. The live band can be heard throughout the 1,672-sq.-m (17,997-sq.-ft.) casino, in spite of the groans of disgust and squeals of delight.

The newest casino at press time is **Cool Casino** (© **297/528-0993;** www.coolcasinogaming.com) at the Riu Palace. It features state-of-the-art video poker and slot machines—meaning that all slots are coinless. Slots open at 10am, and table games start at 2pm.

2 ENTERTAINMENT

A couple of Aruba's stages offer live entertainment, with dancers usually shipped in from Cuba. The popularity of these shows has waned, and subsequently the quality has declined in recent years, and there is even rumor that the Crystal Casino may one day close. You don't have to be a resort guest to see shows at the hotels, but you should make a reservation. Seats for the popular spectacles are likely to book up early, especially during the high season.

ORANJESTAD

Still the island's biggest stage sensation, *Havana Dance!* at the Renaissance's **Crystal Theatre,** L.G. Smith Blvd. 82, Oranjestad (© **297/583-6000**), is reputedly the Caribbean's largest stage production. This show features youthful performers from Cuba's premier dance studios. Combining Latin rhythm, Las Vegas spectacle, and 1950s nostalgia, the 1-hour-and-20-minute show boasts impressive choreography and riveting vocals. Most of the dancers hail from one of Cuba's elite ballet companies, but their moves are more Bob Fosse than Bolshoi. Showtime is 9pm, Monday through Saturday, and tickets at the 430-seat theater are $49 ($26 for children 11 and under). An even better deal is the dinner and show package: for $89, you get a sit-down dinner at their *très* chic steakhouse.

HIGH-RISE AREA

The Occidental Grand's **Las Palmas Showroom,** J.E. Irausquin Blvd. 83, Palm Beach (© **297/586-4500**), boasts the largest stage in Aruba. The theater's multinational performers present different spectacles each week. The shows include *Cir Caribe, Latin Explosion, Broadway, Grease,* and *Viva Las Vegas.* The 45-minute shows start at 9pm and cost $20.

3 CLUBS & BARS

Many hotel bars are cozy and conversation friendly, and most offer live entertainment—a jazz combo, a piano soloist, maybe a chanteuse. If you want higher decibel and energy levels, the trendiest and busiest bars and clubs are in Oranjestad. The strip along L.G. Smith Boulevard on the harborfront abounds with hot spots, making a bar-crawl as easy as saying "bottoms up." Crowds tend to be mixed: Aruban/tourist, gay/straight, young/young-at-heart. Although most bars open at noon, they generally don't get started until 10 or 11pm and stay open until 2am. Clubs open at 10pm, are empty until midnight or 1am, and peak around 2am.

ORANJESTAD

Café Bahia Located on the capital's busiest strip, across from the Royal Plaza Mall, Café Bahia features a tropical ambience, a fishing-boat bar, and hand-painted murals. The kitchen is open until 11pm, so you can snack on Caribbean conch fritters as you drink. After 10pm, the place starts hopping, especially on weekends and holidays, when there's disco dancing. Popular libations include the Chocolate City Black Out and Red Light (ask about their sweet, calorie- and booze-laden ingredients). You can drink and dance until 3 or 4 in the morning. Weststraat 7. © 297/588-9982.

Cuba's Cookin' (Finds) This restaurant offers late-night live music with a Latin beat. The cozy, intimate atmosphere draws everyone to the dance floor for salsa and merengue moves. Try the house *mojito,* a Cuban rum and mint refresher. Wilhelminastraat 27. © 297/588-0627. www.cubascookin.com.

Garufa This clubby, smoky room is a favorite place for jazz- and bolero-loving cigar smokers. It features a premium bar and a humidor for Montecristos and Cohibas. Sip a single malt or port from the comfort of your cigar-motif chair. The food comes from El Gaucho, the Argentine steakhouse across the street. Live music includes a jazz saxophonist and an Argentine guitarist who plays tangos and boleros. Open from 6pm until about 2am, Monday through Saturday. Wilhelminastraat 63. (℡ 297/582-3677. www.garufa-aruba.com.

Jimmy's Place Friday happy hour at this Dutch bar attracts cigar-smoking power brokers who like American rock 'n' roll. After midnight (and until the roosters crow), the restaurant/bar serves hearty soups and sandwiches to a mixed straight and gay crowd of entertainers and insomniacs. Kruisweg 15 (1 block off Caya G.F. Betico Croes or Main St.). (℡ 297/582-2550. www.jimmysaruba.com.

Mambo Jambo Mambo Jambo is sultry and relaxing early in the evening and starts hopping after 9pm. Expect a cosmopolitan blend of Dutch and Latino visitors, and lots of Latin-Caribbean rhythms. There's an array of specialty drinks, served in coconut shells, with colorful straws and chunks of fruit. Wednesday nights feature live music, Thursday is techno night, and the salsa dancers move like pros every other night of the week. Royal Plaza Mall, L.G. Smith Blvd. 94. (℡ 297/583-3632. www.mambojamboaruba.com.

The Paddock This is Aruba's most popular hangout for Dutch residents and vacationers. The Dutch, hip staff serves cocktails, tea and coffee, snacks, and full-fledged meals. Happy hour changes frequently but always attracts a festive crowd, and is sometimes accompanied by casino-style drinking games where you spin the wheel for drink specials. The cow-themed bistro is open until 2am on weekdays, and until 3am on weekends. Wednesday is student night, so bring your college ID if you've got one. L.G. Smith Blvd. 13. (℡ 297/583-2334. www.paddock-aruba.com.

Señor Frog's Party-bus tours bring lots of fun-loving vacationers to this overwhelmingly popular chain establishment for retro music, Mexican food, and, oh yeah, drinks. Twenty-somethings can be seen drinking frozen margaritas to excess just about every night of the week. The first Saturday of every month is Ladies' Night; needless to say the place is even more frenetic than usual with throngs of reveling teens and adults waiting outside for hours to cram into the already-packed venue. Weststraat 1. (℡ 297/582-0355 or 582-0390. www.senorfrogs.com/aruba.

HIGH-RISE AREA

Black Hog Saloon With nightly entertainment that includes motorized bar stools zipping around while riders do tricks and pop wheelies, the Black Hog Saloon takes the term "biker bar" to a new extreme. But the real show starts when staff members mount their shiny chrome Harleys and ride guests around the bar, burning rubber and revving their engines in a biker parade that would make the Hell's Angels proud. Located at Eagle Beach on Sasakiweg at Adventure Golf. ✆ 297/587-6625 or 594-4395. www.blackhogsaloon.com/movie.swf.

Bugaloe This thatch-roofed, tropically colored perch is popular with sunbathers who want to do a little socializing before showering off the sunscreen. And why not? Happy hour lasts from 4 until 5pm. Open from 8am until 2am, the place has lots of good-looking Dutch employees and is the perfect spot to listen to some live music (on a Tues, Fri, or Sat), or just relax, and watch the sunset. De Palm Pier, Palm Beach. ✆ 297/586-2233. www.bugaloe.com.

Café Rembrant This is the new hip place in town for some late-night revelry favored by Dutch locals and frequented by a broad range of ages. South Beach Center, Palm Beach 55. ✆ 297/586-4747.

Mr. Jazz This restaurant and lounge features a 12-piece Latin orchestra that plays mellow jazz during dinner hours, then later plays Latin dance music. While clearly catering to an older clientele, it has a sizeable dance floor so if you go, be ready to show off a few moves. Paseo Herencia, L.G. Smith Blvd. 382-A. ✆ 297/586-3800. www.mrjazzaruba. com.

Moomba Beach Bar & Restaurant This casual, fun spot is essentially a couple of giant *palapas* on the beach with a party every day and night. "No shirts, no shoes, no problem" is the slogan here. On Friday and Saturday nights, live bands play beneath a giant Heineken beer chandelier. Happy hour is from 6 to 7pm daily; the bartenders pour drinks from 10am until very late. Try the Tropical Treasure (melon and banana liqueurs, coconut cream, and pineapple juice). Food is served until 11pm. This may be the only bar on the island that has showers and beach chairs, so don't worry about the tanning lotion and sand. J.E. Irausquin Blvd. 230 (btw. the Holiday Inn and Marriott Surf Club). ✆ 297/586-5365. www.moombabeach.com.

Pinchos Grill and Bar Ⓜⓞⓜⓔⓝⓣⓢ At the Surfside Marina on a pier surrounded by the clear blue waters of Aruba, Pinchos is the ideal place to sip a cocktail and watch the sunset while relaxing at a waterside table or on a cushioned swing. No wonder this was one of the settings for an episode of ABC's *The Bachelor*. L.G. Smith Blvd. 7. ✆ 297/583-2666.

Salt 'n Pepper A mostly tourist crowd comes here for sangria and cocktails, live entertainment in an outdoor courtyard (after 7pm), and a variety of Spanish tapas, sandwiches, and soups. The kitchen closes just before midnight, but the bar's open until 1am every night. J.E. Irausquin Blvd. 368-A (across from the Occidental Grand Aruba). © **297/ 586-3280.** www.saltandpepperaruba.com.

The Sopranos Piano Bar This chic piano bar, tucked away at the end of Arawak Gardens Mall, in front of the High-Rise hotels, takes inspiration for its red-on-red decor from the popular show with the same name. Belly up to the bar for a highball and sing along with the crowd to their favorite tunes, or request your own. L.G. Smith Blvd. 477. © **297/586-8622.** www.sopranospianobar.com/aruba.

4 PARTY & DINNER CRUISES

Tattoo Party Cruises (© 297/586-2010; www.arubaadventures. com/tattoo) follow the coastline, offering views of the island's lights. The triple-deck boat features a full-service bar (with $1, $2, and $3 drinks) and a dinner buffet (barbecue or Italian). The first deck boasts the island's largest floating dance floor, and a live DJ; the second deck is dedicated to imbibing, and the top deck opens to views of the moon's reflection on the water. You're encouraged to don your bathing suit and swing on a rope or slide down a slide into the Caribbean. The crew puts on a show, and guests are invited to join various contests. The crowd is foolish and young (chronologically or at heart), but no one's under 18. The party takes place Wednesday, which is Ladies' Night, and Friday from 8pm until midnight. The ship boards at 7:15pm from the De Palm Pier on Palm Beach between the Aruba Grand and Radisson. The damage is $49 per person.

Jolly Pirates (© 297/586-8107; www.jolly-pirates.com) boards at the Moomba Pier, between the Holiday Inn and Marriott, and offers a very casual evening sea cruise. The buccaneer theme can only mean walking the plank and singing "Yo, ho, ho, and a bottle of rum." The sunset sail features an open bar and rope swing (Mon and Fri 5–7pm; $26 per person).

5 OTHER DIVERSIONS

PARTY BUSES
Kukoo Kunuku (© 297/586-2010; www.kukookunuku.com) invites you to party on a colorfully painted school bus. A bar-crawl on wheels, it's like getting drunk with the Partridge family. The coach has no glass in its windows—the fresh air will do you good—and every

reveler gets maracas. Prepare to sing a solo and do the Macarena. The carousing attracts a mixed crowd with a surprising number of folks over 40; the minimum age is 18. The price of $59 per person includes champagne at sunset, an Aruban dinner under the stars, and the first drink at each of three watering holes. The carousing begins at 5pm and lasts until about 8pm, Monday through Saturday. Pickup and drop-off is at your hotel.

In the same vein but without dinner, the **Banana Bus** (© 297/ **593-0757;** www.bananabusaruba.com) rolls Tuesday through Friday from 8pm until midnight. After your guide and driver rounds up the gang, you zoom away to three local bars. For $37, you get free drinks on the bus, door-to-door transportation to three bars, and a free drink ticket at each destination.

MOVIES

Aruba now has two indoor movie theaters. One is at the **Renaissance Cinema** in the Renaissance Marketplace shopping mall in downtown Oranjestad, L.G. Smith Blvd. 82 (© **297/583-0318;** www.thecinemas. aw). The six-screen complex shows first-run films—mostly Hollywood blockbusters—in English. Midnight flicks are popular on Friday and Saturday. Tickets range from $5 to $7.50. There is also a six-screen multiplex at the Paseo Herencia mall where movies cost $8.25.

A real throwback to a simpler time, the **E. De Veer Drive-In Thea-tre,** on Kibaima, across from the Balashi Brewery on the road to Savaneta and San Nicolas (© **297/585-8355;** www.seaportcinemas. com), is a rare treat. The chance to watch a film (usually American) in a vast field under the stars? In Aruba? That's exotic. Admission is about $4, but Thursday through Sunday are "car-crash" nights—$6 admits an entire carload. Expect tons of Aruban teens, sweethearts, and families with kids in tow. Scheduling information is available online. A ticket at the Paseo Herencia cinemas costs $8.25.

8

A Visit to Curaçao

Just 56km (35 miles) north of Venezuela and a 30-minute flight from Aruba, Curaçao, the "C" of the Dutch ABC islands, is the largest, most populous, and most cosmopolitan of the Netherlands Antilles. Its beaches and resorts cater more to the European tourist, and lack the flashy opulence of the big resorts found in Aruba, but its distinctive cultural offerings are superior, and it too boasts warm people, rich culture and history, shopping, and watersports. It's the least known of the ABCs, but well worth the effort to get there.

Curaçao is 60km (37 miles) long and 11km (6³/₄ miles) across at its widest point. Cacti, spiny-leafed aloe, mesquite, and divi divi trees stud the arid landscape of the desertlike countryside. The charming Dutch colonial waterfront area of **Willemstad,** the capital, featuring centuries-old forts, mansions, and shops, is a designated UNESCO World Heritage Site, and perhaps the most picturesque colonial city in the Caribbean.

Alonso de Ojeda and Amerigo Vespucci spotted Curaçao in 1499. The Spaniards exterminated all but 75 members of a branch of the peaceful Arawaks. However, they in turn were ousted by the Dutch in 1634, who also had to fight off French and English invasions.

The Dutch made the island a tropical Holland in miniature. Peter Stuyvesant ruled Curaçao in 1644. The island was turned into a Dutch Gibraltar, bristling with forts. Thick ramparts guarded the harbor's narrow entrance; the hilltop forts protected the coastal approaches. Today many of these historic buildings have been converted into restaurants, shops, or hotels.

In the 20th century, Curaçao remained sleepy until 1915, when the Royal Dutch/Shell Company built one of the world's largest oil refineries here to process crude oil from Venezuela. Workers from some 50 countries poured onto the island, turning Curaçao into a multicultural, cosmopolitan community of about 171,000. Curaçao has its own governmental authority, relying on the Netherlands only for defense and foreign affairs.

Curaçao, along with Bonaire, St. Eustatius, Sint Maarten, and Saba, make up the Netherlands Antilles, an autonomous part of the Kingdom of the Netherlands. Curaçaons are Dutch nationals and carry European Union passports. The island's 171,000 people have roots in more than 50 countries around the world.

Frommer's Favorite Curaçao Experiences

- **Sitting on the waterfront watching that dang bridge.** No matter how many times you see the Queen Emma Bridge, a floating pontoon bridge, motor its way across the Saint Anna Bay, it's a real showstopper every time. Find a waterside table and order something cool to drink while taking in the outstanding architecture that lines the waterfront. If you're lucky enough to see a cruise ship pass through the narrow inlet, it's a spectacular sight indeed.

- **Exploring the many memorable museums.** Unlike many Caribbean islands where culture and history play a distant second to fun in the sun, Curaçao has a wealth of rich history that has been well-preserved in its many museums, including Kurá Hulanda Museum, the Curaçao Museum, and the Maritime Museum. While exhausting, they are worth a visit, as is a walking tour or a narrated trip aboard the pink trolley that trundles through this historic town.

- **Partying like it's my birthday.** The good people of Curaçao take their parties very seriously and seem determined to have a good time. The nightlife here is great because the locals like to relax as much as or possibly more than the tourists. Live music can be found in varied venues, including Blues on the waterfront, on the sands of Mambo Beach, or on the dance floor of Asia de Cuba in town. Wherever you find it, let the music move you.

- **Being dazzled by dancing dolphins.** The Curaçao Seaquarium is one of the best in the Caribbean, taking advantage of natural coves to accommodate an impressive array of native marine life. Touch tanks, feeding opportunities, and dive encounters allow visitors to get up close and personal with these amazing creatures in a unique way. The educational programs and large enclosures demonstrate that education and animal care are as important as impressing the visitors.

1 ESSENTIALS

VISITOR INFORMATION

The **Curaçao Tourist Board–North America** has an office at One Gateway Center, Ste. 2600, Newark, NJ 07102 (© **800/328-7222**).

You can also get information online at **www.curacao.com**. Once you're on the island, visit the **Curaçao Tourist Board,** Pietermaai 19, Willemstad (© **599/9-434-8200**). The readily available and free glossy magazines *Curaçao Events* and *Curaçao Nights* are published by the tourism board and provide a good overview of where to go and what to see. Also pick up a copy of the weekly dining and entertainment guide *K-Pasa* (www.k-pasa.com) at any tourism office or hotel lobby. It is also available in many shops and restaurants. The board also distributes an island map with useful tips and island facts. A detailed road map of the island is available through the **Curaçao Chamber of Commerce,** Kaya Junior Salas 1, Willemstad (© **599/9-461-1451;** www.curacao-chamber.an), Monday to Friday from 8:30am to 4pm.

GETTING THERE

Tiara Air (© **599/9-839-1234;** www.tiara-air.com), **InselAir** (© **599/9-888-0444;** www.fly-inselair.com), and **DAE** (Dutch Antilles Express; © **599/717-0808;** www.flydae.com) provide 30-minute shuttle service between Aruba, Bonaire, and the modern **Curaçao International Airport,** Plaza Margareth Abraham (© **599/9-839-1000;** www.curacao-airport.com). Flights from North America are often linked to Aruba; **American Airlines** (© **800/433-7300;** www.aa.com) offers daily nonstop flights to Curaçao from Miami. **Air Jamaica** (© **800/523-5585;** www.airjamaica.com) flies nonstop from Montego Bay on Tuesday, Saturday, and Sunday. **Continental Airlines** (© **800/231-0856;** www.continental.com) has nonstop flights to and from Newark on Saturday.

Fun Facts **Special Events**

The big event of the year is the **Curaçao Carnival,** which starts on New Year's Day, with various festivities and dozens of parades extending until Mardi Gras and the **Grand Farewell Parade.** The schedule is available at the tourism office. The most fun events, similar to hoedowns, are called "jump-ups." The highlight of Carnival is the **Festival di Tumba,** the second week in February, in which the island's musicians vie for prizes. Other Carnival events include the crowning of a queen and king, street parades, concerts, and even a children's parade.

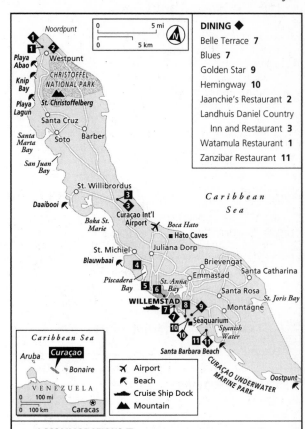

DINING ◆

Belle Terrace **7**

Blues **7**

Golden Star **9**

Hemingway **10**

Jaanchie's Restaurant **2**

Landhuis Daniel Country
    Inn and Restaurant **3**

Watamula Restaurant **1**

Zanzibar Restaurant **11**

✈ Airport
🏹 Beach
⚓ Cruise Ship Dock
▲ Mountain

ACCOMMODATIONS ■

Avila Hotel **7**

Blue Bay Villages **4**

Breezes Curaçao **8**

Chogogo Resort **11**

Curaçao Marriott Beach
    Resort & Emerald Casino **5**

Floris Suite Hotel **5**

Hilton Curaçao Resort **5**

Hotel Kurá Hulanda
    Spa and Casino **6**

Landhuis Daniel Country
    Inn and Restaurant **3**

Lions Dive and Beach
    Resort Curaçao **10**

Lodge Kurá Hulanda
    and Beach Club **1**

Otrobanda Hotel and Casino **6**

Plaza Hotel Curaçao **7**

Renaissance Curaçao
    Resort and Casino **6**

A Word About Carnival

A passing comment from a visitor to Curaçao went something like this: "I don't know what all the fuss is about with regard to Carnival. We were here last year and after hearing all about the lavish parade and festivities, it turned out to be nothing more than a bunch a kids in some costumes dancing around in the street for the afternoon." Ah, had she only known that Carnival is not an event, not a parade, and not an afternoon; it is a full-fledged season, running for months and culminating in a series of elections (to see who will be crowned king and queen of each parade division running from children up to adults), contests, parties, and a series of about 20 different parades, all ending on Carnival Monday. Seeing one parade and making a judgment is much like watching one school play about the Nativity and thinking you understand the frenzy around Christmas.

It really doesn't matter whether you celebrate Carnival in Curaçao (where Carnival is an all-out frenzy), Aruba (where things are even more lavish and extravagant), or Bonaire (where the parties are more subdued and the contests are taken very seriously). On all three islands don't for a moment think you've seen it all if you've seen only one or two parades. Trust me, you haven't seen the half of it!

GETTING AROUND

BY RENTAL CAR   Driving in Curaçao is easy. Valid U.S., British, Australian, and Canadian licenses are honored. The minimum age to rent for many companies is 25. Driving is on the right side, and road signs use international symbols. **Avis** (© **800/331-2112;** www.avis. com), **Budget** (© **800/472-3325** in the U.S., or 599/9-839-1300; www.budget.com), and **Hertz** (© **800/654-3001** in the U.S., or 599/9-868-1182; www.hertz.com) have offices at the airport. Compact cars with manual transmissions start at about $40 per day plus taxes and insurance.

BY TAXI   Most taxis are metered, but drivers in unmetered cabs carry an official rate sheet. Fares rise 20% after 8pm and some go up a few dollars more after 11pm and on holidays. Drivers appreciate a 10% tip. The $20 trip from the airport to Willemstad can be split among four passengers. Each piece of oversize luggage is an extra $1.

In town, taxis are easiest to get on the Otrobanda side of the floating bridge. You can also call ✆ **599/9-869-0752.** Taxi island tours are $50 per hour for up to four passengers. **Taber Tours** (✆ **599/9-868-7012** or 567-6770; www.tabertours.com) specializes in hotel transfers and island tours for big groups.

BY BUS   Most of the large hotels operate a free shuttle to Willemstad's shopping districts, but public transportation is limited. Large yellow buses (also called "convoys") cover the most traveled urban routes, and bus terminals are outside the post office on the Waaigat inlet in Punda and next to the underpass in Otrobanda. Fares in town and east of Willemstad are $1, and may be more to the western end of the island. Buses run most city routes hourly, every 2 hours for points west, and less frequently on Sunday. Shaded bus benches dot the main roads.

ⓕ *Fast Facts*   Curaçao

Banks Bank hours are Monday to Friday from 8am to 3:30 or 4:30pm. Willemstad has several banks and ATMs.

Currency U.S. dollars and credit cards are accepted almost everywhere. The official currency, the Netherlands Antillean florin (NAf), also called a **guilder,** is divided into 100 NA (Netherlands Antillean) cents. The stable **exchange rate** is $1 to 1.77 NAf (1 NAf = 56¢). Credit cards are widely accepted and while American Express, Visa, and MasterCard are preferred, Discover is gaining ground while Diners Club is rarely accepted. Prices throughout this chapter are given in U.S. dollars.

Electricity Electricity is both 220 volts and 110–130 volts/50 cycles, with at least one plug in each hotel room similar to the U.S. standard. Most U.S. electrical appliances will function.

Emergencies Dial ✆ **911** for medics or the police.

Hospital **St. Elisabeth Hospital,** Breederstraat 193 (✆ **599/9-462-4900**), near Otrobanda in Willemstad, is one of the Caribbean's most up-to-date facilities, with a recompression chamber.

Language As in Aruba, Dutch, Spanish, and English are spoken, along with Papiamentu.

Safety Curaçao isn't plagued with crime, but safeguard your valuables.

Taxes Curaçao levies a room tax of 4%, plus a 12% service tax and a $3 daily energy charge. The airport departure tax is usually built into the price of your airline ticket.

Telephone To call Curaçao from the United States, dial **011** (the international access code), then **599** (the country code), and then **9** (the area code) and the local number. In Curaçao, to call another number on the island, dial the local number only; to make off-island calls, dial **021** and then the area code and number. The direct-dial access number for **AT&T** is ✆ **916/843-4685** from your cellphone and ✆ **001-800-872-2881** from pay phones; for **Verizon** it's ✆ **800-8888.** You can reach a **Sprint** operator throughout the Caribbean at ✆ **011-817/698-4199.** Check with your carrier before you leave home to find out if your phone will work on the island, and be sure to ask about rates, which are about $2 per minute. Even local calls from hotels will cost a bomb, so opt for e-mails when possible. Wireless signals are common in hotels, and Internet cafes let you log on for just a few bucks. You can pick up a free signal while in the airport.

Time Curaçao is on Atlantic Standard Time year-round, 1 hour ahead of Eastern Standard Time and the same as Eastern daylight saving time.

Water Water comes from a modern desalination plant and is perfectly safe and clean.

Weather Curaçao's average temperature is 81°F (27°C), and trade winds make the island fairly pleasant. Annual rainfall averages a meager 56 centimeters (22 in.).

2 WHERE TO STAY

Choose from beachfront resorts to inland bed-and-breakfasts in historic Dutch land houses. Hotels cluster in Willemstad and the suburbs 10 to 15 minutes away. The bigger hotels have free shuttle buses into town, and most have beaches and pools. Most quoted prices do not include the 7% room tax or 12% service charge, so make sure to ask when reserving. Some charge a $3 daily energy tax.

Some hotels cater primarily to American and Canadian tourists, while others are occupied almost exclusively by the many Dutch visitors. The latter tend toward a quiet self-service atmosphere, with

kitchenettes in the rooms and shuttles to local shopping markets.
Many of the markets are clustered near the Jan Thiel Beach area.
South Americans are an increasingly significant percentage of the
tourist population, so many hotel desks can greet you in Spanish and
Portuguese. Hotels listed here are a mixture but the larger chain hotels
are really the U.S.-centric ones.

VERY EXPENSIVE

Breezes Curaçao ★ (Kids)   This is Curaçao's first major all-inclusive
resort, boasting the largest casino in Curaçao and one free shore dive
per guest per day. Adjacent to the Undersea National Park and
Seaquarium, this large complex opens onto one of Curaçao's man-
made beaches. This high-energy complex has a large free-form pool and
one of the longest beaches on the island, with decent snorkeling offshore. Catering to both couples and singles, the resort also welcomes
families, with children's programs and an on-site supervised trapeze
school. The most desirable rooms overlook the ocean; others front the
hotel's gardens. Bathrooms have either a shower or a tub/shower combination, and all open onto private patios or balconies. The resort's
active entertainment program includes guest talent shows, the obliga-
tory belly-flop contests and staff "cultural" show, but the staff's true
talent is their friendly attitude. The resort has two specialty restaurants:
an outdoor Japanese steakhouse and an Italian restaurant with some
alfresco tables. The food is plentiful, if patchy in its quality. The outdoor restaurant is cramped but plans are in the works to relocate the
cheesy stage outdoors and make more room for seating.

Dr. Martin Luther King Blvd. 8, Willemstad, Curaçao, N.A. (𝐶) **599/9-736-7888.** Fax
599/9-461-7205. www.breezes.com. 339 units. Dec 21 to early Apr and July–Aug
from $324 double, from $466 suite; mid-Apr to June and Sept–Dec 20 from $308
double, from $439 suite. Rates are all-inclusive. Children 2–13 are an additional
$50 each. AE, MC, V. **Amenities:** 4 restaurants; 3 bars; babysitting; casino; chil-
dren's program and playground; fitness center; 3 pools; room service; spa; 2 tennis
courts; dive shop; deep-sea fishing; snorkeling; windsurfing. In room: A/C, TV, CD
player, fridge (on request), minibar, hair dryer, Wi-Fi ($28 per day).

Renaissance Curaçao Resort and Casino   This new, modern,
and upscale resort is adjacent to the **Rif Fort** (a UNESCO World
Heritage Site) and is responsible for the development of this area,
including the addition of new shops and 15 restaurants and bars. The
rainbow-hued lobby has a colorful frenetic feel that matches the
sound and lights emanating from the hotel's appropriately named
Carnaval Casino. The Nautilus Restaurant and Blue Lobby Bar are
also integrated into the spacious lobby and look out over the outdoor
plaza with additional seating and views of the lobby. The rooms are
spacious, colorful, and loaded with comfortable linens, pillows, and

plush chairs with ottomans. Bathrooms have cheerful colors and are well appointed, though the doors are irritatingly determined to shut on their own. The eternity beach is a new concept and works well in this urban setting, creating a serene respite to swim, sunbathe, and relax before hitting the shops, casino, or abundant nearby bars.

Baden Powellweg 1, Otrobanda. ✆ **800/HOTELS-1** [468-3571] or 599/9-435-5000. Fax 599/9-435-5001. www.renaissancecuracao.com. 223 units. Late Dec to Mar $450–$545 double, $705–$1,650 suite; Apr to mid-Dec $215–$409 double, $380–$1,140 suite. AE, MC, V. **Amenities:** Restaurant; 2 bars; babysitting; casino; room service; free Wi-Fi in lobby; dive shop; rooms for those w/limited mobility. *In room:* A/C, TV, hair dryer, high-speed Internet.

EXPENSIVE

Avila Hotel ★★   The only beachfront hotel in Willemstad proper, the Avila Hotel consists of four separate structures: a beautifully restored 200-year-old colonial mansion; a large extension of deluxe rooms called La Belle Alliance Wing; the Blues Wing, an all-wood complex of deluxe rooms built on a pier off of the beach, each with a private terrace or balcony overlooking the sea; and the new contemporary-style Octagon Wing. Converted into a hotel in 1949, the Avila Hotel regularly hosts members of the Dutch royal family including the queen of the Netherlands. The Blues Wing rooms have a full bathroom, kitchenette, Jacuzzi tub, and a balcony or terrace with an ocean view. Similarly, the recently refurnished La Belle Alliance rooms have full bathrooms and balconies; some have kitchenettes. Rooms in the Octagon Wing have a chic South Beach feel with beige suede headboards, flatscreen TVs, and frosted-glass bathroom walls and doors.

Penstraat 130 (P.O. Box 791), Willemstad, Curaçao, N.A. ✆ **800/747-8162** or 599/9-461-4377. Fax 599/9-461-1493. www.avilahotel.com. 150 units. Dec 16–Apr 15 $430 1 bedroom, $575 2 bedroom; Apr 16–Sept 15 $360 1 bedroom, $475 2 bedroom; Sept 16–Dec 15 $370 1 bedroom, $485 2 bedroom. Meal plans available. AE, MC, V. **Amenities:** 3 restaurants; 3 bars; babysitting; pool; spa/wellness center; tennis court; rooms for those w/limited mobility. *In room:* A/C, TV, hair dryer, high-speed Internet.

Curaçao Marriott Beach Resort & Emerald Casino ★★   The most glamorous and prominent hotel on the island, this resort borders Curaçao's largest and most popular beach. The hotel's three-story ocher buildings reflect traditional Dutch colonial architecture, and the open lobby boasts views of the beach and the property's many fountains. Scattered throughout, unusual, often monumental, artworks by local and international artists, and comfortable, overstuffed chairs add a touch of elegance. Each colorful room offers an ocean view, one king-size or two queen-size beds, and a spacious bathroom. Although never rising to any great imagination or flair, the food here is consistently good, made with quality ingredients. There's an expansive beach with a postcard-perfect beach bar complete with bar swings. There's also a big casino.

Piscadera Bay (P.O. Box 6003), Willemstad, Curaçao, N.A. *©* **800/223-6388** in the U.S., or 599/9-736-8800. Fax 599/9-462-7502. www.curacaomarriott.com. 247 units. Late Dec to Mar $274–$340 double, from $489 suite; Apr to mid-Dec $169–$199 double, from $389 suite. AE, MC, V. **Amenities:** 3 restaurants; 2 bars; casino; children's program; concierge; health club; spa; 2 open-air Jacuzzis; outdoor pool; room service; sauna; watersports; free Wi-Fi in lobby; rooms for those w/limited mobility. *In room:* A/C, TV, hair dryer, minibar.

Hilton Curaçao Resort ★

Originally built in 1965, this former Sheraton is often credited with launching Curaçao's tourism boom. Today, it rises five floors above rocky bluffs that open onto a sandy beach. The large free-form pool and a location convenient to the center of town offset the lack of a wide swath of beach. Glass-enclosed elevators cling to the outside walls, offering a panoramic view as they whisk you to your room, each of which overlooks either the ocean or the garden. Outfitted in tropical colors, each guest room features traditional Caribbean colors, plush furnishings, carpeting, private balconies, and generously proportioned bathrooms.

The food isn't great, but it's varied—everything from Italian trattoria favorites to fresh seafood. A social director organizes theme nights based on Mexican or Antillean food and dance music. There's a lively casino on-site.

Piscadera Bay, John F. Kennedy Blvd. (P.O. Box 2133), Willemstad, Curaçao, N.A. *©* **800/HILTONS** [445-8667] in the U.S. and Canada, or 599/9-462-5000. Fax 599/9-462-5846. www.hiltoncaribbean.com/curacao. 196 units. Late Dec to Mar $188–$264 double, $250–$380 suite; Apr to mid-Dec $150–$170 double, $210–$250 suite. AE, MC, V. **Amenities:** 2 restaurants; 2 bars; babysitting; casino; children's program and playground; 18-hole minigolf course; health club; outdoor pool; room service; smoke-free rooms; 2 tennis courts lit for night play; watersports; rooms for those w/limited mobility. *In room:* A/C, TV, hair dryer, high-speed Internet ($5 for 3 hr.).

Hotel Kurá Hulanda Spa and Casino ★★

Curaçao's most imaginative and unusual hotel in the heart of the city's Dutch colonial historic district is part of the Kurá Hulanda Museum complex (p. 155), and the hotel's Dutch colonial architecture dates from the 18th and 19th centuries. Both the museum and the hotel are the brainchild of Dutch millionaire Jacob Gelt Dekker, whose passion for preserving the architecture of Curaçao and the history and culture of its people is palpable. It's not on a beach, but this hotel offers the Dutch Caribbean's best West Indian character. The gorgeous rooms feature hand-woven linens from India and hand-carved mahogany and teak furniture. A free daily shuttle runs to nearby **Blaubai Beach, Blue Bay Golf Course,** and to Hotel Kurá Hulanda's sister property, the

140 **Lodge Kurá Hulanda** where visitors can escape the city and enjoy an idyllic day at the beach or a relaxed meal at their waterside eatery, Watamula Restaurant.

Langestraat 8, Willemstad, Curaçao, N.A. ✆ **877/264-3106** in the U.S. or 599/9-434-7700. Fax 599/9-434-7701. www.kurahulanda.com. 80 units. Jan 3–Apr 3 from $225 double, from $460 suite; Apr 4–Dec 23 from $139 double, from $415 suite; Dec 24–Jan 2 from $335 double, from $500 suite. AE, DC, MC, V. **Amenities:** 3 restaurants; bar; babysitting; casino; fitness center; 2 pools; room service. *In room:* A/C, ceiling fans, TV, CD player, minifridge, hair dryer, free Wi-Fi, robes.

Lions Dive & Beach Resort Curaçao   This casual beachfront dive resort offers well-appointed comfortable rooms with rattan furniture, outdoor balconies overlooking tropical gardens, and a palm-shaded private beach in a protected cove. All rooms have a shower and bathtub, and family rooms feature kitchenettes. The on-site dive shop is well equipped for divers of all levels. Proximity to the **Seaquarium** is a plus for families, and admission is free for all hotel guests. Baby cots, cribs, and other baby accessories are available on request. The fitness center offers a wide array of classes including spinning, yoga, and kick boxing; and the full-service spa offers massages and body treatments for reasonable prices.

Bapor Kibra z/n, next to the Seaquarium. ✆ **599/9-434-8888.** Fax 599/9-434-8889. www.lionsdive.com. 137 units. Jan 4–Dec 17 $190 double, $389 apt, $525 suite; Dec 18–Jan 3 $282 double, $519 apt, $641 suite. AE, DC, MC, V. **Amenities:** 2 restaurants; bar; babysitting; fitness center; 2 pools; room service; rooms for those w/limited mobility. *In room:* A/C, ceiling fans, TV, CD player, minifridge, hair dryer, high-speed Internet access, robes.

Lodge Kurá Hulanda and Beach Club   On the western tip of the island, this quiet resort offers a retreat from the crowds. As a member of Leading Small Hotels of the World—and as the baby sister of Hotel Kurá Hulanda Spa and Casino back in Willemstad—the formula is one that works: quiet elegance in a unique setting. On a small bluff with a thin beach below, the restaurant and bar afford good vistas, and the cottages are spread out and nestled amid the natural landscape. Don't expect much nightlife—but if you need to get away from it all, this is the right destination. For those seeking a truly rustic experience, there's a treetop safari tent and a mansion on stilts that hearkens to *Out of Africa*. In the Best of Both Worlds packages, a few days at the urban hotel balance the serenity of your time at the lodge. Daily transportation into town is provided.

Playa Kalki 1 Westpunt. ✆ **877/264-3106** or 599/9-839-3600. Fax 599/9-839-3601. www.kurahulanda.com. 74 units. Apr 4–Dec 23 $130–$210 double, $285–$810 suite; Dec 24–Jan 2 $335 double, $440–$1,095 suite; Jan 3–Apr 3 $190–$245 double, $320–$890 suite. AE, MC, V. **Amenities:** 3 restaurants; bar; babysitting; fitness center; pool; room service; dive shop. *In room:* A/C, TV, hair dryer, kitchenette, Wi-Fi.

MODERATE

Blue Bay Villages   Located just steps from the famous Blue Bay Beach, and right next to **Blue Bay Golf and Beach Resort,** Curaçao's best golf course, this collection of duplex villas caters to those who plan to book for a week or more. Each villa has a living room, sleek and fully stocked kitchen, terrace, three bedrooms, and two bathrooms—perfect for families and small groups that are traveling together.

Blauwbaai, Curaçao, N.A. (©) **599/9-888-8880.** Fax 599/9-888-9090. www.blue bay-village.com. 52 units. Late Dec to Mar $285 villa; Apr to mid-Dec $250 villa. AE, MC, V. **Amenities:** Restaurant; bar; babysitting; fitness center; pool; tennis court; Wi-Fi; rooms for those w/limited mobility. In room: A/C, TV, fridge, hair dryer.

Floris Suite Hotel ★   The compound of this all-suites hotel surrounds a lush garden and large pool, offering sleek style and total serenity. A sandy beach is accessible across the street. Each suite in this complex bears the trademark of its designer and creator, Jan des Bouvrie, whose unique designs merge comfort with sleek modern home aesthetics. The combination of smooth stone floors with mahogany doors and window frames erases all sense of being in a chain hotel, as do the spartan bedcoverings, for better or worse. The modern furnishings look like they're straight out of an IKEA catalog. Sleeper sofas, fully equipped kitchens, and spacious balconies accommodate family groups while amenities such as a nearby spa, fitness room, and dive shop make it great for active adults. Because the hotel has adopted an ecofriendly mentality, air-conditioning units turn off when guests leave the rooms.

John F. Kennedy Blvd., Piscadera Bay, Curaçao, N.A. (©) **599/9-462-6211.** www.floris suitehotel.com. 71 units. Dec–Apr $129–$269 suite; off season $149–$289 suite. AE, MC, V. **Amenities:** Restaurant; bar; babysitting; fitness room; outdoor pool; smoke-free rooms; tennis court. In room: A/C, TV, hair dryer, high-speed Internet.

Plaza Hotel Curaçao   Standing guard over the Punda side of Saint Anna Bay, right in the heart of Willemstad, the 14-story Plaza is nestled in the ramparts of an 18th-century waterside fort on the eastern tip of the harbor entrance. As one of the harbor's two "lighthouses," the hotel has to carry marine collision insurance—it's the only hotel in the Caribbean with that distinction. The original part of the hotel was built in 1954, and retains a 1950s look with a quirky lobby complete with a fishpond, enormous rotating ceiling fans, and an open-air terrace next to the small pool. There's also a tower of rooms stacked 15 stories high. Each of the smallish bedrooms is comfortably furnished and contains a small tub/shower combo. The pool, with a bar and sun-tanning area, is inches away from the parapet of the fort. The Waterfort Restaurant serves standard American and Continental dishes.

Plaza Piar (P.O. Box 813), Willemstad, Curaçao, N.A. ℂ **599/9-461-2500.** Fax 599/9-461-6543. www.plazahotelcuracao.com. 252 units. Jan 3–Dec 15 $145–$210 double; Dec 16–Jan 2 $175–$235 double. Rates include breakfast. Children 12 and under stay free in parent's room. AE, DC, DISC, MC, V. **Amenities:** 2 restaurants; 3 bars; casino; outdoor pool; room service; smoke-free rooms; 1 room for those w/ limited mobility. *In room:* A/C, TV, hair dryer, kitchenette (in some).

INEXPENSIVE

Chogogo Resort In Curaçao's east end, a 2-minute walk from the busy and Dutch-dominated Jan Thiel Beach, this resort is for visitors seeking an apartment or a bungalow. It is named after a species of local flamingo and set within an arid landscape between the oceanfront beaches and a shallow saltwater bay southeast of Willemstad. One- and two-story buildings dot the grounds; these contain the guest bungalows, studios, and apartments, each with a kitchenette, airy, unpretentious furniture, and a compact shower-only bathroom.

Jan Thiel Bay, Curaçao, N.A. ℂ **599/9-747-2844.** Fax 599/9-747-2424. www.chogogo.com. 120 units. Dec 17–Mar 31 $135–$146 studio for 2, $147–$158 apt for 2, $252 bungalow for 4; Apr 1–Dec 16 $119–$129 studio for 2, $133–$144 apt for 2, $204 bungalow for 4. 3-night minimum stay. AE, MC, V. **Amenities:** Restaurant; bar; high-speed Internet; outdoor pool; children's wading pool. *In room:* A/C, TV, kitchenette.

Landhuis Daniel Country Inn and Restaurant (Value) Situated on the narrow middle part of the island, this mustard-colored plantation house is a 15-minute drive from the beach, but it offers the best value in Curaçao. Simple but comfortable guest rooms are tidily maintained and have small private bathrooms with showers. Only six rooms are air-conditioned, but all units have ceiling fans. The basic rooms and communal TV room give this simple country inn the aura of a youth hostel; guests can also play billiards.

Weg naar, Westpunt z/n, Curaçao, N.A. ℂ/fax **599/9-864-8400.** www.landhuisdaniel.com. 8 units. $50–$70 double year-round. MC, V. **Amenities:** Restaurant (see review for Landhuis Daniel Country Inn and Restaurant, p. 144); bar; pool; dive shop. *In room:* A/C, Wi-Fi, no phone.

Otrobanda Hotel and Casino Situated in the heart of town, this small hotel is more geared toward local business travelers than American tourists, but it provides an inexpensive way to stay in town for a few nights on the cheap, great for those who just need a crash pad close to the city bustle. The small guest rooms overlook the harbor, and even the pocket-size pool has great views of town. Prices include breakfast at the restaurant, which also affords stupendous photo ops of the waterfront and the mouth of the harbor. The sad casino is not worth more than a glance, but at the other end of town, there are glitzy shops, restaurants, a piano bar, and a new casino at the Renaissance in the Rif Fort.

$250 triple. AE, DISC, MC, V. **Amenities:** Restaurant; bar; pool; small casino. *In room:* A/C, TV, Wi-Fi ($5 per day).

3 WHERE TO DINE

Cheese lovers, rejoice . . . the abundance of Dutch Gouda and the presence of lots of European restaurant owners makes for a gooey and tasty culinary experience for you, from the cheese and ham toasties to the strangely compelling *keshi yena,* a traditional baked dish of spicy chicken, dates, raisins, olives, and velvety Gouda. If you can find it, locally made goat cheese is superb. All restaurants, unless noted, are in Willemstad.

EXPENSIVE

Bistro Le Clochard ★ FRENCH/SWISS   This restaurant fits snugly into the grim ramparts of Rif Fort, at the gateway to the harbor. Its entrance is marked with a canopy leading to a series of rooms, each built under the vaulting of the old Dutch fort. This appealingly formal restaurant has several seating options, including a glassed-in dining room near the entrance and an outdoor terrace. Appetizers such as snails marinated in cognac, frogs' legs, or crepes stuffed with a seafood ragout with a hollandaise sauce seem more appropriate to a Paris bistro than a tropical island. The kitchen staff is at its best when preparing beef dishes; the tenderloin with mushrooms in a cream sauce is recommended. The signature dish is La Potence, a swinging, red-hot metal ball covered with bits of sizzling tenderloin, served with various dipping sauces. The catch of the day always comes with a lemon-butter sauce.

Rif Fort, on the Otrobanda side of the pontoon bridge. ☎ **599/9-462-5666.** www.
bistroleclochard.com. Reservations recommended. Main courses $35–$46. AE,
MC, V. Daily noon–2pm and 6:30–10:45pm. Harborside Terrace daily noon–midnight.

Sustainable Eating

Due to the decline of local species, such as Caribbean lobster and conch, you may want to eschew ordering reef fish such as grouper, snapper, and grunt and opt for equally tasty and more sustainable alternatives that live out in open water such as dorado, wahoo, and barracuda.

Jaipur INDIAN   Within the breezy, European Kurá Hulanda "village" sits this fine Indian restaurant. With its terra-cotta walls, teak chairs, marble tabletops, and location beside the babbling ecopool, Jaipur offers Indian fare with a Pan-Asian flair and an unusually thorough wine list. The food—particularly fresh nan, curries, chicken, and seafood, which emerge steaming from the tandoori oven—is finely honed, with details (bright chutneys, peppery purées) that show unexpected kitchen finesse.

Langestraat 8, within the Hotel Kurá Hulanda complex. ✆ **599/9-434-7700.** www.kurahulanda.com/restaurants-a-bars. Reservations recommended. Main courses $13–$34. AE, MC, V. Wed–Mon 6–11pm.

Landhuis Daniel Country Inn and Restaurant FRENCH/ MEDITERRANEAN/CREOLE   This restaurant serves a unique combination of loosely French and Mediterranean flavors using a lot of fresh produce organically grown on the premises. Surrounded by arid scrubland about 3km (2 miles) south of Westpunt, near the island's most northwesterly tip, this place was originally built in 1711 as an inn and tavern. Today, its mustard-colored facade, white columns, terra-cotta roof, and old-fashioned green-and-yellow dining room are carefully preserved and historically authentic. Menu items are cooked slowly, to order, in a setting of sea breezes and sunlight streaming in the big windows. Start with the spicy Caribbean seafood bisque, and then order the Dover sole or rabbit in stewed pears. The four-course surprise menu, costing $43, changes weekly.

Wegnaar, Westpunt. ✆ **599/9-864-8400.** www.landhuisdaniel.com. Reservations recommended. Main courses $19–$31. MC, V. Daily 8am–10pm.

La Pergola ★ ITALIAN   Nestled in the Waterfront Arches, this trattoria has thrived for more than a decade. The eatery's centerpiece is a Renaissance-style pergola, or arbor, which is indoors and overlooks the seafront. The outdoor seating is along the edge of the fort and overlooks the sea. The menu changes daily but might include a pasta dish such as tagliatelle with pesto and shrimp or pumpkin ravioli with ricotta and bacon. Some dishes have a touch of island panache, such as grilled salmon with béarnaise sauce.

Waterfort Straat, in the Waterfront Arches. ✆ **599/9-461-3482.** Reservations recommended. Main courses $11–$29. AE, DISC, MC, V. Mon–Sat noon–11pm.

Wine Cellar ★ FRENCH   Close to the center of town, this restaurant boasts an extensive wine list and old-fashioned European ambience. The kitchen turns out excellent lobster salad and sole meunière in butter-and-herb sauce. Other good choices include poached Norwegian salmon and U.S. beef tenderloin with goat-cheese sauce.

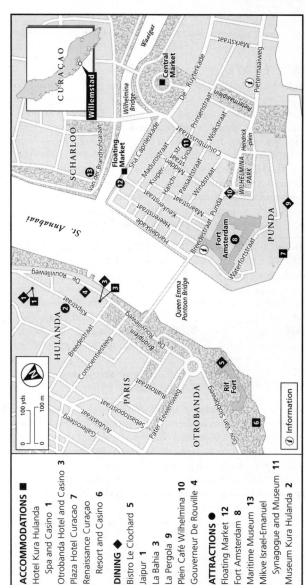

ACCOMMODATIONS ■

Hotel Kura Hulanda
Spa and Casino **1**
Otrobanda Hotel and Casino **3**
Plaza Hotel Curacao **7**
Renaissance Curaçao
Resort and Casino **6**

DINING ◆

Bistro Le Clochard **5**
Jaipur **1**
La Bahia **3**
La Pergola **9**
Plein Café Wilhelmina **10**
Gouverneur De Rouville **4**

ATTRACTIONS ●

Floating Market **12**
Fort Amsterdam **8**
Maritime Museum **13**
Mikve Israel-Emanuel
Synagogue and Museum **11**
Museum Kura Hulanda **2**

Game dishes, imported throughout the year from Holland, include venison roasted with mushrooms.

Ooststraat/Concordiastraat. ✆ **599/9-461-2178.** www.winecellar.an. Reservations required. Main courses $15–$38. AE, MC, V. Mon–Fri noon–3pm and 6–11pm; Sat 6–11pm.

MODERATE

Belle Terrace ★ INTERNATIONAL   This open-air restaurant in a 200-year-old mansion overlooking the sea offers satisfying food in a relaxed atmosphere. Sheltered by an arbor of flamboyant branches, the restaurant features Scandinavian, Continental, and local cuisine with specialties such as pickled herring and smoked salmon. Local dishes include the ever-popular *keshi yena*. The fish is always fresh, and the chef prepares a weekly special to perfection: grilled, poached, or meunière. On Saturday night there's a mixed grill and a serve-yourself salad bar, all accompanied by live music.

Penstraat 130, in the Avila Hotel. ✆ **599/9-461-4377.** Reservations required. Main courses $15–$27. AE, MC, V. Daily 7–10am, noon–2:30pm, and 7–10pm.

Blues SEAFOOD/INTERNATIONAL   Perched over lapping water on a pier, this restaurant features platters of fresh seafood that challenge even the heartiest appetite. The sapphire and aqua tile interior is accented with oversize blues and jazz album covers, echoing the live entertainment. Blue mussels are cooked in wine sauce with shallots and herbs; dorado comes with mustard-flavored beurre blanc (white butter). The freshly caught "seafood challenge" may include tuna, salmon, squid, langoustine, and scallops. Live jazz is offered Thursday and Saturday.

Penstraat 130, in the Avila Hotel. ✆ **599/9-461-4377.** Reservations recommended. Main courses $16–$31. AE, MC, V. Tues–Sun 7–11pm.

Gouverneur De Rouville INTERNATIONAL   Overlooking the waterfront, this spectacular three-story structure was the residence of the original governor of Willemstad. Whether you sit on the balcony overlooking the water, in the courtyard next to the fountain, or inside the main dining room beneath the ornate chandelier, you will likely appreciate the charming Dutch architecture almost as much as you'll enjoy the well-prepared local and international food and professional service. The *keshi yena* is worth the wait, and the mixed grill is cooked to perfection.

De Rouvilleweg 9-F. ✆ **599/9-462-5999.** www.de-gouverneur.com. Reservations recommended. Main courses $17–$28. AE, MC, V. Daily 10am–midnight.

Hemingway INTERNATIONAL   The fact that this themed eatery's namesake never ate or drank here—or anywhere else in Curaçao—should not dissuade you. Casual beachside dining at its best can be experienced here at wooden tables right in the sand. The expansive menu includes everything from fried calamari, burgers, and pizza, to Asian beef salad and Mediterranean salad with grilled tuna. The large dessert menu includes Dutch apple pie with pecans and, of course, Key lime pie.

Bapor Kibra at Lions Dive and Beach Resort. (𝓒 **599/9-434-8888.** www.hemingway beach.com. Main courses $10–$23. AE, MC, V. Daily 10am–10pm.

Jaanchie's Restaurant CREOLE   Ask any local or tour guide and they can point the way to this eclectic and rustic eatery. A family business for two generations, this old farmhouse-turned-restaurant serves up local dishes such as iguana soup (no, it does not taste like chicken); goat stew; and okra, tripe, or cactus soup. More-approachable options include fresh conch, wahoo, grouper, or shrimp cooked in garlic and served with rice and beans, *funchi,* or *tu tu* (local polenta with beans). Be prepared to wait for a meal, but the dozens of little yellow bananaquits that flock to the sugar-filled bird feeders will keep you amused with their busy chatter.

Westpunt 15. (𝓒 **599/9-864-0126.** Reservations recommended. Main courses $14–$20. AE, MC, V. Daily noon–7pm (last seating).

Rijsttafel Indonesia INDONESIAN   This is the only place in Curaçao to sample Indonesian rijsttafel, the traditional rice table with various zesty appetizer-size dishes. At lunchtime, the selection is comparatively modest, but for dinner, Filipino cooks prepare rijsttafel with 16, 20, or 25 dishes. There's even an all-vegetarian option. Season your plate with condiments rated hot, very hot, or palate melting. The spicy feast is a good change of pace after a week of seafood and steak.

Mercuriusstraat 13, Salinja. (𝓒 **599/9-462-6361.** Reservations recommended. Main courses $16–$25; rijsttafel $22 for 16 dishes, $27 for 20 dishes, $43 for 25 dishes; vegetarian $23 for 16 dishes. AE, MC, V. Tues–Sun noon–2pm and 6–10pm.

Watamula Restaurant SEAFOOD/INTERNATIONAL   Perched over azure water with views of the beach below, this breezy open-air restaurant features fresh local food prepared with a Continental flair. The seared tuna or shrimp tempura appetizers work well to open your palate before the ostrich filet with teriyaki sambal or blackened swordfish with blue-cheese mashed potatoes. Seafood is not the only option; the jerk chicken, spiced New Zealand rack of lamb, and wild-forest-mushroom linguine are just as satisfying. For dessert, tease your palate with the banana crepe, flavored with local rum and served with rum raisin ice cream.

Playa Kalki 1, Westpunt, at the Lodge Kurá Hulanda. (𝓒 **599/9-839-3600.** Reservations strongly recommended. Main courses $20–$48. MC, V. Daily 6–10:30pm.

Zanzibar Restaurant INTERNATIONAL   This stylish beach bar and restaurant caters to patrons at Jan Thiel Beach on the east side of the island. It has a global vibe and features Moroccan decor, under a large open African hut, and serves an international menu, with a Mediterranean flair, to mostly Dutch patrons. Shish kabob and seafood are good, but pizza is the specialty.

Jan Theil Beach. ✆ **599/9-747-0633.** www.zanzibar-curacao.com. Reservations recommended. Main courses $12–$19. AE, MC, V. Daily 8:30am–11:30pm.

INEXPENSIVE

Golden Star CREOLE   With the air of a Caribbean roadside diner, this restaurant is simple, but its Antillean dishes are tasty. Choose from *bestia chiki* (goat meat stew), *bakijauw* (salted cod), and *concomber stoba* (stewed meat and spiny cucumbers). Everything comes with a side order of *funchi,* a cornmeal polenta. Diners are locals for the most part, with an occasional tourist.

Socratesstraat 2, at Dr. Hugenholtzweg and Dr. Maalweg, southeast of Willemstad. ✆ **599/9-461-9633.** Main courses $10–$30. AE, MC, V. Daily 11am–10pm.

La Bahia SEAFOOD/STEAKHOUSE   The old adage of location, location, location applies here. The second-story restaurant offers spectacular alfresco views of narrow Saint Ann Bay, the floating pontoon bridge, the gingerbread gabled architecture of Punda across the water, and the cruise ships that dock in town. The menu is vast and ranges from salads, pizza, and burgers to lobster, steak, and burritos. The chef even creates combinations such as steak salad or fajita pizza, but it's best to stick with the simple classics. When it comes to dessert, go straight for a mudslide, lava flow, or Key lime pie—from the specialty cocktail menu.

Breederstraat z/n. ✆ **599/9-462-7400.** Main courses $12–$34. AE, MC, V. Daily 7am–midnight.

Plein Café Wilhelmina DUTCH   A great place to stop for lunch after a hard morning of shopping. The locals come for the hip urban vibe, cold beer in a wide assortment of brands and brews, and great people-watching opportunities. The food is simple fare with a Dutch flair and consists of hearty breakfasts, large salads, hot and cold sandwiches, chicken satay, burgers, and local favorites such as *frikendel* (breaded deep-fried sausages) or *bitterballen* (breaded deep-fried puréed meatballs).Yum (I think).

Wilhelminaplein 19–23, Punda (next to Wilhelmina Park). ✆ **599/9-461-9666.** www.pleincafewilhelmina.an. Main courses $10–$30. AE, MC, V. Daily 7:30am–11pm.

4 HITTING THE BEACHES & ACTIVE PURSUITS

BEACHES

Although Curaçao's beaches are inferior to Aruba's, there are nearly 40 of them, ranging from hotel sands to secluded coves. The northwest coast's rugged waters make swimming difficult, but the more tranquil waters of the west coast have sheltered bays that are good for swimming and snorkeling. The best beaches are along the southern coast, west of Willemstad.

Man-made **Seaquarium Beach** (or **Mambo Beach**), just east of central Willemstad, charges $3 for beach-chair rental, changing facilities, and showers. Two bars, two restaurants, and a watersports shop are on-site. The calm waters are ideal for swimming.

Northwest of Willemstad, **Blauwbaai** is the island's largest and most popular beach. The $3 entrance fee is well worth it. Along with showers and changing areas, facilities include a bar and restaurant as well as plenty of shade. Head toward Juliandorp, then bear left for Blauwbaai and San Michiel.

Farther down the west coast, about 30 minutes from Willemstad in the Willibrordus area, **Daaibooi** draws crowds of locals on Sunday. Wooden umbrellas provide shade, but there are no showers or changing rooms. Rainbow-hued fish and coral attract snorkelers.

Family-friendly **Playa Lagun,** in the fishing village of Lagun, hides in a narrow cove and boasts tranquil, shallow water, which is excellent for swimming. Snorkelers and divers appreciate the plentiful marine life. Concrete huts provide shelter, and the snack bar, dive center, and changing rooms are open on weekends.

Knip Bay, north of Playa Lagun, has white sand, rocky sides, and turquoise waters, making it suitable for snorkeling, swimming, and sunbathing. The beach is crowded on weekends, often with locals.

Playa Abao, or Playa Grandi, at the northern tip of the island, is one of Curaçao's most popular strands. Thatched shade umbrellas provide some protection, and the small snack bar and restroom in the parking lot address other needs.

On the northwestern tip of the island, **Westpunt** is known for the Sunday divers who jump from its cliffs into the ocean—an amazing sight. Colorful boats and fishermen's nets adorn the area, which has no facilities or shade trees. The calm waters are great for swimming.

One of the most spectacular and picturesque beaches in the world is found on the uninhabited island of **Klein Curaçao (Small Curaçao),** 13km (8 miles) off the southern tip of Curaçao. Sometimes referred to as **Castaway Beach,** this picturesque stretch of white sand is only accessible by boat and is entirely unpopulated save for some seriously gnarly shipwrecks, a quaint old lighthouse, and plenty of wildlife, including hatchling turtles (May–Aug). A shaded food stand with tables and chairs is where lunch is served as part of the day trip. It's a full-day's commitment but worth the 2 plus–hour rocky journey. A 60-passenger ship called *The Mermaid* (© 599/9-560-1530; www.mermaidboattrips.com) picks up passengers at the Fishermen's Pier on Wednesday, Friday, and Sunday at 6:45am and shuttles them out and back again at 4pm.

OUTDOOR PURSUITS

CRUISES   The two-masted *Bounty,* Sarifundy Marina (© 599/9-767-9998; www.bountyadventures.com), operated by Bounty Adventures, offers 4-hour snorkel, swim, and swing outings that include lunch, an open bar, a rope swing, snorkel gear, and a guided snorkel safari at both a tugboat wreck and shallow reef. *Bounty* sails every Wednesday, Friday, and Sunday from 10am to 2:30pm. The fare is $69 for adults and $35 for children 12 and under. Bounty Adventures also has a catamaran that sails to Klein Curaçao on Tuesday, Wednesday, Thursday, and Sunday; the cost is $89 for adults and $45 for children 4 to 12. The trip includes BBQ lunch, open bar, and snorkel gear. All boats leave from the Boathouse, Brakkeput Ariba z/n. Hotel pickup and drop-off can be arranged for an additional charge.

Travelers looking for an experience similar to the sailing days of yore should book a trip on the *Insulinde,* Handelskade (© 599/9-560-1340; www.insulinde.com). This 37m (121-ft.) traditionally rigged clipper offers afternoon snorkel, scenic tour, beach swim, and sail safaris for $50 for adults ($30 for children), and day trips to the island of Klein Curaçao for $90 (children $50). These trips depart at 6:30am and return at 6:30pm and include breakfast and lunch. Boats leave from right next to the Queen Emma Bridge in town. Occasional

---

(Moments   Coral Above and Below

After emerging from an awe-inspiring dive to a healthy reef that was a patchwork of pink, purple, and green corals, waving fans containing a Carnival of topaz, yellow, and pink fish, I glanced skyward. As if to not be outdone, a flock of pink flamingos silently glided overhead in a perfectly synchronized single-file display. Thank goodness salt water conveniently masked the tears of awe. Awwww.

DIVING & SNORKELING   Curaçao offers spectacular underwater treasures when it comes to marine environments, where scuba divers and snorkelers can enjoy healthy reefs and good visibility. Stretching along 20km (12 miles) of Curaçao's southern coastline, the **Curaçao Underwater Park ★★** features steep walls, shallow wrecks, gardens of soft coral, and more than 30 species of hard coral. A snorkel trail with underwater interpretive markers is laid out just east of the Breezes resort and is accessible from shore.

The two most spectacular dive sites are the **Mushroom Forest** and **Sponge Forest** where oversize coral heads and sponges abound. Two good wreck dives are the *Superior Producer,* a sunken vessel near Willemstad Harbor, and the **tugboat** near Caracas Bay. Dramatic vertical drops abound and can be explored at **Knipbai** and **Blauw-baai.** Due to the abundance of marine life, night dives are particularly rewarding in Curaçao.

(Tips)   Sustainable Diving & Snorkeling

Touching any coral—including soft corals such as sea fans—is forbidden in any marine protected area and should be avoided at all costs everywhere. Even the lightest contact is deadly to the coral and can scrape and cut you as well, leaving rashes and stings much like that of a jellyfish (coral's free-floating cousin). Divers and snorkelers are also not permitted to touch, pet, or otherwise harass any fish, including eels and rays, whose delicate skin is coated with antibacterial slime, which protects them from potentially deadly skin infections.

Feeding fish is similarly dangerous, however innocuous it seems. It can alter natural feeding behavior or, worse, cause the fish to sicken or die from ingesting unfamiliar food.

But wait, there's more. By applying sunscreen or insect repellent before entering the water, divers release harmful chemicals to the water and can mimic the coral's hormones causing them premature death and illness.

It seems the more scientists learn, the more delicate these systems appear. Want to make up for past infractions? Check out **REEF,** the **Reef Environmental Education Foundation** (www.reef.org), a volunteer monitoring program that allows divers to log in and add their fish sightings to a gobal data-base used by scientists to monitor populations.

Ocean Encounters Diving (© 599/9-461-8131; www.ocean encounters.com) offers the most complete dive facilities and services at many hotels, including Breezes, Lions Dive & Beach Resort, Hilton Curaçao Resort, and both Kurá Hulanda properties. It offers daily two-tank dives for $87 and afternoon snorkel trips for $44; wreck dives and night dives run $65. Ocean Encounters can even arrange interactive open-water dolphin dives together with the Dolphin Academy for $242. Weekly trips to Mushroom Forest and East Punt and Klein Curaçao are also offered for $130 with its fleet of seven custom dive boats. The Kid's Sea Camp offers underwater educational activities for children.

FISHING Proximity to the continental shelf of South America and wanton overfishing significantly limit the likelihood of catching large pelagic fish, and their rarity significantly limits the pleasure of hauling these spectacular top predators from the sea as either a prize or a meal—it also ain't cheap. Deep-sea fishing costs $350 for a half-day tour (six-person maximum) and $525 for a full-day tour, with drinks and equipment included. **Let's Fish** (© 599/9-561-1812; www. letsfish.net) offers small-scale fishing charters, including bonefishing trips on the flats, which are strictly catch and release, and therefore much more sustainable.

GOLF Blue Bay Golf and Beach Resort (© 599/9-868-1755; www.bluebaygolf.com) provides 18 holes close enough to the Blue Bay Beach that you can leave the spouse and kids there for the day and still meet for lunch at the adjacent restaurant. This par-72 course at 6,815 yards opened in 1999 and takes advantage of the island's natural terrains and arid landscape. Designed by Rocky Roquemore, it's a challenging course, with some holes over water, but it provides stunning views of the Caribbean. Greens fees start at $85, including cart rental. It's open from 7am to 7pm daily.

HORSEBACK RIDING Criadero El Hijo de David, Seru Lora naast 175 (© 599/9-465-1166), can arrange 2-hour tours along scenic trails that pass by Salt-Lakes near Jan Theil Bay for $50, or 3-hour tours to Caracasbaai for $75. It also offers beginner lessons in an outdoor ring. Call ahead for an appointment.

MOUNTAIN BIKING Curaçao hosted the Union Cycliste Internationale's 2006 Mountain Bike World Cup, so it should come as no surprise that the trails here can be pretty challenging. **Wanna Bike** (© 599/9-527-3720; www.wannabike-curacao.net) offers guided tours for riders of all levels. In addition to well-equipped bikes and helmets, the knowledgeable guides provide an insightful historic narrative of key historic sites and ruins. Bike tours lasting from 8am to 11pm cost $32.

arranged through **Eric's ATV Adventures,** Martin Luther King Boulevard across from Lion's Dive (© **599/9-524-7418;** www.curacao-atv.com).The cost for a half-day tour is $90 for a single and $140 for a two-person machine suitable for two adults or one adult and one child. These hefty four-wheel behemoths, reminiscent of a large tractor mower, can take on the steepest and rockiest terrain. The vehicle is relatively easy to operate, if rather loud and extremely hot underneath you. Goggles and helmets are provided. Sunscreen, eye protection, long pants, and closed shoes are highly recommended. A valid U.S. or international driver's license is required, and all drivers must be at least 16 years of age. The **Bike Shop Curaçao,** Sta. Rosawegn 27a (© **599/9-560-3882;** www.thebikeshop.nl), also rents motorcycles and scooters.

---

5 EXPLORING THE ISLAND

Venture out into the countryside and explore the towering cacti and rolling hills topped by *landhuizen* (plantation houses) built more than 3 centuries ago. For those who prefer a guide, contact **Island Tours** (© **599/9-465-2703** or 561-5368; www.petertrips.com). Half- and full-day tours of the island range from $22 to $45, including soft drinks and admission fees.

WILLEMSTAD ★★
Originally founded as Santa Ana by the Spanish in the 1500s, Willemstad was renamed in the 17th century by Dutch traders, who found the natural harbor a perfect hideaway along the Spanish Main. Willemstad's historic pastel-colored, red-roofed town houses and natural harbor are on UNESCO's World Heritage List. Hemmed in by the sea, a tiny canal, and an inlet, the narrow streets are cross-hatched by still narrower alleyways.

Saint Anna Bay runs through the heart of Willemstad. This narrow span belies its natural depth, which is sufficient to allow even cruise ships to berth directly in town. Two bridges span the bay: the pedestrian-only **Queen Emma Bridge,** a pontoon bridge that floats on the water and opens about every half-hour to allow boats to pass by, and the more modern 50m-high (164-ft.) **Queen Juliana Bridge,** which has a four-lane modern highway and is high enough to allow even the most ostentatious mega–cruise ships to sail below.

Orientation
Downtown Willemstad has two central districts on either bank of the bay. **Punda** ("The Point" in Papiamentu) is the name given to the

eastern side, noted for its Dutch colonial architecture that lines the front street, Handelskade. This is the oldest part of town and was the original Dutch settlement where ship merchants built structures that served a dual purpose, with shop and warehouse on the ground floor and residence above. Shaded porches and galleries offered protection from the sun, and ample windows on all stories cooled interiors with cross breezes from the trade winds. Tile floors were also designed to cool rooms off.

The western side of town is called **Otrobanda** ("The Other Bank" in Papiamentu) and is marked by the historic **Rif Fort.** Built to protect the mouth of the bay, the fort was run by the U.S. Army during World War II. Nazi submarines were kept out by a large chain-link net that was drawn across the harbor. Now the fort houses a variety of high-end retail shops and restaurants and is home to the posh **Renaissance Curaçao Resort and Casino.**

Guided Tours

Take the 75-minute **trolley tour,** which visits the city's highlights. The open-sided cars, pulled by a tiny pink "locomotive," make several trips each week. The tours begin at Fort Amsterdam near the Queen Emma Bridge. The cost is $25 for adults, $20 for children 2 to 12. Call ahead (© 599/9-461-0011) for availability.

Walking tours of the city can be arranged as well, and are a nice alternative if the trolley is not operating on the day you are visiting. Contact **Jopi Hart** for a historic walk of Otrobanda (© 599/9-767-3798) or **Eveline van Arkel** (© 599/9-747-4349) in Punda. For a walking tour of the town's architecture, call **Anko van der Woude** (© 599/9-461-3554). **Gigi Scheper** (© 599/9-697-0290) offers 3-hour tours focusing on the Jewish heritage of Willemstad for $55 per person, which includes tours of the Jewish cemetery, the liquor distillery, and more.

What to See

On Otrobanda the architecture is more reflective of a later stage of development and has a stronger Spanish influence. As it was a repository for all types not desirable in Punda, it is more of a jumbled mix of architectural and cultural styles, with narrow streets and winding alleys. The low profile of many buildings was intended to afford a view of the harbor in the event of an attack. Some of this architectural "nonstyle" can be observed in the labyrinth that makes up the historic Hotel Kurá Hulanda (which translates to "Holland Yard" in Papiamentu) complex. After the Queen Emma Bridge was built in 1888, wealthy merchants bought up cheap land on the Otrobanda side and built up lavish mansions. Once in disrepair, many of these historic homes have been preserved and restored.

The **statue of Pedro Luis Brion** dominates the square known as Brionplein, at the Otrobanda end of the pontoon bridge. Born in Curaçao in 1782, Brion became the island's favorite son and best-known war hero. Under Simón Bolívar, he was an admiral and fought for the independence of Venezuela and Colombia.

Fort Amsterdam, site of the Governor's Palace and the 1769 Dutch Reformed Church, guards the waterfront. The church still has a British cannonball embedded in it, and the arches leading to the fort were tunneled under the official residence of the governor.

A few minutes' walk from the pontoon bridge, at the north end of Handelskade, the **Floating Market** features scores of schooners tied up alongside the canal. Boats arrive here from Venezuela and Colombia, and from other West Indian islands, to sell tropical fruits and vegetables, as well as handicrafts. Repeat visitors will note that the faded wooden tarps that once provided shade have been replaced by modern rainbow-hued sun shades.

Near Fort Amsterdam, at the corner of Columbusstraat and Hanchi di Snoa, the **Mikve Israel-Emanuel Synagogue ★** (© 599/ 9-461-1067) dates from 1732 and is the New World's oldest Jewish congregation. Joaño d'Illan led the first Jewish settlers to the island in 1651, almost half a century after their expulsion from Portugal by the Inquisition. Following a Portuguese Sephardic custom, sand covers the sanctuary floor, representing the desert where Israelites camped when the Jews passed from slavery to freedom. It also serves as a reminder of the custom of quieting footsteps with sand while hiding from Germans during World War II. The highlight of the east wall is the Holy Ark, rising 5m (16 ft.); a raised *banca* (balustraded dais), canopied in mahogany, is on the north wall.

Next door, the **Jewish Cultural Historical Museum,** Kuiperstraat 26–28 (© 599/9-461-1633), occupies two buildings dating from 1728. On display are ritual and cultural objects, many dating from the 17th and 18th centuries but still used by the congregation. The synagogue and museum are open Monday through Friday from 9am to 4:30pm. They are closed on High Holidays. Services are Friday at 6:30pm and Saturday at 10am. Admission to both the museum and synagogue is $6, children 12 and under enter free.

Museum Kurá Hulanda ★★, Kipstraat 9 (© 599/9-434-7765), is one of the most unusual and largest museums in the Caribbean. Housed in once-dilapidated 19th-century buildings, the exhibits here reflect the passion of Jacob Gelt Dekker. After making his fortune when he was young, Dekker quickly built up an astounding collection of prehistoric, historic, and cultural artifacts from the Middle East, Africa, and the Americas. His collection includes a life-size reconstruction of a slave ship that once sailed from the Ivory Coast, fossils, wood masks, fertility dolls, stone sculptures, and musical instruments. Guided tours start out slow and unfocused but quickly become fascinating as the dismal history of slave trading on the island comes into focus. Actual and re-created slave quarters house scores of rusted shackles, chains, and other forms of restraint, and the white KKK hoods and cloaks are easily as disturbing as the specters they resemble. On Wednesday evenings a live reenactment of slave trading and subsequent rebellion takes the reality one step further. Hours are daily 10am to 5pm, and the entrance fee is $9 for adults, $7 for students, and $6 for children and seniors.

WEST OF WILLEMSTAD

You can walk the distance inland or take a short cab ride from the Queen Emma Bridge to the sleepy **Curaçao Museum,** Van Leeuwenhoekstraat (© **599/9-462-3873;** www.curacaomuseum.an). Built in 1853 by the Royal Dutch Army Corps of Engineers as a military quarantine hospital, the building has been restored and now houses paintings, art objects, and antique furniture. There's also a large collection of indigenous Amerindian artifacts. It's open Monday to Friday from 8:30am to 4:30pm, and Sunday from 10am to 4pm. Admission is $4.50 for adults, $2.50 for children 11 and under.

The **Maritime Museum,** Van De Brandhof Straat 7 (© **599/9-465-2327;** www.curacaomaritime.com), in the historic Scharloo district, just off the old harbor of Saint Anna Bay, boasts 40 permanent displays that trace Curaçao's history. Admission is $10 for adults, $7 for children 12 to 16, and free for children 11 and under. Hours are Tuesday to Saturday from 9am to 4pm.

On Schottegatweg West, northwest of Willemstad, **Beth Haim Cemetery** is the oldest European burial site still in use in the Western Hemisphere. Consecrated before 1659, the 1.2-hectare (3-acre) site has 2,500 graves, some with exceptional tombstones.

Toward the western tip of Curaçao, a 45-minute drive from Willemstad, 4,500-acre **Christoffel National Park ★★** in Savonet (© **599/9-864-0363**) features cacti, bromeliads, and orchids, as well as the Dutch Leewards' highest point, Saint Christoffelberg (369m/1,211 ft.). Donkeys, wild goats, iguanas, Curaçao deer, and many species of birds thrive in the arid countryside, and Arawak paintings adorn a coral cliff near two caves. The 32km (20 miles) of one-way trail-like roads pass the highlights, but the rough terrain makes even the shortest trail (8km/5 miles) a 40-minute drive. Hiking trails include a 2-hour climb to the summit of **Saint Christoffelberg.** The park is open Monday to Saturday from 7:30am to 4pm and Sunday from 6am to 3pm, but go early, before it gets too hot. The $10 entrance fee includes admission to the one-room museum, which currently houses a few whale skeletons; however, the museum is slated for a complete overhaul.

Next door, the park has opened the **National Park Shete Boka** (Seven Inlets National Park; ✆ **599/9-864-0363**). This turtle sanctuary contains a cave with pounding waves off the choppy north coast. Admission to this park is $3 per person.

To learn more about nature, conservation, and history in Curaçao, and to participate in exciting nature exploration for the whole family, such as deer spotting, a pickup truck safari, or a day hike up the mountain, log onto the **Caribbean Research and Management of Biodiversity Foundation's** website, www.carmabi.org.

NORTH & EAST OF WILLEMSTAD

Just northeast of the capital, **Fort Nassau** was completed in 1797 and christened Fort Republic. Built high on a hill overlooking the harbor entrance to the south and Saint Anna Bay to the north, it was fortified as a second line of defense in case the waterfront gave way.

The **Curaçao Liqueur Distillery,** Landhuis Chobolobo, Saliña Arriba (✆ **599/9-461-3526;** www.curacaoliqueur.com), operates in a 17th-century *landhuis* (villa) where Curaçao's famous liqueur is made. Distilled from dried Curaçaon orange peel, the cordial is spiced with several herbs. The tour, offered Monday to Friday from 8am to noon and 1 to 5pm, ends with a free snifter of the liqueur. Some recently introduced flavors are chocolate, coffee, and rum raisin, but the original orange flavor (regardless of the color) remains a favorite. Another interesting product made from the orange oil is a cooling spray called **Alcolodo Glacial,** which is great to sooth hot skin and ward off insects; it is reputed to have many curative properties.

The **Curaçao Ostrich Farm** (✆ **599/9-747-2777;** www.ostrich farm.net) is one of the largest breeding facilities for these enormous birds outside of Africa. An open-sided safari-style tour bus leaves every hour on the hour to give visitors an up-close and personal introduction to ostriches that range in age from newly hatched chicks to fully plumed adult males. Feeding, petting, and even riding an ostrich may make visitors decide not to sample the ostrich meat served in the adjacent restaurant. The farm is open Tuesday to Sunday 9am to 5pm.

For those who swear by the curative properties of aloe, a visit to the **Aloe Vera Plantation** (✆ **599/9-767-5577;** www.aloecuracao.com) may be just what the doctor ordered. Not surprisingly, all guided tours, which describe the production process from plantation to shelf, conveniently end in the factory gift shop. The plantation is open Monday through Friday 8am to 4pm and Saturday 8am to noon. Admission is free, but you may be inclined to purchase an aloe product even though there is no sales pressure from the friendly staff.

Curaçao Seaquarium ★★, off Dr. Martin Luther King Boulevard at Bapor Kibrá (☎ **599/9-465-6666;** www.curacao-sea-aquarium. com), displays more than 400 species of local marine invertebrates as well as nurse sharks, sea lions, dolphins, and sea turtles. Created in 1984, it is the largest aquarium in the Caribbean and takes advantage of an on-site natural lagoon and coral reef. Located a few minutes' walk along the rocky coast from the Breezes resort, and marked by a looming wooden minesweeper from World War II (wooden so it would not attract the magnetic mines that destroyed steel vessels), the Seaquarium is open daily from 8:30am to 4:30pm. Admission is $19 for adults and $9.50 for children 5 to 12. Special features of the aquarium are sea lion and dolphin encounters, costing $99 to $300 for divers or $39 to $149 for snorkelers. Divers, snorkelers, and experienced swimmers can feed, film, and photograph sharks through a large window with feeding holes, and swim with stingrays, tarpons, and parrotfish in a separate controlled environment, or even do an open-water encounter with dolphins outside their enclosures. The less adventurous can watch a dolphin show and pet marine invertebrates in a kid-friendly touch tank. The Seaquarium also presides over access to Curaçao's nicest full-facility, palm-shaded, white-sand beach.

Note: While swimming with dolphins can be an amazing experience, there are real downsides that you may not learn while at the Seaquarium. One of them is that the dolphins used in Seaquarium's programs were captured from the wild as a result of loopholes in protection of wild species from international trade. Dolphins are often captured through inhumane methods and transported great distances to marine parks and aquariums throughout the world. Furthermore, as a result of national policy, the Seaquarium has been allowed to display wild-caught dolphins on the promise that it is conducting legitimate research on dolphin ecology that will ultimately contribute to their conservation. The problem is that little actual research has been carried out to date. Concerns from the scientific community have also been raised about the damage to wild dolphin populations that are often robbed of key members of their social group through capture proceedings that can leave entire groups vulnerable and disoriented, and relegate once high-ranking wild individuals to a life of servitude and tricks. Log on to **www.wdcs.org** to learn more about threats to wild dolphins.

Guides at the **Hato Caves ★**, F.D. Rooseveltweg (☎ **599/9-868-0379**), take visitors through the stalagmites and stalactites of Curaçao's highest limestone terrace. Featuring an underground lake, large rooms, and ancient Indian petroglyphs, the caves are open daily from 10am to 4pm; admission is $6.50 for adults and $5 for children ages 4 to 11.

6 SHOPPING

Willemstad's shops concentrate along Heerenstraat and Breedestraat in the **Punda** shopping district. Most stores are open Monday through Saturday from 8am to noon and 2 to 6pm (some stay open at midday). When cruise ships are in port, many shops open for a few hours on Sunday and holidays as well.

Good buys include French perfumes, Dutch Delft blue china, Italian silks, Japanese and German cameras, jewelry, watches, linens, leather goods, and liquor, especially Curaçao liqueur. The island is famous for its 2.2-kilogram (5-lb.) wheels of Gouda and Edam cheeses, and you'll also see decorative wooden shoes, lacework, wood-carvings, and paintings from Haiti and the Dominican Republic.

Every garment at **Bamali,** Breedestraat 2 (© **599/9-461-2258**), is designed and, in many cases, crafted by the store owners. Based on Indonesian patterns, the airy women's clothing includes V-neck cotton pullovers and linen shifts.

Boolchand's, Breederstraat 50 (© **599/9-461-6233;** www. boolchand.com), sells cameras and camera accessories as well as other electronics and watches.

Curaçao Creations, Schrijnwerkerstraat 14, off Breedestraat (© **599/9-462-4516**), showcases authentic handicrafts made at the on-site workshop.

Fine watches from nearly every maker plus a wide selection of jewelry can be found at any of **Freeport's** five locations: Handelskade 9, Heerenstraat 25–27 (© **599/9-461-3764**); Handelskade 23 (© **599/9-461-2399**); Heerenstraat 8 (© **599/9-461-5361**); and Heerenstraat 13 (© **599-9/461-2399**).

Little Holland, Breedestraat 37 (© **599/9-461-1768**), reputedly changed hands, but still specializes in silk neckties, Panama hats, Nautica shorts and shirts, Swiss Army knives, and, most important, a sophisticated array of cigars. Crafted in Cuba, the Dominican Republic, and Brazil, they include some of the most prestigious names in smoke, including Montecristos, Cohiba, and Churchills. *Remember:* It's still illegal to bring Cuban cigars into the United States; smoke them here.

As the name implies, **Mr. Tablecloth,** Handelskade 3, on the waterfront (© **599/9-462-9588**), is where the finest linens on the island can be found.

Gandelman Jewelers, Breedestraat 35, Punda (© **599/9-461-1854**), is the island's best and most reliable source for diamonds, rubies, emeralds, sapphires, and other gemstones. You'll also find watches and leather goods at **Baba's Jewelers,** Breedestraat Punda 39 (© **599/9-465-7161**).

For some truly unique nature-inspired jewelry and artistic prints, head over to the boutique called **Maravia** (© **599/9-461-9866;** www.maraviagallery.com) at Handelskade 1 in Punda near the swing bridge.

Penha & Sons, Heerenstraat 1 (© **599/9-461-2266**), is known for perfumes, cosmetics, and designer clothing for men and women.

The **Art of Nena Sanchez** (© **599/9-461-2882;** www.nena sanchez.com) displays the artist's vibrant Caribbean still lifes and striking portraits as well as affordable prints.

Wulfsen & Wulfsen, Wilhelminaplein 1, at the Promenade Shopping Center (© **599/9-461-2302**), sells fashionable ladies' clothing from Germany and Holland and men's shirts in every color of the rainbow.

Zylo, Wilhelminaplein 25 (© **599/9-461-5500**), sells jewelry, perfume, sunglasses, pens, and cosmetics.

In Otrobanda, there are a slew of high-end shops in Rif Fort Village next to the new Renaissance including **Brietling, Tiffany,** and a **Little Switzerland.**

8

7 CURAÇAO AFTER DARK

The large population and diverse culture mean that Curaçao's nightlife is without a doubt the best in the ABC islands. The best time of year to visit for the die-hard reveler is during Carnival, which runs for several weeks, ending on Mardi Gras, and features about two dozen parades through the main streets of Willemstad. During this time, the sides of the road are lined with chairs and makeshift spectator stands. The parade route is about 5km (3 miles) long, and the seemingly endless parties start early and end late.

During the rest of the year, the island nightlife works on a time-share system: Each club has its unofficial "night" when the crowds gather under its roof and the fun lasts long into the early morning hours. Pick up a copy of the weekly dining and entertainment guide *K-Pasa* at any tourism office or hotel lobby, or log on to www.k-pasa. com to find out what's happening where.

Because the island is densely populated with a happy, social bunch of locals, the nightlife scene is geared for the residents as well as the tourists. The hot spots move around like shifting dunes, and the locals all have their fingers on the pulse of each evening's beat. The **Salinja** district is the heart of Curaçao nightlife, but ask a Curaçaoan for the best place to go on any given night. If so inclined, you can stay out late and dance till dawn to great live music. The local brothel even has a ladies' night that's apparently quite popular among local women and men.

One of the island's best and most memorable venues is **Blues,** a restaurant and bar (see "Where to Dine," earlier in this chapter) in the Avila Beach Hotel, Penstraat 130 (© 599/9-461-4377). Perched over the water, this tiny treehouse of a bar is packed every night except Monday, when it is closed. Live jazz plays Thursday from 10pm to midnight and Saturday from 9pm to 1:30am—and you won't ever have to pay a cover charge. **Mambo Beach,** at the **Seaquarium Beach** (© 599/9-461-8999; www.mambobeach.com), features food, music, and a great beach bar that, on slow nights, shows classic movies under the stars a mere stone's throw from the water. Sunday night is salsa night, and the place is usually packed. While the revelry can be heard and seen from the far end of the **Breezes resort,** unless you are a good swimmer, it's a long walk or a short cab ride to this perennial hot spot. Another longtime favorite, especially for happy hour, is **Hook's Hut** (© 599/9-462-6575; www.hookshut.com), on the beach of the same name at Piscaderabaai z/n. **Asia de Cuba,** Zuikertuintjeweg z/n (© 599/9-747-9009), has live Cuban music and a Pan-Asian decor and cuisine. Grab a *mojito* and belly up to a high-top table near the dance floor to watch the locals as they show off Latin moves so good you'll think you're in old Havana. The **Sopranos Piano Bar,** in Rif Fort Village (© 599/9-567-0007; www.sopranospianobar.com), has nightly dancing, cocktails, and live music. The bar is open from noon to 3am (or later).

You'll find plenty of gaming action in the island's **casinos.** The fun usually starts at 2pm, and some places stay open until 4am. The **Princess Casino** at the **Breezes Curaçao resort,** Dr. Martin Luther King Blvd. 8 (© 599/9-736-7888), is the liveliest on the island. The **Emerald Casino,** at the Curaçao Marriott Beach Resort, Piscadera Bay (© 599/9-736-8800), features 149 slot machines, six blackjack tables, two roulette wheels, two Caribbean stud poker tables, and a craps table. The **Holiday Beach Hotel & Casino,** Pater Euwensweg 31, Otrobanda (© 599/9-462-5400), also offers gaming. The newest and flashiest casino on the island is the **Carnaval Casino** (© 599/9-435-5087) at the **Renaissance Curaçao Resort and Casino,** which features flashing lights and noise from the slot machines (including hilarious themes such as Betti the Yetti and Revenge of the Moolah, featuring cows in spaceships). Nightly live music is a nice touch.

9

A Taste of Bonaire

Eighty kilometers (50 miles) north of Venezuela and 138km (86 miles) east of Aruba, Bonaire is the "B" of the ABC islands. There's no better place to find out what's going on under the Caribbean's azure waters than this "Diver's Paradise," as the island's license plate boasts. Bonaire is slightly larger than Aruba, just 39km (24 miles) long and 5 to 11km (3–7 miles) wide. Bonaire has none of Aruba's glitzy diversions, but avid divers have flocked to this unspoiled treasure for years. With its pristine waters, stunning coral reefs encircling the island just feet from shore, and vibrant marine life, Bonaire is one of the best places in the Caribbean for both diving and snorkeling.

The island also offers hiking, mountain biking, kayaking, and first-rate windsurfing and kiteboarding. Bonaire has some of the Caribbean's best bird-watching and it's also one of the best places to spot the endangered and highly protected sea turtles.

The 15,000 people of Bonaire claim Dutch, South American, and African roots. Bonaire along with Curaçao, Sint Maarten, Sint Eustatius, and Saba form the Netherland Antilles. These are represented on the Bonairan flag as five stars (once six but Aruba ceded in the mid-1980s). Bonaire, along with the remaining stars, remains a formal part of the Netherlands and its lieutenant governor is appointed directly by the queen of the Netherlands.

1 ESSENTIALS

VISITOR INFORMATION

Before you go, contact the **Bonaire Government Tourist Office** (or TCB for short; ✆ **800/BONAIRE** [266-2473]) or check out their informative website, **www.tourismbonaire.com**, for links to other helpful sites. On the island, the **Tourism Corporation Bonaire** is at Kaya Grandi 2 in Kralendijk (*crawl*-en-dike), the capital and major town (✆ **599/717-8322**).

Pick up a copy of *Bonaire Affair, Bonaire Nights,* and *Bonaire Dining Guide* and *Bonaire Update* for information on where to

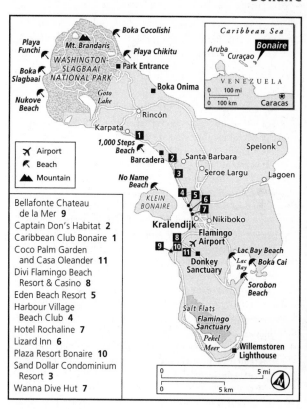

Legend:
- ✈ Airport
- ⌐ Beach
- ▲ Mountain

Bellafonte Chateau
de la Mer **9**
Captain Don's Habitat **2**
Caribbean Club Bonaire **1**
Coco Palm Garden
and Casa Oleander **11**
Divi Flamingo Beach
Resort & Casino **8**
Eden Beach Resort **5**
Harbour Village
Beach Club **4**
Hotel Rochaline **7**
Lizard Inn **6**
Plaza Resort Bonaire **10**
Sand Dollar Condominium
Resort **3**
Wanna Dive Hut **7**

shop, play, eat, and stay. The *Bonaire Dive Guide* provides up-to-date information on the best dive and snorkel sites.

GETTING THERE

The airlines in Bonaire change with alarming frequency, so call the **airport** directly (℗ **599/717-5600**) to confirm your carrier. Be aware that flights between Bonaire and Aruba are considered international so whether you are flying back to Aruba or home, you will be charged a $35 airport tax upon departure.

Currently **DAE** (℗ **599/717-0808;** www.flydae.com) connects Aruba and Bonaire by air. All flights stop in Curaçao with several departures per day. The entire journey takes about 1½ hours. Two

Frommer's Favorite Bonaire Experiences

- **Dive, dive, dive.** This will spoil you for all other dive experiences. Every dive operator is top-rate, so go with the one closest to your resort for convenience's sake. Some of the best diving is near Klein Bonaire, and boat dives are easier than navigating the roads and rocky shores on your own. Try a night dive to see the reef in an entirely new light (or lack thereof).

- **Snorkle with scads of sea turtles.** Not a diver? No problem. Don a mask and flippers and meet Captain Mike at Karel's Beach Bar. He'll take you to the best turtle snorkel spot in the Caribbean with an expert turtle spotting guide. I lost track after my sixth sighting of these graceful beauties, and that was after only half an hour in the water!

- **Dally with the darling donkeys.** Where else can you get so much lovin' from so many furry admirers? The donkey sanctuary is a veritable hotbed of happy donkeys whose only goal in life is to stick their nose in your face and say hello. Young and old alike can't resist the urge to smile, pat, and giggle when bombarded by a bustling band of bold burros.

- **Marvel at the mangroves.** Kayaking through the unspoiled mangrove forest and exploring this unique ecosystem is a relaxing yet exhilarating way to spend an active afternoon. Snorkels and fins allow you to really see what goes on beneath the surface. Keep an eye out for birds, crabs, fish, and snails.

- **Descend into the darkest depths.** Inside the many caves that permeate the island, stalactites and stalagmites come in fanciful shapes while new formations sparkle like a mountain of sugar crystals. The occasional bat adds to the excitement; and if you do some cave snorkeling, you'll get to meet the friendly shrimp that reign in this kingdom.

other local carriers serving the ABC islands are **Tiara Air** (© 599/717-3008; www.tiara-air.com) and **Insel Air** (© 599/717-2004; www.fly-inselair.com), so compare rates and schedules. **Continental Airlines** (© 800/231-0856; www.continental.com) flies nonstop from Newark and Houston to Bonaire on weekends during the high season. Through its American Eagle subsidiary, **American Airlines** (© 800/433-7300; www.aa.com) has nonstop service from San Juan, Puerto Rico, on Tuesday, Thursday, and Saturday.

BY RENTAL CAR Bonaire is flat, and the roads are fine, except for the rocky trails in the outback and in Washington-Slagbaai National Park, where a four-wheel-drive vehicle is a must. Highway signs are in Dutch and English, with easy-to-understand international symbols. Driving is on the right, and a valid driver's license is all that's needed to rent and drive a car. Car-rental agencies include **Avis** (© 800/230-4898 in the U.S., or 599/717-4700; www.avis.com), **Budget** (© 800/527-0700 in the U.S., or 599/717-4700; www.budget.com), or **Hertz** (© 800/654-3001 in the U.S., or 599/717-7221 or 717-6020; www.hertz.com). Rates start at $40 per day, $60 to $70 for a four-wheel-drive vehicle.

Island Car Rentals, Flamingo Airport 12 (© **599/717-2100;** www. islandcarrentalbonaire.com), rents soft-top jeeps for $24 a day. Your valid U.S., British, or Canadian driver's license is acceptable for driving jeeps on Bonaire. You must be between the ages of 25 and 70 to rent a car. Remember to drive on the right and keep an eye out for goats, chickens, and donkeys that frequently dart out in front of cars.

BY TAXI The set fare from the airport to most hotels is $9 to $20 regardless of whether you are one person or four. Fares increase by 50% after midnight. Most drivers give tours of the island for $25 per hour for up to four people. For more information, call **Taxi Central Dispatch** (© **599/717-8100**).

BY SCOOTER, MOTORCYCLE, OR ATV If you're not venturing too far, scooters and mopeds are practical alternatives. At the **Bike Shop,** J.A. Abraham Blvd. 30 (© **599/560-7000;** www.thebikeshop. nl), scooters are $18 a day; and two seaters are $38 per day. **Bonaire Motorcycle Shop,** Kaya Grandi 52 (© **599/717-7790**), offers Harley-Davidson motorcycles and three-wheel bikes for rent, and off-road island tours via ATV.

Fast Facts   Bonaire

Banks Banks are open Monday through Friday from 8am until 4pm. ATMs are along Kaya Grandi in Kralendijk and at the airport.

Currency Bonaire's official currency is the Netherlands Antillean florin (NAf), but the U.S. dollar is as widely accepted as the local currency. The exchange rate is 1.78 florins to US$1 (NAf 1 = 56¢). Most stores and businesses convert at 1.75 florins to the dollar. Traveler's checks and credit cards are widely accepted, though American Express and Diners Club are not as popular as Visa and MasterCard, while Discover is gaining popularity. Prices throughout this chapter are given in U.S. dollars.

Electricity Bonaire's electricity (127 volts/50 cycles) is slightly different from North America's (110 volts/60 cycles). Most North American appliances function without a transformer but older ones may run warm or burn out if left plugged in for a long time. *Warning:* Electrical current used to feed or recharge finely calibrated diving equipment should be stabilized with a specially engineered electrical stabilizer. Every diving operation on the island has one of these as part of its standard equipment for visiting divers.

Emergencies Call ☎ **911** for the police or ☎ **912** for an ambulance.

Hospital **San Francisco Hospital,** Kaya Soeur Bartola 2, Kralendijk (☎ **599/717-8900**), has a hyperbaric recompression chamber and handles most emergencies, but an evacuation plane provides backup.

Internet Access Most hotels have Wi-Fi in the lobby and many have it in the guest rooms too. **Chat 'n' Browse,** in the Sand Dollar Shopping Plaza (☎ **599/717-2281;** www.chatnbrowse.com), as well as **Bonaire Access,** in Harborside Mall (☎ **599/717-6040**), provide access for about $10 per hour.

Language English is widely spoken, but you'll hear Dutch (the official language), Spanish, and Papiamento (the tongue spoken in Aruba).

Safety Bonaire is safe, but keep an eye on your valuables and use your hotel's safe.

Taxes Virtually all goods and services are subject to a 5% tax. A room tax of $5.50 to $6.50 per person per day is also charged. Upon leaving Bonaire, you'll be charged an airport departure tax of $35.

Telephone To call Bonaire from the United States, dial **011** (the international access code), **599** (the country code), **717** (the area code), and then the four-digit local number. On Bonaire, dial **717** plus the four-digit local number only. It's often difficult to make international and toll-free calls from hotel rooms, and lines aren't always clear. If you're having a problem, contact **TELBO** (☎ **599/717-7000**), the central phone company on Kaya

Libertador Simón Bolívar. The direct-dial access number for **AT&T** is ✆ **916/843-4685** from your cellphone and ✆ **800-8000** from pay phones; for **Verizon** it's ✆ **800-8888.** You can reach a **Sprint/Nextel** operator throughout the Caribbean at ✆ **011-817/698-4199.** Check with your carrier before you leave home to find out if your phone will work on the island and be sure to check the fees, which are about $2 per minute. **Prepaid phone cards** can be purchased from convenience stores. **Cellphone rentals** go for about $5 per day plus the cost of minutes. There is a $200 deposit. Local calls cost about 40¢ per minute and international calls run about 60¢ per minute. Allegedly, you won't be billed for incoming cellphone calls. **Bonaire Access** has an office in the **Harborside Mall** (✆ **599/717-6040**) but the best place to rent is **Chat'n'Browse** (✆ **599/717-2281**). You can also buy phone cards and make international calls from **Chippie,** a local cellphone carrier in town.

Time Bonaire is on Atlantic Standard Time year-round, 1 hour ahead of Eastern Standard Time and the same as Eastern daylight saving time. Due to the difference in electrical current, U.S. clocks may run slow and PDA's won't always update to local time.

Tipping Tipping is much the same as in the U.S., with some restaurants adding a 10% to 15% service charge automatically. Tip taxi drivers and dive masters 10%.

Water Drinking tap water is perfectly safe.

2 WHERE TO STAY

VERY EXPENSIVE

Harbour Village Beach Club ★★   Easily Bonaire's most luxurious resort, Harbour Village caters to an ultra-upscale clientele. The cluster of Dutch Caribbean–style one- and two-bedroom suites rests in lush tropical gardens bordered by a sandy beach and picturesque marina. Most guests come from the U.S., many to dive but a good number come to pamper themselves at the spa, which boasts a comprehensive array of massages and other treatments. Each suite has a spacious balcony or terrace (with hammock) and beach or marina views. The stylish rooms boast teak and rattan furniture and four-poster beds. Other features include commodious closets, large glass-enclosed showers, separate claw-foot tubs, an iPod docking station, and fully equipped kitchens with state-of-the-art appliances. Another plus: The resort is never packed so there's ample peace and quiet.

Kaya Gobernador N. Debrot 71, Bonaire, N.A. ℂ **800/424-0004** in the U.S. and Canada, or 599/717-7500. Fax 599/717-7507. www.harbourvillage.com. 42 units. Early Jan to mid-Apr $330 courtyard room, $365 marina-front room, $590 beachfront 1-bedroom suite, $805 beachfront 2-bedroom suite; mid-Apr to late Dec $275 courtyard room, $295 marina-front room, $460 beachfront 1-bedroom suite, $645 beachfront 2-bedroom suite; Dec 19–Jan 3 $385 courtyard room, $415 marina-front room, $645 beachfront 1-bedroom suite, $855 beachfront 2-bedroom suite. Children 15 and under stay free in parent's room. Packages available. AE, DISC, MC, V. **Amenities:** Restaurant; bar; babysitting; bike rentals; fitness center & spa; outdoor pool; smoke-free rooms; 4 tennis courts lit for night play; resident tennis pro; watersports; clubhouse; member's lounge; marina. *In room:* A/C, TV, fridge, hair dryer, microwave, Wi-Fi (in suite).

Plaza Resort Bonaire ★ Bonaire's only large-scale resort, the Plaza sprawls over nearly 5 hectares (12 acres) of tropical grounds bordered by a saltwater lagoon and a long stretch of natural beach. The nine two-story buildings have white walls and terra-cotta roofs, creating a sunny village connected by a pair of bridges that cross the lagoon, the site of a full-service dive and boat shop. The sparsely appointed rooms have terra-cotta tile floors, rattan furniture, and spacious balconies or terraces that emphasize the tropical locale. Although the units referred to as "suites" have no room dividers, they boast 56 to 65 sq. m (603–700 sq. ft.) of space. Suites feature fridges, and the larger one- and two-bedroom villas boast kitchenettes. All units have grand bathrooms, with the toilet located in a separate "water closet."

J.A. Abraham Blvd. 80, Bonaire, N.A. ℂ **800/766-6016** in the U.S. and Canada, or 599/717-2500. Fax 599/717-7133. www.plazaresortbonaire.com. 174 units. Jan 2–Apr 9 $240–$270 suite, $290 1-bedroom villa, $370 2-bedroom villa; Apr 10–Dec 18 $190–$220 suite, $230 1-bedroom villa, $300 2-bedroom villa; Dec 19–Jan 1 $280–$300 suite, 1-bedroom villa $320, 2-bedroom villa $390. Packages available. Children 12 and under stay free in parent's room. AE, MC, V. **Amenities:** 3 restaurants; bar; babysitting; bike and scooter rentals; children's program; concierge; exercise room; large outdoor pool; children's pool; room service; spa; 4 tennis courts lit for night play; dive and watersports center; rooms for those w/limited mobility. *In room:* A/C, TV, hair dryer (on request), kitchenette (in some).

EXPENSIVE

Bellafonte Chateau de la Mer As you enter the courtyard, you are greeted by a *bella fonte* (beautiful fountain) surrounded by three-story buildings that replicate a small Mediterranean villa. Though it is on the waterfront, the hotel has no beach—only a pool and a long pier over the water good for sunbathing and swimming in the sea below. Except for its pool, it lacks the amenities of the larger resorts, but is a bastion of comfort, style, and grace in all other respects. The rooms are decorated with taste and a sense of glamour, with teak wood and stainless steel. The limited space and lack of guardrails indicate that the destination is more suited to couples than families. The richly appointed units with balconies or terraces will lure honeymooners whose desire is to relax and escape from the crowds.

EEG Blvd. 10, Bonaire, N.A. (𝓒 **599/717-3333.** Fax 599/717-8581. www.bellafonte bonaire.com. 22 units. Dec 12–Apr 9 $145–$275 double, $325 2-bedroom suite; Apr 10–Dec 11 $125–$235 double, $275 2-bedroom suite. AE, DISC, MC, V. **Amenities:** Outdoor pool; Jacuzzi; grocery service. In room: A/C, TV, kitchen, free Wi-Fi.

Captain Don's Habitat ★   Built on a coral bluff overlooking the sea just north of Kralendijk, this informal, congenial dive resort was created by Captain Don Stewart, Caribbean legend, former Californian, and the godfather of Bonaire's passionate protection of its marine environment. More than 90% of guests come on vacation-length dive packages, so side-trip stays of 1 or 2 nights are hard to arrange. The accommodations, which include cottages and one- and two-bedroom villas, are bright and airy. Some have a balcony or patio, many feature fully equipped kitchens, and some have phones. All rooms have air-conditioning. The resort's tiny beach is good for snorkeling, and the on-site **Intermezzio Day Spa** (𝓒 **599/717-8290**) is great for relaxing. One-hour massages, body wraps, or facials start at only $75.

Kaya Gobernador N. Debrot 103, Bonaire, N.A. (𝓒 **800/327-6709** in the U.S. and Canada, or 599/717-8290. Fax 599/717-8240. www.habitatbonaire.com. 63 units. Dec 19–Mar 31 $190–$259 double; Apr 1–Dec 18 $149–$216 double. Children 11 and under stay free in parent's room. AE, DISC, MC, V. **Amenities:** Restaurant; pizza bar; outdoor bar; babysitting; outdoor pool; free Wi-Fi throughout the property; dive center; rooms for those w/limited mobility. In room: A/C, TV, hair dryer (on request), no phone (in some).

Divi Flamingo Beach Resort & Casino ★   Divi is the comeback kid, having reinvented itself after a massive restoration that began at the beginning of the millennium. Modern furnishings, paint, tiles, and rejuvenated air-conditioning have made this once-tired waterfront hostelry more comfortable than it's been in years. Originally a cluster of flimsy wooden bungalows used to intern German prisoners during World War II, today the resort consists of individual cottages and seafront rooms with private balconies. These accommodations rest on piers above the surf so you can stand on your balcony and watch rainbow-hued tropical fish in the waters below. The resort's original rooms are supplemented timeshare units, forming Club Flamingo. These are the best accommodations, and each can be rented by the day or week. The timeshare units are clustered in a neo-Victorian pavilion facing a curving pool, and each comes with a kitchenette. The two on-site restaurants, Chibi-Chibi and Calabas, provide satisfying, straightforward meals featuring fresh local seafood and Continental specialties.

J.A. Abraham Blvd. 40, Bonaire, N.A. ℂ **800/367-3484** in the U.S. and Canada, or 599/717-8285. Fax 599/717-8238. www.diviflamingo.com. 129 units. Dec–Apr $165–$199 double, $219 studio; May–Nov $125–$149 double, $165 studio. Children 14 and under stay free in parent's room. Packages available. AE, DISC, MC, V. **Amenities:** 2 restaurants; 2 bars; babysitting; casino; fitness center; 2 outdoor pools; spa; rooms for those w/limited mobility. *In room:* A/C, TV.

MODERATE

Caribbean Club Bonaire
This small resort complex nestled in the rugged green hills is perfect for those who want to mix diving and watersports with bird-watching, kayaking, biking, or caving. The charming villas were originally built as a brothel for employees of an oil company that was never opened. The rooms are clean and cheerful with very private porches or balconies. A communal room offers reading material and the opportunity to socialize, and the outdoor veranda is used for group gatherings as well. Since the hotel is well off the beaten track, car rental is necessary; ask about dive and explore packages that include a car rental.

Blvd. Santa Barbara 50 (north of Kralendijk), Bonaire, N.A. ℂ **800/906-7708** in the U.S. or 599/717-7901. Fax 599/717-7900. www.caribbeanclubbonaire.com. 33 units. Dec 19–Apr 10 $70–$90 studio, $89–$99 1-bedroom cottage, $128 2-bedroom cottage; Apr 11–Dec 18 $60–$80 studio, $79–$89 1-bedroom cottage, $108 2-bedroom cottage. AE, MC, V. **Amenities:** Restaurant; bar; pool. *In room:* A/C, TV, free Wi-Fi.

Eden Beach Resort ★ (Kids)
Located directly on one of Bonaire's nicer beaches, this tiny resort provides all the essentials and more at a price that's right. The clean and spacious rooms, studios, and apartments feature simple decor; tile floors; a functional, well-equipped kitchen; and plenty of comfort. Most units have their own private porch or terrace and are only steps away from the beach, pool, patio, restaurant, and bar. A dive shop is located on the premises and an activity center offers bike, kayak, and windsurf rentals.

Kaya Gobernador Nicolaas Debrot 73, Bonaire, N.A. ℂ **599/717-6720.** Fax 599/717-6710. www.edenbeach.com. 46 units. Apr 16–Dec 14 $130 studio, $140 1 bedroom, $220 2 bedroom; Dec 15–Apr 15 $140 studio, $150 1 bedroom, $220 2 bedroom. AE, MC, V. **Amenities:** Restaurant; bar; babysitting; fitness center; pool. *In room:* A/C, TV, kitchen.

Sand Dollar Condominium Resort ★ (Kids)
The comfortable, casual Sand Dollar is a favorite with repeat visitors. Almost all guests are from the U.S., and the hotel's extensive children's programs attract

families. Decor varies in each of the individually owned studios and in the one-, two-, and three-bedroom apartments. All units feature a terrace or balcony, full kitchen, and good-size bedrooms, but no phones. The huge bathrooms in the larger units have showers and tubs. At high tide, water engulfs the tiny beach, but most people are here to dive, and the resort's dive shop is one of the island's best. The on-site tour operator offers an array of island adventures.

Kaya Gobernador N. Debrot 79, Bonaire, N.A. © **800/288-4773** in the U.S. and Canada, or 599/717-8738. Fax 599/717-8760. www.sanddollarbonaire.com. 75 units. Dec–Apr $198 double, $208 1 bedroom, $288 2 bedroom, $369 3 bedroom; May–Nov $168 double, $193 1 bedroom, $233 2 bedroom, $356 3 bedroom. Children 11 and under stay free in parent's room. Packages available. AE, DISC, MC, V. **Amenities:** Restaurant; 2 bars; babysitting; bike rentals; children's program; outdoor pool; 2 tennis courts lit for night play; watersports/rentals. *In room:* A/C (in bedrooms only), ceiling fans, TV, kitchen, no phone.

INEXPENSIVE

Coco Palm Garden & Casa Oleander   Although this "self-catering" assemblage of studios and villas has few amenities, it offers attractive dive, windsurfing, and adventure packages in a quiet residential area. The large rooms feature bright yellow walls, Southwestern accents, rattan furniture, tile floors, and plenty of privacy. Each unit has its own private porch and garden space with sun bed and hammock, as well as a full kitchen. Only bedrooms have air-conditioning, and the only TV is at the bar. Beaches for swimming, snorkeling, and scuba diving are a 5-minute walk away.

Kaya Statius van Eps 9, Bonaire, N.A. © **599/717-2108.** Fax 599/717-8193. www. cocopalmgarden.org. 10 units. $66–$76 studio; $76–$86 1 bedroom; $96 2 bedroom; $116 4 bedroom year-round. Children 11 and under stay for $10 in parent's room. Dive and windsurf packages available. AE, DISC, MC, V. **Amenities:** Restaurant; bar; babysitting; pool. *In room:* A/C, kitchen.

Hotel Rochaline   Located in the heart of town and attached to the popular City Café, the Rochaline is Bonaire's take on an urban backpacker/youth hostel. (The name is a merging of the names of the owner's four children.) The rooms upstairs are sparse but clean. Noise from festivities below can be an issue, so bring earplugs if you are a light sleeper. There is a dive shop next door, and ample dining and shopping options nearby.

Kaya Grandi 7, Bonaire, N.A. © **599/717-8286** or 717-8286. Fax 599/717-6060. www.hotelrochaline.com. 17 units. $60 single; $69 double year-round. AE, DISC, MC, V. **Amenities:** Restaurant; bar. *In room:* A/C, TV.

Lizard Inn   This whitewashed compound is in a residential neighborhood. The clientele is mainly Dutch, Aruban, Curaçaoan, and Venezuelan; it's also popular among backpackers and budget travelers.

The rooms feel somewhat stark, though they are immaculately clean. The abundant hot water and extensive cable channels are definite highlights. Single and double rooms at this one-story complex all open onto a central thatch-roofed patio and pool. Studios offer full kitchenettes.

Kaya America 14, Bonaire, N.A. ⓒ **599/717-6877.** Fax 599/786-0277. www.lizard innbonaire.com. 12 units. $65 double; $80 studio year-round. Packages available. Children 11 and under stay free in parent's room. AE, MC, V. **Amenities:** Limited food and beverage menu; Wi-Fi. *In room:* A/C, TV, fridge.

Wanna Dive Hut Bonaire Don't expect more than the bare essentials—the basic accommodations in this tiny three-level budget complex are intended for those who come here primarily to dive. The large rooms with tile floors each open onto an outdoor walkway via large sliding-glass doors. Apartments have two bedrooms and are fully furnished, but have no hot water for your post-dive shower. Beaches for swimming, snorkeling, and scuba diving are a 10-minute walk away.

Kaya Gobernador N. Debrot z/n, Bonaire, N.A. ⓒ **599/717-8850** or 786-8850. Fax 599/717-8860. www.wannadivehutbonaire.com. 14 units. $60–$70 double; $80 apt year-round. Dive packages available. AE, DISC, MC, V. **Amenities:** Restaurant; bar; dive center. *In room:* A/C, TV, fridge, Wi-Fi.

3 WHERE TO DINE

While most restaurants on this island serve up gourmet meals, the atmosphere is always friendly and relaxed. While some things such as french fries are clearly frozen, you can't go wrong if you opt for local favorites or the chef's specials. Most desserts are homemade.

> ### ⓘ Tips Sustainable Eating
>
> Due to the decline of local species, many restaurants have made a choice to stop serving Caribbean lobster and conch. It's also recommended that reef fish (such as grouper, snapper, and grunt) be avoided—even if the server tells you its okay. Tasty, fresh, and ecofriendy alternatives are pelagic species that live out in open water, such as dorado, wahoo, and barracuda. If seafood isn't your game, don't be afraid to try some local goat cheese or goat stew; while cute, the island's goats are quite abundant!

Capriccio ★★ NORTHERN ITALIAN   One of Bonaire's most popular restaurants, Capriccio has served impeccably fresh Northern Italian cuisine on the harborfront for almost 30 years. Originally from Padua and Milan, the restaurateurs offer savory salads, homemade pastas, straight-from-the-oven focaccia, and thin-crust pizzas. More-substantial fare includes flavorful mahimahi braised in onion, olives, and sun-dried tomatoes or braised duck in port-wine sauce. The 8,000-bottle wine cellar holds Italian, Californian, and French vintages, and the grappa and brandy list, although not as extensive, is formidable. Dining areas include an alfresco terrace, a cozy air-conditioned interior bathed in flickering candlelight, and elevated dimly lit alcoves for special occasions.

Kaya Isla Riba 1, Kralendijk. ✆ 599/717-7230. www.emporiocapriccio.com. Reservations recommended. Main courses $20–$25; pizzas and pastas $10–$21. AE, MC, V. Mon and Wed–Sat noon–2pm and 6:30–10:30pm; Sun 6:30–10:30pm.

It Rains Fishes ★ SEAFOOD   At the far end of the strip, you can't (and shouldn't) miss this chic restaurant with a South Beach vibe, which is both relaxed and elegant. The seafood is impeccably fresh and always prepared to order. The Japanese salad with fresh tuna, spinach, avocado, and wasabi ginger dressing is a healthy treat while the garlic shrimp (peeled or unpeeled) are a sinful indulgence.

Kaya Jan N.E. Craane 24. ✆ 599/717-8780. www.itrainsfishesbonaire.com. Main courses $18–$32. AE, MC, V. Daily 5–11pm.

La Balandra INTERNATIONAL/SEAFOOD   Shaped like a Spanish schooner and dangling over the water right next to an exclusive beach, this outdoor restaurant exudes a romantic ambience. Menu highlights include seared tuna crusted in sesame seeds with wasabi cream or wild boar tenderloin. For dessert, indulge in the warm chocolate cake. To go over the top, a private candlelight dinner can be arranged upon request.

Kaya Gobernador N. Debrot 71, at the Harbour Village Beach Club. ✆ 599/717-7500. Reservations recommended. Main courses $20–$29. AE, MC, V. Daily 7:30–10:30am, noon–3pm, and 7–10:30pm.

Mona Lisa FRENCH/INTERNATIONAL   This popular restaurant, tucked away in the shopping district and barely noticeable when passing by, makes fresh French food with generous portions. Perennial favorites include the French onion soup, fresh seafood such as wahoo, or meat dishes like rack of lamb and sirloin steak. The dark bar has an old-world European feel and is frequented by local, Dutch, and Caribbean diners alike.

Kaya Grandi 15. ✆ 599/717-8717. Reservations recommended. Main courses $17–$27. AE, MC, V. Restaurant Mon–Fri 6–10pm. Bar Mon–Fri 4pm–2am.

Sunset Bar and Grill SEAFOOD   Located next to the Sand Dollar Condominium Resort, the tables are set on a breezy terrace where you can watch the waves hit the small beach or watch the ethereal underwater glow as night divers emerge from the sea with their powerful lamps. The restaurant is relatively new but its owner is a veteran restaurateur on the island and makes it his goal to serve some of the freshest seafood in Bonaire. There are also meat and vegetarian options. The local goat-cheese fritters will make you thank those pesky critters, and the beef carpaccio is top-notch. Follow with a trio of seafood brochette in smoked tomato and crab butter sauce or fresh tuna steak prepared to order (try it blackened for a spicy option). Select from the extensive wine list that includes bottles from almost every continent. Cheesecake topped with passion-fruit coulis ends the meal on a tangy note.

Kaya Gobernador N. Debrot 77, Kralendijk. ✆ **599/788-2698.** Main courses $17–$31. DISC, MC, V. Thurs–Tues 11:30am–3pm and 5–10pm.

MODERATE

Casablanca Argentine Grill ARGENTINE STEAKHOUSE   This restaurant is known for its steaks, including a mixed grill for two, and every meal comes with a hefty side of rice, potatoes, and vegetables. Be sure to come hungry and be prepared to ask for a doggy bag to take home the leftovers. Locals abound and all prefer the outdoor seating, though indoor air-conditioned tables are also available. A wide selection of wines is offered.

J.A. Abraham Blvd. 6. ✆ **599/717-4433.** www.restaurantcasablanca.com. Main courses $14–$31. MC, V. Sun–Mon 6–10:30pm; Tues–Sat 11:30am–2:30pm and 6–10:30pm.

La Guernica Fish and Tapas TAPAS/SEAFOOD   Specializing in tapas and seafood, this chic corner restaurant has seating indoors and out as well as casual lounge seating. The hacienda decor blends well in the 150-year-old architecture. Tapas with an Italian flair and fried calamari make for a good appetizer or main course. Then again, why not try the coconut shrimp with ginger sauce or the fresh tuna sashimi?

Kaya Bonaire 4C. ✆ **599/717-5022.** Reservations recommended. Main courses $19–$23. AE, MC, V. Daily 11am–5pm and 6–11pm.

The Lion's Den Beach Bar and Restaurant INTERNATIONAL   This outdoor restaurant corners the market when it comes to great views. Here, you can gaze out over both the sea and the stars as you dine. The grilled shrimp and asparagus in lemon butter sauce is a rich yet tasty starter. The Bombay duo of shrimp and scallops is in a sweet, creamy curry sauce and served over a mountain of pasta. The grilled fish with delicious homemade pesto is served with roasted root vegetables that are surprisingly light and flavorful. The Key lime pie is creamier than most and not too tart.

Kaya Gobernador Debrot 77, at Buddy Dive Resort. ✆ **599/788-2698.** www. buddydive.com. Main courses $9–$31. DISC, MC, V. Daily 5–10pm.

INEXPENSIVE

Bistro De Paris FRENCH   This tiny roadside restaurant with indoor and outdoor seating has a casual European feel. The sandwiches are made on fresh-baked bread, the salads are fresh and flavorful, and the main courses add a healthy twist to traditional French recipes, with plenty of vegetarian options. The apple tarte tatin, with caramelized sugar and served a la mode, is exquisite.

Kaya Gobernador N. Debrot 46. ✆ **599/717-7070.** Main courses $10–$22. AE, MC, V. Mon–Sat 11am–3pm and 6–10pm.

Kon Tiki ★ (Finds) INTERNATIONAL   If you're headed to Lac Bay to windsurf, make a point of stopping at this charming oasis in Bonaire's outback. Kon Tiki offers casual dining at its best: beach-bum cheerful decor, pleasant ambience, stunning vistas, cool breezes, and scrumptious food. On a hot day, wash down a smoked-salmon sandwich with a mango shake. The dinner menu changes frequently and features vegetarian pastas, Argentine steak, and fresh seafood; a special menu caters to kids. The deep-fried crispy crepe with hot chocolate sauce is as good as the Dutch apple pie with vanilla ice cream. Regularly, local artists hold exhibitions at Kon Tiki and several times a year local musicians play on the outdoor patio.

Kaminda Sorobon 64, Sorobon. ✆ **599/717-5369.** www.kontikibonaire.com. Dinner reservations recommended. Dinner main courses $8–$20. MC, V. Daily 8am–10pm.

Le Flamboyant INTERNATIONAL   After an arduous afternoon of shopping, duck into this eclectic storefront boutique to uncover the hidden gem of a restaurant at the back. The airy outdoor patio with casual tables is the perfect child-friendly spot for a tasty bite or a full meal. The chef has a flair for originality and likes to keep the menu both literally and figuratively fresh. At press time, he was experimenting with new flavors of ice cream including mint, basil, cinnamon, and anise. The eucalyptus ice apparently wasn't a big hit but he gets points for creativity.

Kaya Grandi 12. ✆ **599/717-3919.** www.flamboyantbonaire.com. Main courses $10–$22. AE, MC, V. Daily noon–3pm and 6–10pm.

Rum Runners ★ INTERNATIONAL/SEAFOOD   This casual waterfront restaurant has a breezy yet intimate feel and sits above the tranquil water (which is inhabited by a school of enormous tarpon attracted by the lure of leftovers). The pizza is said to be the best on the island. For starters, try the calamari or beef yakitori. Seafood lovers should sample the shrimp and scallop skewers served with beurre blanc. The filet mignon with a red-wine sauce has strong nutmeg overtones and gets rave reviews from carnivores. Save room for the heavenly fiesta de frutas: Bavaros crème topped with strawberry coulis, bathed in a melon soup and garnished with a fresh fruit kabob. It sounds weird but is a fruit lover's delight.

At Captain Don's Habitat. (𝄽) **599/717-8290** or 717-7303. Reservations recommended. Main courses $12–$23. AE, MC, V. Daily 7–10am, 11:30am–2pm, and 5:30–10pm.

Zeezicht Seaside Bar and Restaurant SEAFOOD This prominent landmark, in front of Karel's Beach Bar on the main waterfront, has indoor and outdoor seating with a salty nautical theme. Serving up standard fare since 1900, menu options include deep-fried firecracker fish rolls, hearty seafood chowder, and *keshi yena,* a local dish of meat, olives, and raisins served in a ramekin and topped with cheese. The dinerlike menu also offers pasta, steaks, burgers, and other comfort food. If these don't tickle your taste buds, the owner, who aims to please everyone, also lays claim to the steakhouse upstairs and the Japanese restaurant next door.

Kaya J.N.E. Craane 12. (𝄽) **599/717-8434.** Main courses $10–$22. AE, MC, V. Daily 8am–11pm.

4 DIVING & OTHER OUTDOOR PURSUITS

DIVING & SNORKELING

Bonaire has 86 marked dive sites and a rich marine ecosystem that includes brain, elkhorn, staghorn, mountainous star, and soft corals; anemones, sea cucumbers, and sea sponges; parrotfish, surgeonfish, angelfish, groupers, blennies, frogfish, and yellowtails; not to mention sea horses, sea turtles, moray eels, and sea snakes. Sixty of the sites are accessible by shore and are marked by painted yellow rocks along the roadside. **Forest,** with an abundance of black coral, and **Hands Off,** with its abundant marine life, are two favorite boat dive sites, both near Klein Bonaire, the small, uninhabited island off the west coast.

Created in 1979 to protect the island's coral-reef ecosystem, **Bonaire National Marine Park** ★★ incorporates the entire coastlines of both Bonaire and Klein Bonaire, the small, uninhabited

(Fun Facts   "The Hooker"

The waters off the coast of Bonaire received an additional attraction in 1984. A 79-foot long rust-bottomed general cargo ship was confiscated by the police, along with its contraband cargo, about 25,000 pounds of marijuana. Known as the *Hilma Hooker* (familiarly dubbed "The Hooker" by everyone on the island), it sank unclaimed (obviously) and without fanfare one calm day, in 27m (89 ft.) of water. Lying just off the southern shore near the capital, its wreck is now a popular dive site.

island opposite Kralendijk. Collecting shells or coral is prohibited, as are spearfishing and anchoring (boats use permanent moorings). Visitors are asked to respect the marine environment and to refrain from activities that may damage it, including sitting, standing, leaning, or walking on the coral. Even a thin layer of silt can prove fatal to these delicate colonial marine animals that make up the fragile living surface of the coral formations. Feeding the fish is also illegal not to mention unhealthy for the fish. Due to safety regulations since the September 11, 2001, terrorist attacks in the U.S., diving or snorkeling near any commercial piers requires an additional permit from the harbor master (in other words, you really should go elsewhere).

Because protecting nature is taken seriously, all divers, snorkelers, windsurfers, and swimmers are required to pay a **nature fee** of $10 to $25. Tags are good for 1 calendar year and also permit admission into Washington-Slagbaai National Park. A 1-day pass can also be purchased for $10 for divers and $2 for nondivers. Nondivers 11 and under and Netherlands residents are exempt. Tags can be purchased at all dive shops as well as the Tourism Office at Kaya Grandi 2. An orientation dive is required for all divers. For more information, contact **STINAPA Bonaire** (© 599/717-8444; www.stinapa.org).

Dive shops are numerous and highly professional. Expect to pay $45 to $50 for a one-tank dive and $70 to $80 for a two-tank dive (equipment extra) and about $100 for an introductory resort course (equipment included). Every operation offers multiple dive packages that are a much better value than the a la carte options.

Divi Dive Bonaire, K.A. Abraham Blvd. 40, at the Divi Flamingo Beach Resort & Casino (© 800/367-3484 in the U.S., or 599/717-8285; www.diviflamingo.com), has a well-stocked shop, 24-hour access to tanks, and a reef only 18m (59 ft.) away. Divi Dive Bonaire is also fully equipped for travelers with disabilities.

Great Adventures at Harbour Village, Kaya Gobernador N. Debrot 71 (© 800/868-7477 in the U.S. and Canada, or 599/717-7500), is the island's poshest operation. It's upscale but unpretentious and friendly. In addition to two of the island's most beautiful boats, it boasts a first-class photo shop that rents underwater still and video cameras.

Bonaire Dive & Adventure, Kaya Gobernador N. Debrot 77a (© 599/717-2229; www.bonairediveandadventure.com), offers Ocean's Classroom, a discovery-based program for children that combines snorkeling with hands-on learning about the ocean and its inhabitants. Bonaire Dive & Adventure also arranges other activities such as cycling, kayaking, and nature tours.

Wanna Dive (© 599/717-8884; www.wannadive.com) has five locations, but its biggest place is at Eden Beach Resort where you can dive right off the beach or hop on a boat and head out to the spectacular double reef at Klein Bonaire.

Thanks to shallow-water coral reefs, snorkelers can enjoy Bonaire's awesome marine environment, too. The island's **Guided Snorkeling Program** includes a slide-show introduction to reef fishes, corals, and sponges; an in-water demonstration of snorkeling skills; and a guided tour of one of several sites. The cost is $25 per person. Equipment rental is about $10 more. Families may want to enroll with **Sea and Discover** (© 599/717-5322; www.seandiscover.com) for a marine education experience. A real marine biologist will teach you reef ecology, fish behavior, and critter identification both in a classroom and in the water for $45. The Reef Explorers program for kids offers a half-day hands-on discovery experience for $30 per child, including transportation.

You can arrange a guided snorkeling tour through any of the dive shops listed above or through **Buddy Dive Resort,** Kaya Gobernador N. Debrot 85 (© 599/717-5080; www.buddydive.com); or **Dive Inn,** Kaya C.E.B. Hellmund 27 (© 599/717-8761). The more adventurous can purchase a map that marks all the dive sites off Bonaire, most of which are excellent for snorkeling (as well as diving) and can be reached by wading into the water.

If you are an experienced diver and have training doing reef cleanups, you can participate in a cleanup dive through **Bonaire Marine Park** (© 599/717-8444; www.bmp.org). You must send an e-mail to marinepark@stinapa.org to make special arrangements. Additionally, every few months, **Dive Friends Bonaire** (© 599/717-2929; www.dive-friends-bonaire.com), together with NetTech NV, organizes cleanup dives. If the timing is wrong and you still want to "do your part" for the reef, check out the **Reef Environmental Education Foundation** (REEF; www.reef.org), a volunteer monitoring program where divers can log in and add their fish sightings to a global database used by scientists to monitor populations.

ⓘ Tips Sea Turtle Etiquette

The sea turtle is one of the most highly endangered species in the oceans. Catching even a passing glimpse of one is a magical experience, but you'll blow the chance unless you heed some basic guidelines. When you first spot a sea turtle, resist the urge to move in and get a closer look; you will only scare it off and ruin the opportunity for others to see it. Instead, stay still and watch at a respectful distance as it goes about its business, searching for food or gliding along gracefully. Keep an eye out for identification tags on their flippers or shells—a sure sign these fellas are being closely studied and well protected. You should never approach a turtle or its nest, and never touch or try to touch one—for your safety and theirs. While it seems harmless to humans, it is in fact quite stressful for the turtles (how'd you like to be chased around the grocery store by strangers all day?). **Warning:** Do not swim above the turtles; it will prevent them from surfacing to breathe and subject them to undue respiratory stress.

And of course, if someone offers you a sea turtle shell, egg, or meat products, just say no; then immediately call the number below to file a report.

To learn more about sea turtles or to learn about current conservation efforts and how you can participate, volunteer, or make a donation, contact **Sea Turtle Conservation Bonaire** (ⓒ **599/717-2225;** www.bonaireturtles.org).

For a relaxing morning or afternoon sail and snorkel trip, board the *Woodwind* (ⓒ **599/786-7055;** www.woodwindbonaire.com). For $30 per person, the 3-hour trip includes snorkel gear and nonalcoholic beverages. Or try **Pirate Cruises** (ⓒ **599/780-9933**) with Captain Mike, aboard a 56-foot private ship that offers half-day sail and snorkel trips as well as sunset or dinner cruises daily. If you are eager to see one of Bonaire's rarest inhabitants, Mike offers a turtle lover's snorkel trip aboard a 36-foot (11-meter) dive boat to some of the best sites for turtle encounters. All trips leave from Karel's Beach Bar Pier downtown on the waterfront, and reservations can be made there or at Zeezicht Restaurant across the street.

BEACHES

Bonaire's beaches are narrow and full of coral, but they're clean, intimate, and uncrowded. Swimming on the tranquil leeward coast is never a problem, but the east coast is rough and dangerous. Be careful venturing into the water barefoot; the coral chunks and jagged coral bottom can be sharp, and sea urchins like to hide in crevices, where it's easy to step on them by accident. If that happens, local doctors are practiced at removing these brittle and easily broken spines, but if segments remain, they will soon dissolve on their own.

The water at **Lac Bay Beach and Sourbon ★** is only .6m (2 ft.) deep, making it popular with families and windsurfers. In a protected area of Bonaire's southeast coast, it boasts windsurfing concessions and snack bars on one end and quiet, safe shallow waters toward the point. Trees and the makeshift platform for viewing windsurf competitions provide shade. A taxi from town will cost you $20 each way so it may be more economical to rent a car or go in a group of four.

Klein Bonaire ★, less than a mile west of Kralendijk, boasts **No Name Beach,** which features Bonaire's only classic white-sand strip. Parrotfish and yellowtail snappers patrol the finger, brain, and mustard hill corals, attracting snorkelers and divers. A water taxi from the town pier costs about $20 round-trip and leaves at 10am, noon, and 2pm. No facilities and little shade exist on the island, so bring water, a snack, and a coverup. One can also go for a quick dip a few steps south of the cruise dock at the postage-stamp-size **Playa Chachacha,** named in honor of a woman who once lived across the street. It's calm and safe for young children.

For a more traditional beach experience with all the amenities, try the 112m (367-ft.) stretch called **Eden Beach ★** just north of Kralendijk. The shallow water is loaded with marine life, so bring a snorkel and mask, and watch where you step. The dive shop at the south end maintains a small pier from which you can spot fish, sponges, and coral. There are both a restaurant and a beach bar that provide snacks and refreshments.

North of Kralendijk, stairs descend a limestone cliff to the white sand and bleached coral chunks of **1,000 Steps Beach,** which offers good snorkeling and diving. There are only about 75 steps down to the picturesque coves, craggy coastline, and tropical waters of changing hues, but there are no facilities to be had.

Farther north, Washington-Slagbaai National Park boasts a number of beaches. **Boka Slagbaai ★**, once a plantation harbor, draws snorkelers and picnickers. A 19th-century building houses toilets, showers, a restaurant, and a breezy bar. If so inclined, contact the park headquarters (**© 599/717-8444**) to find out about overnight rentals of a room or one of the historic buildings, which are about the size of a cottage. Aside from a solar-powered lamp and cold running water, the buildings are virtually empty so you'd be roughing it in paradise for certain.

The island's northernmost beach, **Boka Cocolishi,** is a perfect spot to picnic, but it's not safe to swim. Algae make the water purplish, and the sand, formed by coral and mollusk shells, is black. The water's treacherous at **Playa Chikitu,** but the cove, sand dunes, and crashing waves are secluded and beautiful. If the East of Eden vibe overcomes you with romantic inclinations, be wary of a surprise visit by the park rangers, who may pass by on their daily patrol.

OTHER OUTDOOR PURSUITS

BIRDING   Bonaire is home to over 200 bird species, including endemic lora parrots, pelicans, frigate birds, and one of the world's only breeding colonies of Caribbean flamingos. **Bonaire Dive & Adventure,** Kaya Gobernador N. Debrot 77 (© **599/717-2227**), offers expertly guided trips to Washington-Slagbaai National Park's bird havens for $45.

FISHING   Accessibility, calm waters, and abundant fish have always made Bonaire an attractive fishing destination. However, due to global declines, the catch rate has dropped off somewhat even here, in what seems an unspoiled paradise. The catch varies by season but includes marlin, sailfish, dorado, wahoo, amberjack, yellowfin, and bonito. **Piscatur Fishing,** Kaya H.J. Pop 4 (© **599/717-8774;** www. piscatur.com), and **Multifish Charters,** Kaya Pikuditu (© **599/ 717-3648**), offer deep-sea, reef, and bonefishing (catch-and-release) options. A half-day deep-sea or reef charter (up to 5 hr.) with up to six people runs $400; a three-quarter day (6¹/₂ hr.) is $475 and a full day (8 hr.) is $550. A half-day wading trip is $250 for one or two people up to 4 hours, and a half-day shore trip is $300 for three people up to 5 hours. If your group has more than six people, they can be added for $25 each. Strict regulations on fishing and size limits and high levels of concern about the reef fish mean that catch and release may be the best way to go even if your guide says otherwise.

HIKING   **Washington-Slagbaai National Park's** terrain is interesting and varied. Climbs up the steepest hills are rewarded with panoramic views, while cliff-side beaches with crashing waves make ideal picnic sites. After going on patrol with a ranger, we could see that this is a big park and it's surprisingly easy to get lost, injured, or dehydrated, so it may be best for beginners to go with a guide. **Outdoor Bonaire** (© **599/791-6272;** www.outdoorbonaire.com) can arrange hiking, free climbing, and overnight camping adventures in the park.

KAYAKING   While kayaking through the mangroves of Lac Bay, take time to observe the baby fish and bizarrely shaped tree roots. Bring protection from the sun and the ravenous mosquitoes. Guided trips and kayak rentals are available from **Bonaire Dive &**

Adventure/Discover Bonaire, Kaya Gobernador N. Debrot 79 (© 599/717-2229). In Sorobon, **Jibe City** (© 599/717-5233; www.jibecity.com) rents one-man kayaks by the hour for $10; double kayaks are $15 per hour and stand-up paddle boards are $15 per hour. A half-day guided tour through the mangroves can be arranged through **Mangrove Info and Kayak Center** (© 599/780-5353; www.mangrovecenter.com). A 1-hour tour is $25, and a 2-hour tour costs $45. For those who are not able to kayak but still want to see the ecosystem, tours on a solar-powered boat for $23 per hour are available. The center is closed on Sunday. **Outdoor Bonaire** (© 599/791-6272 or 785-6272; www.outdoorbonaire.com) offers both day and night kayaks and specializes in small groups. The owner Hans will even take you kayaking to Klein Bonaire, but it's farther than it looks so be prepared for a workout if you go.

KITEBOARDING This extreme sport combines windsurfing with kite flying and allows boarders to sail, leap, and flip along the water's surface. On Atlantis Beach, at the southern end of the island, **Kiteboarding Bonaire** (© 599/786-7138 or 786-6138; www.kiteboarding bonaire.com) helps beginners get started with 3-hour intro lessons or multiday packages. Those who've already taken an intro course and received certification are allowed to rent equipment and go it alone, though it often takes several weeks to master this challenging sport.

LAND SAILING ★ With less than 5 minutes of instruction and even less experience, you can be cruising at top speed around the largest land-sailing track in the world. This fun sport requires little knowledge of sailing and just a rudimentary understanding of physics. Let the natural trade winds speed you along an 823m (2,700-ft.) oval track. **Landsailing Bonaire** (© 599/786-8122 or 717-8122; www.landsailingbonaire.com) can be found on the road to Rincon. An hour rental plus a 15-minute lesson will cost $50 for adults and $35 for children.

MOUNTAIN BIKING Explore Bonaire's scenery on its 290km (180 miles) of trails and dirt roads. Ask at the tourist office for a trail map that outlines the most scenic routes. You can check with your hotel about arranging a trip, or call **Bonaire Wellness Connexions** (© 599/785-0767; www.bonairewellness.com), which offers guided bike excursions for every skill and endurance level from the leisurely pedal pusher to the grit-in-your-teeth, mud-splattered enthusiast. **Outdoor Bonaire** (© 599/791-6272 or 785-6272; www.outdoorbonaire.com) also offers cross-island bike excursions for $65. Mountain bikes can also be rented from a number of other locations, including the **Bike Shop** (© 599/560-7000). **Buddy Dive Resort** (© 599/717-5080; www.buddydive.com), has mountain bike rentals for $15 and mountain bike tours for $40. Mountain bikes can also be rented at the entrance of Washington-Slagbaai National Park, though you must arrive before noon, place a $100 retainer on your credit card, and return before 5pm. The bikes rent for $20 per day.

TENNIS   Several hotels have courts lit for night play, but the best facilities are at **Harbour Village Beach Club,** Kaya Gobernador N. Debrot (© 599/717-7500; www.harbourvillage.com), which offers clinics, racket services, and a resident pro. Courts are $15 an hour; a 1-hour private lesson is $50.

WINDSURFING   Shallow protected waters and steady breezes make Lac Bay perfect for beginners and pros. Sorobon has two equipment-rental centers: **Jibe City** (© 599/717-5233; www.jibecity.com) and **Bonaire Windsurf Place** (© 599/717-2288; www.bonairewindsurf place.com). Boards and sails are $45 for a half-day, $60 for a full day. Beginner lessons at 9:30am, 11am, 2pm, and 3:30pm cost $50 each, including equipment. Packages are available.

5 EXPLORING THE ISLAND

Bonaire Tours and Vacations, Kaya Gobernador N. Debrot 67, at Harbor Village Market Square (© 599/717-8778; www.bonaire tours.com), offers island tours, nature and history walks, snorkeling, fishing, mountain biking, sailing, or kayaking expeditions, as well as day and evening sailing excursions. **Outdoor Bonaire ★** (© 599/791-6272 or 785-6272; www.outdoorbonaire.com) offers more adventurous outdoor pursuits, such as cave snorkeling, rock climbing, night kayaking, hiking and camping in the national park, and even rappelling down from the top of the historic lighthouse.

KRALENDIJK

Because Bonaire has always been off the beaten track, highlights are modest and few. You can walk the length of sleepy Kralendijk—the name translates literally into "dike made of coral"—in less than half an hour. Stroll along the seafront, with its views and restaurants, and along Kaya Grandi, the major shopping district. The town has some charming Dutch Caribbean architecture—gabled roofs painted ocher and terra cotta. If you've got a yearning for fruit, visit the waterfront food market with daily produce deliveries from Venezuela.

Bonaire's minuscule **Fort Oranje** takes more time to find than to explore, but provides a pleasant diversion. The tiny fort, Bonaire's oldest building, is quaint and makes for a pleasant walking destination. Around the corner, **Yenny's "museum"** is simply the owner's collection of quasi-creepy life-size rag dolls dressed and surrounded by a backdrop of island scenes. As you meander through her yard, the forlorn turtles, lonely flamingos (rescued when found as orphans), and boisterous dogs are all part of the experience. The cheerful hand-painted decorations are reasonably priced, unique gifts. The owner is usually seated in the front yard on a nice afternoon, but if not, you may want to drop by another day.

A 10-minute walk away, the **Museo Boneriano (Bonaire Museum),** at Kaya J. v/d Ree 7 (© **599/717-8868**), displays a hap-hazard collection of shells from local species, excavated human remains from a Caicetto burial site, and various antiques and artifacts of European settlement that offer clues into the island's colonial his-tory. With few signs to make sense of the collection, a guided tour is recommended. It is open weekdays 8am to noon and 2 to 4:30pm. Admission is $1.50 for adults and $1 for children.

NORTH OF KRALENDIJK

The coastal road north of Kralendijk is one of the most beautiful in the Antilles. Turquoise, azure, and cobalt waters stretch to the horizon on the left, while pink and age-blackened coral cliffs loom on the right. Towering cacti, intimate coastal coves, strange rock formations, and panoramic vistas add to the beauty.

Starting in 2010, there are plans to erect giant white windmills to harness the abundant wind power and reduce dependency on oil, which is currently imported via massive oil tankers from Venezuela. The long-term goal is to reduce dependence on fossil fuels by as much as 80%. While this initiative may impact some of the island's scenic vistas, it will be a net gain for this ecofriendly island.

Just north of Kralendijk, **Barcadera** is an old cave once used to trap goats. Take the stone steps down to the cave and examine the stalac-tites. Farther north, just past the Radio Nederland towers, **1,000 Steps Beach** offers picturesque coves, craggy coastline, and tropical waters of changing hues.

ⓕun Facts   Name That Street Theme

As you meander along in Bonaire, read the street signs and try to figure out their theme. Each town will designate a certain theme (such as musical instruments, women's names, gem-stones, fish). This makes it easy to figure out someone's loca-tion if you only know their **street name.**

Turn right on Kaya Karpata for **Rincon,** the island's original Spanish settlement. Today, the quiet village is home to Bonaire's oldest church. Stop for a traditional lunch of *stoba* (stew) and *funchi* (polenta) or slimy but tasty cactus soup at the famous **Rose Inn,** Kaya Buyaba 4 (© 599/717-6420), Thursday to Monday noon to 6pm.

On the outskirts of Rincon, a large white building marks the spot of a new and not-to-be-missed highlight of any island tour. **Magazina di Rei** (© 599/786-2101) translates as the King's Warehouse, and is the second-oldest building on the island. Once used to store provisions for slaves, it has been restored and transformed into a small museum and cultural center that preserves and depicts the culture, history, architecture, and traditions of early Bonaire. Drop by for a tour, or wander through the gardens where re-creations of houses from different eras are on display. Local children learn traditional crafts, dances, and recipes from elders, so don't be surprised if you're offered some homemade tamarind juice or limeade and invited to try a few local dance steps. The center is open Monday to Saturday from 9am to 5pm.

On the way back to Kralendijk, take the road along the northeast coast to **Boka Onima,** the site of 500-year-old Caiquetio Indian petroglyphs. Stop at the home of **Sherman Gibbs,** on Kaminda Tras di Montaña. Sherman combines plastic bottles, boat motors, buoys, car seats, and just about everything to create an outsider-art fantasyland.

WASHINGTON-SLAGBAAI NATIONAL PARK

Washington-Slagbaai National Park ★★ (© 599/717-8444; www.washingtonparkbonaire.org) occupies the island's northern end. It's easy to find; just look for the yellow and green lizards painted on telephone poles along the road. They lead you to the park entrance. Formerly plantation land producing aloe, salt, charcoal, and goat meat, the 5,463-hectare (13,500-acre) reserve showcases Bonaire's geology, animals, and vegetation. Residents include 203 bird species, thousands of organ-pipe and prickly-pear cacti, endemic parrots, parakeets, flamingos, iguanas, and blue lizards. Feral goats and donkeys, left over from the colonial period, continue to roam the hills grazing voraciously on rare native and endemic plant species. For this reason, the park is attempting to remove these animals over time. The scenery includes stark hills, quiet beaches, and wave-battered cliffs. Take either the 24km (15-mile) or the 35km (22-mile) track around the park. Admission is $10 for adults, $5 for children 11 and under. Purchase of a **nature tag** (the mandatory pass costs $10 for all swimmers and $25 for divers) gets you complimentary entry into the park. The park is open from 8am to 5pm daily except for major holidays. You must enter before 2:45pm. Guide booklets, maps, and a small museum are at the gate. The unpaved roads are well marked and safe, but rugged; jeeps trump small cars here. For those looking to leave the island just a tad tidier than it was when they arrived, volunteer opportunities to paint, prune, and mend park infrastructure can be arranged by sending an e-mail to washingtonpark@stinapa.org.

Just past the gate, the **Salina Matijs** salt flat attracts flamingos during the rainy season. Beyond the salt flat on the road to the right, **Boka Chikitu's** cove, sand dunes, and crashing waves provide a splendid seascape. A few miles farther up the coast, **Boka Cocolishi,** a black-sand beach, is perfect for a private picnic, and the calm, shallow basin is perfect for close-to-shore snorkeling. **Boka Slagbaai** has a picturesque beach and positively charming restaurant where you can cool off with a bite, a beer, and a view of the ocean on one side and a serene lake teeming with shorebirds such as flamingos, egrets, and herons on the other side.

Back along the main road, **Boka Bartol's** bay is full of elkhorn coral, sea fans, and reef fish. Nearby **Poos Mangel,** a popular watering hole, is good for twilight birding, while the remote reef of **Wajaca** harbors sea turtles, octopuses, and triggerfish. Immediately inland, 235m (771-ft.) **Mount Brandaris** is Bonaire's highest peak. At its foot, **Bronswinkel Well** attracts dozens of bird species including pigeons and parakeets.

SOUTH OF KRALENDIJK

Just south of town, next to the airport, down a dirt road, the **Donkey Sanctuary ★** (© **599/9-560-7607;** www.donkeysanctuary.org) provides a safe haven for many of the island's 400 or so wild donkeys that previously roamed the entire island and fell victim to car accidents with increasing frequency. The park is open daily from 10am to 5pm, but the last drive through is at 4pm. The entrance fee is $6 for adults and $3 for children, but additional donations are welcome, as is a volunteered hour or two helping to clean out a few stalls, or feed and brush these adorable orphans. If you encounter a donkey outside of the sanctuary, remember it's illegal to feed them and advisable to not approach or touch as they can kick or bite if frightened. Not touching is particularly important when encountering a colt whose mother is probably nearby. Females may abandon their young if your smell masks its natural odor, which is used to help the mother recognize her baby.

A little farther south, dazzlingly bright **salt pyramids** dominate the horizon. Looking more like snowdrifts than sodium mounds, they're the product of the nearby salt pans.

Farther from the road, saltworks serve as a **flamingo sanctuary.** Bonaire is one of the world's few nesting places for Caribbean pink flamingos, and the island's spring flamingo population swells to

5,000. Because the birds are wary of humans, the sanctuary is off-limits, but from the road you can see the birds feeding in the briny pink and purple waters.

At the island's southern tip, restored **slave huts** recall the island's dark past. Each hut, no bigger than a large doghouse, provided night-time shelter for African slaves brought over by the Dutch West Indies Company to work the salt flats. Four cement obelisks, each painted a different color along the shore, were used as flagpoles to indicate to passing ships when the salt was ready for export.

Near the island's southern tip is **Willemstoren Lighthouse,** which was built in 1837. It's fully automated today and closed to visitors, but is classically picturesque.

A few minutes up the east coast, **Lac Bay's** shallow water and steady breezes are ideal for windsurfing. Deep inside the lagoon, mangrove trees with dramatic roots lunge from the water. Nearby **Sorobon Beach** is idyllic for frolicking in the calm surf.

Hungry after your adventures? Follow the signs to **Maiky Snack** (© 599/786-0086 or 700-6785) for a local lunch under the shade of a divi divi tree. The papaya and cucumber stews *(stoba)* with goat meat are served with rice or *funchi* (polenta) and the fresh fish of the day is topped with a sweet creole sauce. It's open Friday to Wednesday for lunch from noon to 3pm.

6 SHOPPING

Aruba has more stores and better prices than Bonaire, but dive-related items such as dive watches, underwater cameras, and marine-themed jewelry are more abundant here. Most shops are in Harborside Mall and on Kaya Grandi in Kralendijk. Shops are usually open 9am to noon and 2 to 6pm. *Tip:* When a cruise ship is in harbor, shops stay open longer, and small stands selling local wares and affordable jewelry magically appear in the town square.

For high-end (Tag-Heuer, Rolex, Omega) dive watches, and quality jewelry, try **Littman Jewelers,** Kaya Grandi 33 (© **599/717-8160;** www.bonairelittmanstores.com). *Tip:* Avoid purchasing any jewelry made with black coral. It is a globally protected species and may raise eyebrows at Customs, which could ask to see proof of its origin. **Atlantis,** down the street at Kaya Grandi 32B (© **599/717-7730;** www.atlantisbonaire.com), has a similar selection of jewelry and watches.

Perfume Palace (© **599/717-5288**), in Harborside Mall, carries perfume and a few high-end cosmetics. **Bonaire Gift Shop,** Kaya Grandi 13 (© **599/717-2201;** www.bonairegiftshop.com), sells a wide assortment of wine, liquor, T-shirts, and assorted souvenirs. **Jewel of Bonaire,** Kaya Grandi 38 (📞 599/717-8890), sells assorted gifts as well as beautifully crafted jewelry with an underwater theme.

For handmade and truly unique gifts, **Littman's Anything Artistique ★** (📞 599/717-8160), inside the Harborside Mall, sells unique and colorful paintings, prints, woodcarvings, jewelry, and home decor; Littman's other two locations in the Harborside Mall (the **Perfect Gift** and **Littman's Lifestyles**) sell casual jewelry, hand-blown glassware, figurines, and other decorative knickknacks.

Benetton, Kaya Grandi 49 (📞 599/717-5107), has smart men's and women's casual wear. For souvenir T-shirts for adults and children as well as affordable freshwater-pearl jewelry try **Best Pearls Bonaire,** Kaya Grandi 32 (📞 599/796-7451; www.bestpearlsbonaire.com). **Bamali ★,** Kaya Grandi 26A (📞 599/717-4833), sells men's and women's clothing, silver jewelry and accessories imported from Indonesia, and buttery leather handbags and belts from South America. The best place for dressier women's clothing is the **Shop at Harbour Village,** Kaya Gobernador N. Debrot 72 (📞 599/717-7500).

Cultimara Supermarket, Kaya L.D. Gerharts 13 (📞 599/717-8278), stocks Dutch cheeses and chocolates, fresh-baked goods, and products from the Caribbean, Europe, South America, and the United States. **Warehouse Bonaire,** Kaya Industria 24 (📞 599/717-8700; www.warehousebonaire.com), sells American and Dutch products as well as fresh meats, produce, cheese, and chocolates, and even delivers to your hotel room or resort. It is closed on Sunday.

7 BONAIRE AFTER DARK

Bonaire's nightlife is for the most part subdued and relaxed. Head out along the waterfront in Kralendijk and follow the small crowd to find the fun; then order the island's signature beer, Heineken Bright, or try a Polar, brewed in Venezuela.

Local musician Moogie plays bongos while serenading the crowd with familiar favorites and original tunes. His sound is distinctive and he lends a fun, relaxed vibe to every venue. He plays during dinner on Wednesday at **Cactus Blue** restaurant (📞 599/717-4564; www.cactusbluebonaire.com) and Thursday at **Rum Runners** (📞 599/717-8290).

Look in the back of *Bonaire Nights* for dates, times, and locations of evening slide and video shows, given by local experts. It's a great way to learn more about Bonaire's spectacular marine life, or just pass an hour or two with fellow nature lovers and dive enthusiasts. They usually take place around 6:30pm about once a week, and are commonly held at either **Captain Don's Habitat** or **Buddy Dive.** Best of all, they are free and open to the public.

City Cafe, Kaya Isla Riba 3 (no phone), the island's most popular hangout, and is the place to see and be seen, whether you're a tourist, a local, or a resident American med student taking a well-earned study break. The **Divi Flamingo Casino,** J.A. Abraham Blvd. 40 (© 599/717-8285), offers blackjack, roulette, poker, wheel of fortune, video games, and slot machines, all of which are popular with the locals. Its hours are Monday to Saturday from 8pm to 4am, and Sunday 7pm to 3am. If the slots don't inspire you, or you're overwhelmed by the cloying smell of cigarette smoke, walk over to the beach bar and indulge in a glass of house wine.

Karel's Beach Bar and Cappuccino Bar, on the waterfront (© 599/717-8434), features high ceilings and sea breezes. At press time, the cappuccino bar had been blown away by tropical storm Omar, but was in the process of being rebuilt. Sit at the long bar with the island's dive professionals, or take a table overlooking the surf. Local bands entertain on Friday, and you can watch games on the flatscreen TV.

Little Havana ★, Kaya Bonaire 4 (© 599/786-0717), with its dark-wood furniture and Cuban feel, is the current hot spot of the island's tiny nightlife scene. Live jazz on weekends and mellow jazz vinyls spun by a DJ all week long attract people to the indoor and outdoor tables just steps away from the waterfront. Enjoy a Cuban cigar on the veranda or find a spot inside to boogie down.

To really get away from it all, try some romance on the high seas aboard the *Samur* (© 599/786-5592; www.samursailing.com), an authentic Siamese junk that offers starlight evening sails with champagne, appetizers, or a full seven-course homemade Thai dinner. Charters leave from the pier in between the Sand Dollar Condominium Resort and Den Laman Restaurant at Kaya Gobernador N. Debrot 77.

Fast Facts

1 FAST FACTS: ARUBA

AREA CODES To call Aruba from the U.S., dial **011** (the international access code), then **297** (Aruba's country code), then **58** (the area code) and the five-digit local number. When in Aruba, dial only the five-digit local number.

BANKS Banks are open Monday to Friday from 8am to 4pm. Oranjestad and Noord, the town inland from Palm Beach, have many branches. The most centrally located bank is **Aruba Bank** at Caya Betico Croes 41 (© **297/527-7777**). It's not hard to find an ATM (since there are over 50 on the island and they dispense money in either florins or U.S. dollars depending on your preference).

BUSINESS HOURS Stores open from 8am to 6pm (Mon–Sat); some close noon to 2pm. Shops in malls and shopping centers are open 9:30am to 6pm. When cruise ships are in port, some stores in Oranjestad are open on Sunday and holidays. Office hours are 9am to 5pm (Mon–Fri).

CURRENCY The coin of the realm is the **Aruban florin (AWG),** but U.S. dollars are universally accepted. See "Money & Costs," in chapter 1.

DRINKING LAWS The legal drinking age in Aruba is 18 for beer, wine, and spirits. While drinking alcoholic beverages is allowed on the beaches, be careful to remove all empty bottles as the Aruban authorities are stringent about their littering laws.

DRIVING RULES See "Getting There & Getting Around," p. 14.

ELECTRICITY Like the U.S. and Canada, Aruba uses 110–120 volts AC (60 cycles).

EMBASSIES & CONSULATES The **Royal Netherlands Embassy,** Washington, D.C. (© **202/244-5300;** www.netherlands-embassy. org), is responsible for Aruba. Other embassies that may be useful are the **Embassy of Canada,** 501 Pennsylvania Ave., Washington, DC 20001 (© **202/682-1740;** www.canadianembassy.org); the **British Embassy,** 3100 Massachusetts Ave. NW, Washington, DC 20008

(© **800/443-8882;** www.britainusa.com); and the **Embassy of Australia,** 1601 Massachusetts Ave. NW, Washington, DC 20036 (© **202/797-3000;** www.australianvisasdc.com).

There is a **U.S. consulate** in Curaçao (P.O. Box 158, J.B. Gorsiraweg 1; © **599/9-461-3066;** fax 599/9-461-6489; http://curacao. usconsulate.gov; infocuracao@state.gov). The office is open from Monday to Friday from 8am to 5pm. Consular walk-in hours are only Monday, Wednesday, and Friday from 9 to 11am.

EMERGENCIES As in the United States, dial © **911** for police, medical, and fire emergencies. See "Health," in chapter 1.

GASOLINE (PETROL) Despite being so close to Argentina and refining a heck of a lot of oil, Aruba doesn't have cheap gasoline. At press time, the price was AWG 1.63 per liter, which is about 94¢ or $3.56 per gallon.

HOLIDAYS Most stores and restaurants close on official holidays. If you stay near the resort areas, however, you may not be affected at all. Here's a list of Aruba's holidays: January 1 (New Year's Day); January 25 (Betico Croes Day); February 15, 2010 (Carnival Monday); February 24, 2010 (Fat Tuesday); February 25, 2010 (Ash Wednesday); March 18 (National Anthem and Flag Day); April 2, 2010 (Good Friday); April 10, 2010 (Easter Sunday); April 30 (Queen's Birthday); May 1 (Aruba's Labor Day); May 13, 2010 (Ascension Day); December 25 (Christmas Day); and December 26 (Boxing Day). For more information on holidays see "Aruba Calendar of Events," in chapter 1.

HOSPITALS Horacio Oduber Hospital, L.G. Smith Boulevard, near Eagle Beach (© **297/587-4300**), is modern and well equipped, with 280 beds. See "Health," in chapter 1.

INSURANCE For information on traveler's insurance, trip cancellation insurance, and medical insurance while traveling please visit www.frommers.com/planning.

INTERNET ACCESS Many hotels have either dataports or Wi-Fi in rooms and/or the lobby. In downtown Oranjestad, **Inter Transfer** (© **297/588-6626**), in the Port of Call Marketplace, offers Internet access from 7:30am to 9pm Monday to Saturday and 10am to 2pm on Sunday. The rate is about $3.10 per hour.

LANGUAGE Official languages are Dutch and Papiamento, a local tongue that combines European, African, and indigenous American languages, but practically everybody speaks English. Spanish is also widely spoken.

MAIL Aruba created its own postage stamps in 1986. The post office (© **297/582-1900**) is located at J.E. Irausquinplein 9 in Oranjestad. Postcard stamps to the U.S. are 1.25 AWG (71¢).

NEWSPAPERS & MAGAZINES The *News, Aruba Today,* and *Aruba Daily* are the three leading English-language newspapers in Aruba.

PASSPORTS See www.frommers.com/planning for information on how to obtain a passport.

POLICE Police respond to emergency calls to (C) **911.** The main station ((C) **297/582-4000**) is at Wilhelminastraat 33, Oranjestad.

SMOKING Many restaurants have smoking sections which are usually at the bar or outside. Generally, in hotel lobbies, smoking is restricted to inside the casino or in bar areas. Hotels have smoking and nonsmoking rooms.

TAXES & SERVICE CHARGES The government of Aruba charges an 11% room tax as well as 5% to 7% for service. Restaurants often add service charges of 10% to 12%; see "Money & Costs," in chapter 1. A 3% sales tax that was implemented in 2007 may be added to purchases, or it may be absorbed into the ticket price of merchandise. Store owners have the option to decide whether the tax is added to the price or if it is built into the original price, so be sure to ask before you make any big purchases.

TELEPHONES To make a local call from a pay phone, purchase a phone card in $5, $9, or $18 denominations from a hotel desk, gas station, or convenience store. You can also dial (C) **121** to place a collect call. Most cellphones will work in Aruba, but call your carrier first to be sure. Rates are usually on the order of $2 per minute, even if you're dialing an 800 number. **AT&T** customers can dial (C) **916/843-4685** to reach an operator from your cellphone, or call (C) **800-8000** from special phones at the cruise docks and airport. **Verizon's** global customer service number is (C) **908/559-4899. Sprint** customer service in Aruba is (C) **888/211-4727.** Local cellphones can be rented at the airport by the day or week. The two main carriers are **Digicel** ((C) **297/522-2222;** www.digicelaruba.com) and **SETAR** ((C) **297/583-4000;** www.setar.aw). Rates are $8 per day for the first 5 days and $5 for each subsequent day. Additional charges for outgoing and incoming calls apply and a deposit is usually required.

TIME Aruba is on Atlantic Standard Time year-round. For most of the year, the island is 1 hour ahead of Eastern Standard Time. When the United States is on daylight saving time, the time in New York and Aruba is the same.

TIPPING See "Money & Costs," in chapter 1.

VISAS Americans, Canadians, Australians, New Zealanders, and E.U. nationals can stay in Aruba for up to 1 month without a visa. Timeshare and home owners are allowed to stay on island up to 180 days without one. If you plan to stay longer, get a visa application from the **Institute of Vigilance & Security Aruba (IASA)** in Aruba (© 297/587-7444; fax 297/587-1077) or at a Dutch embassy or consulate. In the U.S., the embassy of the Netherlands is located at 4200 Linnean Ave. NW, Washington, DC 20008 (© **877/388-2443**; www.netherlands-embassy.org).

VISITOR INFORMATION Contact the **Aruba Tourism Authority** (© **800/TOARUBA** [862-7822]; www.aruba.com), which has offices in major cities such as Chicago, Miami, Houston, and Atlanta. Their main location in the U.S. is 100 Plaza Dr., first floor, Secaucus, NJ 07094 (© **201/558-1110**; ata.newjersey@aruba.com), and in the U.K., the Copperfields, 25 Copperfield St., London SE1 0EN (© **020/7928-1600**; aruba@saltmarshpr.co.uk).

You also can gather tons of information from other Internet sources. A couple of Aruba's greatest fans compile **Aruba Bound!** (www.arubabound.com), a noncommercial collection of hard facts, informed opinions, and numerous Web links. **Visit Aruba** (www. visitaruba.com) has commercial links, practical information, news items, and a snappy gossip column. For a lively exchange of information and opinion, visit **Aruba Bulletin Board** (www.aruba-bb.com), where you can post questions to seasoned Aruba-vacation veterans and search for great deals on a timeshare rental.

Once you're on the island, go to the **Aruba Tourism Authority** at L.G. Smith Blvd. 172, Oranjestad (© **297/582-3777**). It is open Monday to Friday 8am to 5pm. But if you miss the office hours, you can find the authority's many free local magazines, like *Destination Aruba, Aruba Experience, Island Temptations, Aruba Nights, Aruba Ta Hot!, Bon Bini,* and *Island Gourmet* at restaurants, shops, and hotels. Two English-language dailies—*Aruba Today* and the *News*—provide entertainment listings.

WATER The water comes from the world's second-largest desalination plant, which is considered one of the best water supplies in the world. Bottled water is widely available but highly discouraged due to the environmental cost of importing it, as well as the island's mounting garbage disposal problem.

---

2 AIRLINE, HOTEL & CAR RENTAL WEBSITES

MAJOR AIRLINES

American Airlines
www.aa.com

Continental Airlines
www.continental.com

Delta Air Lines
www.delta.com

JetBlue Airways
www.jetblue.com

Martinair
www.martinair.com

United Airlines
www.united.com

US Airways
www.usairways.com

LOCAL AIRLINES THAT SERVICE BONAIRE & CURAÇAO

DAE (Dutch Antilles Express)
www.flydae.com

InselAir
www.flyinselair.com

Tiara Air
www.tiara-air.com

MAJOR HOTEL & MOTEL CHAINS

Divi Aruba
www.diviaruba.com

Hilton Hotels
www.hilton.com

Holiday Inn
www.holidayinn.com

Hyatt
www.hyatt.com

Marriott
www.marriott.com

Occidental Hotels & Resorts
www.occidental-hotels.com

Radisson Hotels & Resorts
www.radisson.com

Renaissance Hotels & Resorts
www.renaissancehotels.com

Riu Hotels & Resorts
www.riu.com

Westin Hotels & Resorts
www.starwoodhotels.com/westin

CAR RENTAL AGENCIES

Ace Car Rental
www.acearuba.com

Alamo
www.alamo.com

Amigo Rent-a-Car
www.amigocar.com

Auto Europe
www.autoeurope.com

Avis
www.avis.com

Budget
www.budget.com

Dollar
www.dollar.com

Economy Car Rental
www.economyaruba.com

Enterprise
www.enterprise.com

Explore Car Rental
www.explorecarrental.com

Hertz
www.hertz.com

National
www.nationalcar.com

Payless Car Rental
www.paylesscarrental.com

Smart Rent a Car
www.smart-rent-a-car.com

Thrifty
www.thrifty.com

INDEX

See also Accommodations and Restaurant indexes, below.

RESTAURANTS